TWAYNE'S
RULERS AND STATESMEN OF THE WORLD
SERIES

Hans L. Trefousse, Brooklyn College
General Editor

NEVILLE CHAMBERLAIN

(TROW 11)

TWAINE'S
RULERS AND STATESMEN OF THE WORLD
SERIES

Hans L. Trefousse, Brooklyn College
General Editor

NEVILLE CHAMBERLAIN

(TROW 11)

Neville Chamberlain

By WILLIAM R. ROCK

Bowling Green State University

Twayne Publishers, Inc.   ::   New York

TO
Stephen, Anne, and Brian

Preface

HISTORY HAS A CURIOUS WAY OF ATTACHING TO MAJOR PERSON-
alities one or two important events, ideas, or policies upon which
their reputations rise or fall; and all the other facets of their lives
notwithstanding, the reputation so affixed becomes deeply im-
bedded with the passing of time and the inevitable emergence of
historical generalization. So it is with Neville Chamberlain, whose
futile pursuit of appeasement—most commonly, if somewhat er-
roneously, symbolized by the now-wretched term "Munich"—has
come to overshadow everything else that is known about the man.
There is no doubt, of course, that appeasement was the single
most important "thing" in Chamberlain's entire career (at least
as the historian finds it useful to survey it). But a fair and mean-
ingful life of the man cannot be written in terms of appeasement
alone—no more, for example, than the life of Martin Luther can
be written solely in terms of the ninety-five theses or the life of
Abraham Lincoln can be written entirely in terms of the eman-
cipation of slaves. Consequently, one half of this study has been
devoted to Chamberlain's life before he became prime minister.
The second half deals with the latter (better known and highly
controversial) segment of his career.

Throughout the first half of the volume, Chamberlain has been
referred to by his Christian name. This is not meant to imply
disrespect. Rather, its use has made it possible to distinguish him
from his famous father and brother without employing cumbrous
clarifying phrases. In the second half of the book the more traditional practice of using the family name is followed.

This work makes no pretense at being definitive on any aspect
of Chamberlain's life. It attempts simply to provide a useful
summary, incorporating the latest scholarship, for the general
reader or the apprentice historian of the subject and period under
consideration. Uncertainties still exist, especially with regard to
Chamberlain's attitudes and thought and the process of decision-
making. Further study and later evidence will undoubtedly reduce the uncertainties. But it must also be said that the historian

is sometimes unable to trace roles, evaluate influences, assign motives, and allocate responsibilities with unerring precision—nor indeed should he be expected always to do so.

As is usual, responsibility for the opinions and judgments in this study rests solely with the author. The following persons, however, deserve special recognition for their assistance in its preparation: my wife Suzanne, who offered encouragement, patience, and understanding; Professor Stuart R. Givens, who read the first half of the manuscript and made many helpful suggestions; and Mrs. Phyllis Wulff, who typed and proof-read the manuscript with uncommon efficiency.

W. R. R.

Contents

Chronology

1854   Joseph Chamberlain settles in Birmingham.

1869   Arthur Neville Chamberlain is born, the first child of Joseph Chamberlain's second marriage. Joseph Chamberlain's political career is launched by his election to the Birmingham City Council.

1875   Neville's mother dies in childbirth.

1876   Neville's father is elected to Parliament.

1877   Neville enters school at Southport.

1880   The Chamberlain family moves to Highbury, which remains Neville's home for thirty years.

1878–   Neville attends Rugby.
1886

1886–   Neville attends Mason College, a business school, in Birmingham.
1888

1889   Neville begins a short-lived apprenticeship with Howard Smiths', a firm of public accountants. He makes his first travels abroad.

1891–   Neville undertakes a six-year residence on Andros Island,
1896   Bahamas, as the manager of a sisal plantation.

1897   The Andros adventure collapses and Neville returns to Birmingham. He resumes residence at Highbury, purchases Hoskins and Son (a manufacturing concern), and begins the life of a young, public-spirited businessman.

1900   Neville campaigns in the general election for Unionist candidates in the Midlands; thereafter he is drawn increasingly toward political involvement.

1904   Neville serves on fourteen Birmingham city committees. He develops special interests in city hospitals and Birmingham University. He travels to India.

1906   Neville serves as a link between his incapacitated father in Birmingham and his brother Austen in London.

1911   Neville marries Anne Vere Cole. He enters the Birmingham city government.

1912   Neville serves as vice-chairman of a committee restating the meaning of Unionism. He chairs the Town Planning Committee in Birmingham.

1914 Neville is elected alderman in Birmingham. His Housing Committee recommendations are tabled by the outbreak of war.

1915 Neville becomes Lord Mayor of Birmingham.

1916 The Birmingham Municipal Bank is established through Neville's efforts. He is re-elected Lord Mayor of Birmingham.

1917 Neville serves eight months in London as Director of the Department of National Service.

1918 Neville is elected to Parliament from the Ladywood division of Birmingham.

1919 Neville serves on a number of important Parliamentary committees.

1922 Neville becomes Post-Master General in Bonar Law's Cabinet following the collapse of the Coalition Government.

1923 Neville becomes Minister of Health. A short time later he is named Chancellor of the Exchequer in the first Baldwin Government.

1924 Neville achieves reunion of the Conservative Party. He develops a policy secretariat in the Conservative Central Office. He returns to the Ministry of Health in the second Baldwin Government.

1924– Neville compiles an outstanding record at the Ministry of
1929 Health. He gradually emerges as an important influence in the Conservative Party. He develops a lasting antipathy for the Labor Party.

1929 Neville achieves passage of the highly significant Local Government Act. He is sent into opposition by the Labor victory in the national election.

1930– Neville devotes his efforts, first as chairman of the Con-
1931 servative Party's Research Department, then as party chairman, to party reorganization and reconstruction.

1931 Neville becomes Chancellor of the Exchequer in Ramsey MacDonald's National Government.

1932 Neville presents a tariff bill (the culmination of one of his father's pet projects) to the House of Commons. He attends the Lausanne and Ottawa Conferences as a member of the British delegation.

1932– Neville compiles a substantial record as Chancellor of the
1935 Exchequer. He becomes increasingly concerned with foreign affairs and defense.

Chronology

1935 Neville continues as Chancellor of the Exchequer in Baldwin's new Government. He becomes still further involved in foreign affairs and defense.

1936 Neville is acknowledged as Baldwin's "heir apparent."

1937 Chamberlain becomes Prime Minister. He initiates the policy of appeasement. Lord Halifax visits Germany.

1938 Chamberlain pursues conversations with Italy. Eden resigns as Foreign Secretary in protest. The Austrian *Anschluss* occurs. Chamberlain concludes the Anglo-Italian Agreement. The Czechoslovak crisis develops. Chamberlain visits Hitler at Berchtesgaden, Godesberg, and Munich and signs the Munich Agreement. The Anglo-Italian Agreement is put into force. Chamberlain and Halifax visit Paris.

1939 Chamberlain and Halifax visit Rome. The "golden age" of appeasement quickly passes. The German destruction of Czechoslovakia occurs. Britain and France extend guarantees to Poland. Italy seizes Albania. Britain and France guarantee Greece and Romania. Britain and France pursue negotiations with Russia; a British military mission goes to Moscow. The Nazi-Soviet Pact is announced. Chamberlain fails in last-ditch efforts to preserve peace. World War II begins.

1940 The Chamberlain Government falls following the German invasion of Norway. Chamberlain becomes Lord President in Churchill's Cabinet. He is stricken with cancer and rapidly fails in health. Chamberlain dies.

PART I

PART I

CHAPTER I

Birmingham Beginnings

THE EXTENT TO WHICH A MAN'S ADULT LIFE IS AFFECTED BY HIS parentage, his environment, and the experiences of youth is a matter which has long intrigued, and often vexed, those who attempt to write biography. History is strewn with figures who seem, on the surface at least, easy to understand in terms of their family background and upbringing. It is equally filled with persons whose views and actions seem to belie almost everything associated with their past. There are obvious dangers involved in attempting an overview of a man's early years in order to seek insight into his general character and nature, especially the temptation (so often misleading) to seek neatly-packaged explanations of later attitudes in the experiences of early life. But a man cannot escape the imprint of his past entirely, even if he wills it—and Neville Chamberlain certainly did not wish to do so. Consequently, a review of his Birmingham beginnings is a fruitful, if altogether traditional, point of departure for this book.

It appears at first glance—and this view is strengthened by deeper study of the man—that Chamberlain was one whose parentage, environment, and experiences of youth were a positive influence in shaping his general nature and outlook of later years. In a very real sense (though this term is sometimes too loosely used by historians) he was a product of his times, the late Victorian era, to which he showed in later years, both knowingly and unknowingly, considerable attachment. He was also a product of his city, Birmingham, and his family, which by the time of Neville's birth had already attained prominence.

Although the "great days" of the Chamberlain family began with the arrival of Neville's father Joseph in Birmingham in 1854, the family could trace its ancestry, with modest pride, for generations. It sprang from yeoman stock in Wiltshire, from which William Chamberlain went to London when apprenticed to his uncle, a confectioner, in 1733. For more than a century (1755–1863) William and his descendants were associated with a respectable, if not especially profitable, shoemaking business in

Milk Street, Cheapside, London. During that period six Chamberlains became Masters of the Cordwainers Company, as the business was known, and there was hardly a time when a Chamberlain did not sit on the Company Court. Living modestly over their warehouse, worshipping at the Unitarian chapel in Carter Lane, and doing their civic duty as churchwardens of St. Lawrence Jewry, they were described in 1829 as "the highest sort of tradesmen, plain, honest, and sincere." [1] Among their other attitudes, they showed complete devotion to civil and religious liberty, though always in combination with sturdy patriotism. Thus typical of thousands of other British families, their ancestral closeness to one of the main streams of English thought provided innate strength to those members of the family who later rose to political prominence.

Joseph Chamberlain, Neville's father, went to Birmingham in 1854 "on business." Having left school at age sixteen and put in two years with the Milk Street enterprise, he was attracted to the rising provincial city by his uncle, John Sutton Nettlefold, who had taken his small screw manufacturing business there from Holborn in the 1840s. There he invested both money and effort— in the long run his tireless zeal and shrewd mind proved far more important to the enterprise—in what became Nettlefold and Chamberlain, a firm which, through efficient operation and the acquisition of English rights to American-patented machinery, gradually bested its competition and developed a near monopoly in the trade. For this great business success Joseph Chamberlain was primarily responsible, and his reputation spread through Birmingham and beyond. Over a period of fifteen years he achieved a new affluence, became increasingly involved in civic affairs, and developed some of the interests and activities which were to lead to a brilliant political career.[2]

He also acquired a heavy domestic responsibility, twice marrying into the Kenrick family of Birmingham, which had migrated from North Wales some years before. His first wife, Harriet, died while giving birth to their second child, Austen, in 1863. (Beatrice was born the year before.) Five years later, he married her first cousin, Florence, and that union produced four children, the mother again dying in childbirth in 1875. Neville, born on March 18, 1869, was the eldest child and only son of the second marriage (Ida, Hilda, and Ethel following in that order). Of Neville's mother, Austen was later to write: "Between them [her own children] and us [her stepchildren] she made no distinction, and amidst all the cares of this growing family and of my father's public life . . . she always found time to play with us, to read to us, and to watch over us with all a mother's love." [3] She was never very strong, but her spirit was indomitable; idleness was something she abhorred.

Although the "source" of a man's characteristics can be defined with no more certainty than the impact of his early life upon his later years, it seems as if Neville owed a good deal to his mother's family. Indeed, his "official" biographer, Feiling, declares that "by the evidence of all who knew him best, Neville's strongest characteristics came from the Kenricks." [4] Beyond the realm of inherited traits, there was ample opportunity for the Kenrick influence to exert itself on him. In addition to his father's two marriages into the Kenrick family, his uncle Arthur Chamberlain had married his mother's twin "Louie," and his aunt Mary Chamberlain had wed Harriet Kenrick's brother William. These unions produced a total of nineteen children, and herein lay the nucleus of a very compact clan.

The Kenricks had come to Birmingham in late eighteenth century. Though distinctly Welsh, with a trace of Scot and Huguenot, they were in many ways like the Milk Street Chamberlains. Their background was primarily one of solid Unitarian respectability, and although the line produced several learned divines, they retained an intense nonconformity. They had made a respected name as iron-founders in West Bromwich after Archibald Kenrick, Neville's great grandfather, had turned from the manufacture of shoe buckles about 1791. Making money quickly for that day and spending it generously, they had assumed civic duties, backed social reform, and promoted the new independence which Birmingham was coming to feel. Their general political outlook was reflected in their fierce resentment of Pitt's war to force (as they saw it) tyranny upon France and, some years later, their ardent support for Lord Grey in the Reform Bill controversy.

One of Chamberlain's biographers points to Neville's grandmothers as a likely source of the new vitality which helps to explain "the sudden eruption of a worthy pedestrian family into business success and political brilliance within a generation." Caroline Harben, Joseph Chamberlain's mother, came from a Sussex family whose record was colorful, if checkered, and seems to have possessed real wit and imagination. Florence Kenrick's mother, Maria Paget, was remembered as "full of vitality, bright, and lively, and fascinating." [5] While this proves nothing, of course, with regard to Neville, it does suggest the appearance of a new spark in the family line in the generation or so before his birth.

Since Neville's mother died when he was just six years old, he spent most of his childhood years in a motherless home, and, in part because of that, a home from which his father was frequently absent. The same year that Neville was born, his father was elected to the Birmingham City Council; his three-year mayoralty (1873–76), which made Birmingham the pioneer of a planned society, ensued; and in 1876, he was elected to Parliament. He sold his business interests and became engrossed in politics. His wife's death encouraged him to lose himself in his work, and he became quite separated from his children. "For a good many years I respected and feared him more than I loved him," Neville later explained.[6] Neville was thus deprived—for whatever this might imply—of parental affection during his childhood.

But the Chamberlain children were not, of course, neglected. To their suburban home, Southbourne in Augustus Road, Edgbaston, came their father's younger sisters, Caroline first, and after her marriage, Clara, to perform the task of foster parent. The latter was perhaps too young to bring the proper kind of understanding to her assignment. For example, her greeting, "Neville, your cap's crooked," upon his return home from a term at Rugby led him to vow privately that he would never kiss her again.[7] But she performed her work faithfully until Neville was sixteen. At that point the selfless Beatrice, eldest of the children, was able to take charge. Joseph Chamberlain had realized £120,-000 from the sale of his business interests in 1874, so few of the material needs of the family went unsatisfied.

When Neville was eleven, the family moved to "Highbury" on Moor Green, a newly-constructed home (as later described) "in the hideous roomy Victorian-Gothic style, with vast hall of arches, stained glass, and inlaid woods." [8] This was Neville's home for the next thirty years. Highbury's sumptuous surroundings— water, woods, and ample open spaces—were a delight to the Chamberlain children, and it is easy to picture Neville, who had early developed an interest in nature study, climbing trees, chasing moths and butterflies, and camping in the bluebell woods.

Highbury's location was important in another way. Within easy reach of other clan houses (including those of Arthur Chamberlain with nine children, and William Kenrick with four), Neville matured in a circle of sisters and cousins which was exclusive and self-sufficient. Sharing almost everything from pets to governesses to holidays in Scotland, they were so content with their own company that they rarely sought company from the outside. Within the group, Neville appears to have been a happy and normal boy; indeed, inasmuch as the girls far outnumbered the boys, and since Austen was far ahead of him in age, Neville, usually the eldest boy around, was the natural leader. But outside the group he was uncomfortable, unsociable, or as he himself later said, bedeviled by "accursed shyness"—which in fact he never fully overcame. The exclusiveness of the clan, which had an adult counterpart to its adolescent variation, probably contributed to this; so content within the family circle, he was simply unhappy and uneasy outside it.

His schoolboy experiences seemed to deepen this side of his nature. His first year away from home, at a small school in the sandhills at Southport, where he went at age eight, went well enough. But it was a very different story in the preparatory school at Rugby, and in Rugby School, which he entered in the spring of 1882. He did "good-level" work, became head of his house, and participated in games (though he rather disliked them). But he was most unhappy through it all. There were specific problems: laboring in the shadow of his brother Austen, now about to enter Cambridge; bullying by other boys; suffering under a housemaster whose nickname, "Slops," indicates his reputation, perhaps unmerited, with the students; and experiencing wounded pride at being transferred, at his father's request, to a group of smaller boys. But the chief problem seems to have been his absence from family and clan, where he knew he was safe and loved. He was, in short, lonely, and the upshot of this was that he went his own way, seeking refuge within himself, especially through the development of an intense interest in music and literature and a passion for natural history.

Looking back from the vantage point of a half century later, it is tempting to see the two faces of Neville Chamberlain, so apparent in his later political career, already present. To a few close associates and to his family, he was a simple, warm, understanding person; to most others he was stiff, reserved, aloof—so much so that many who knew him well found him hard to understand. It is tempting also, if a casual memory is worth anything at all, to detect his passion for positive action. Surprised at Chamberlain's mastery of a complex theorem in algebra, his mathematical master was told: ". . . as it was clear that I should have to learn it sometime, I concluded I might as well do it at once." [9]

Positive action of another kind followed soon thereafter: Neville left school at the beginning of the 1886–87 term. Some years before, his father had apparently made a decision, with the acceptance if not the full concurrence of his sons: Austen being groomed for a career in politics, Neville should go into business. Accordingly, he entered Mason College, Birmingham (later converted to Birmingham University), where he took commercial courses and studied, quite without distinction, metallurgy and engineering design. Ironically, it was during this two-year experience as a commuter to a business-technical school that he became intrigued with the far-ranging thought of Darwin, Huxley, and Wallace, in which his sisters, though not his father and brother, also showed great interest. He had time to read, certainly, for during this period he was left largely to himself, his father in London, his sisters at school, and his classmates at Mason College not really his own sort.

A successful apprenticeship with a firm of public accountants (Howard Smiths') seemed to launch Neville, in quite orthodox fashion, on a business career in Birmingham. He did well. His mental alertness and quick mastery of financial problems were noticed almost at once, and he apparently enjoyed traveling around the Midlands on auditing assignments. But his association with the firm was short-lived, for in 1890 his father summoned him to another kind of work which took him very far afield, geographically and in other ways as well.

The period 1887–1890 might appear to have been "lost years" for Neville, but this was certainly not the case. In one sense, it provided his most liberal education. As a result of his father's meteoric rise in British politics, his vast interests and many connections, both national and local, Highbury was the scene of exciting activity. Here came many of the great figures of the political and journalistic world to discuss a variety of matters with Joseph Chamberlain, widely regarded as one of the best talkers and hosts in Europe. Here, as one writer has put it, the "ruthless efficiency of the caucus" was fashioned, and the "Radicalism that was to split the Liberal party was fostered. Here the new Birmingham was charted, and an even newer concept of Empire born." [10] The Chamberlain children were admitted freely to the company and conversations of these visitors, especially those at the dinner table. National political strategy, projects for slum clearance, campaigns for schools and hospitals, and various matters of social reform were all frequent topics of discussion, and Neville was almost inescapably drawn into the "big issues" of the day. His political conscience and awareness of a social duty, long taken for granted in the Chamberlain family, were certainly sharpened. (In a lesser way, the latter was also advanced by a stint of Sunday school teaching, undertaken perhaps more from a sense of social duty than religious faith, in the Church of the Messiah in Broad Street, which conducted active mission work in the nearby slums of Ladywood.)

It was during this period that he made his first trip abroad, visiting Paris for the Exposition in June, 1889, then, during the winter, journeying to Venice and Egypt in the company of his father and other members of the clan. Traveling with his father involved a rather extensive encounter with officialdom, but according to biographer Feiling, Neville's record of the trip reveals a thorough sightseer, much more absorbed with little things (donkey-racing and gaudy Arab dress, for example) than with official functions.[11]

Life at Highbury changed in one important respect in this period, too. In late 1888, Joseph Chamberlain brought home from New England his third wife, Mary Endicott, a daughter of the Secretary of War in President Grover Cleveland's Cabinet. He had met her while in America as a special envoy to discuss the problem of fishing rights in Canada. Though very young (younger than Beatrice and Austen), she succeeded admirably in bringing happiness and an even greater sense of unity to the family. She and Neville seem to have gotten on very well, and it must have been with at least some slight misgivings, despite the "hard core" he now observed in himself, that he temporarily departed Highbury at age twenty for an adventure overseas.

CHAPTER II

Andros Adventure

ANDROS IS AN ISLAND IN THE BAHAMAS. SISAL IS A FIBER-PRODUCING plant from which hemp is made. The two of them together claimed the next six years of Neville Chamberlain's early adult life.

The Andros adventure began in Montreal in the autumn of 1890. Traveling to the Canadian city during a visit with his wife's family in New England, Joseph Chamberlain encountered, much by chance it would seem, Sir Ambrose Shea, governor of the Bahamas. Sir Ambrose was at that moment ecstatic over the virtues of sisal, which, he was convinced, would grow readily in the shallow soil covering the coral rocks of the Bahamas, produce fiber of high quality, and thus provide a new and thriving industry sorely needed in the poverty-stricken island group. And since he was familiar with Manila hemp from an earlier business connection, he spoke with some authority. In Joseph Chamberlain he found a ready listener. Since the sale of his interest in Nettlefold and Chamberlain, his capital had depreciated somewhat, and politics was expensive, especially since he had been in opposition for four years. Colonial advocate that he was, the idea of making a second fortune in the colonial empire apparently intrigued him. It is also probable that he saw in this a suitable business venture for Neville. In his own youth, at his father's bidding, he had successfully forsaken London and shoes for Birmingham and screws. Now his son might profitably trade statistics for sisal. Thus it was that Neville received a cable summoning him to meet his brother Austen (who was traveling with their father) in New York, from where they would hasten to Nassau to investigate the possibilities of establishing a sisal plantation.

The brothers reached their destination by mid-November. Their father having reserved an option on 20,000 acres of land, their task was essentially two-fold: to evaluate the prospects themselves, on the basis of an exhaustive questionnaire provided by their father, and to find a suitable tract of land on which to begin operations. Despite the interference of festivities in their honor—

the presence of Joseph Chamberlain's sons was a "big thing" in the islands—Austen and Neville moved quickly to accomplish their mission. From extensive and sometimes grueling boat trips to explore the many out-islands, interviews with all kinds of people, and a thorough inspection of existing facilities, they compiled information which they submitted to their father, in true Chamberlain fashion, in frequent and detailed letters. In late January, 1891, they returned home with a full report.

Their findings denied Sir Ambrose's claim that the first sisal crop (coming in the fourth year, since it took that long for the plant to produce) would repay all initial production costs, thus leaving ensuing crops, less current expenses, as clear profit; but their own calculations produced, nevertheless, a highly favorable prospect. No one site had been decided upon, though they apparently leaned toward Mayaguana, some distance from Nassau, where the harbor was good, the land promising, and quite incidentally (as Neville recorded it), the flamingoes eye-catching. In detailed family discussion Joseph Chamberlain's brothers advised against so risky a venture. But the issue was never really in doubt. Consequently, April, 1891, found Neville on his way back to the Bahamas, this time alone. A youth just turned twenty-two, he was solely responsible for the establishment and operation of the new enterprise.

Within a few days of his arrival, he settled upon a site for the plantation. It was on Andros island, not Mayaguana; Andros' relatively short distance from Nassau (20 miles) was apparently decisive. A week of exploring and prospecting through rough terrain and dense thicket, during which he exhausted two companions (Forsyth, a surveyor, and Michael Knowles, whom he had engaged as an experienced overseer), pointed to a section of land on the north side as the best available. Neville quickly arranged terms with the governor—and very favorable ones they were, in view of Sir Ambrose's interest in having the prestige of the Chamberlain name in the new industry.[1] Thus began the Andros Fiber Company, and with it six years of anxious toil for Neville Chamberlain.[2]

There was, in short, everything to be done: land cleared and planted, roads fashioned, houses constructed, labor engaged and fed, food and materials imported, accounts kept, and so on. This would have been a formidable undertaking in favorable circumstances, but conditions on Andros hardly merited such a description. The soil was rocky and matted with undergrowth; the temperature torrid (especially between April and October); the insects most bothersome; local resources (except for labor) almost non-existent; the native population sparse, backward, and disease-ravaged. But Neville carefully planned what he would do and did it with a vigor and competence which quite belied the nature of the task and the inexperience of youth.

After a rigorous pioneering period of about six months, during which he worked twelve hours a day, lived in a small native hut, and suffered a variety of hardships and annoyances, he had the satisfaction of knowing that his enterprise was at last under way. His own home, sitting atop a small rise near the shore at Mastic Point, and that of his manager, Knowles, were completed; 580 acres of land had been cleared and 320 of them planted; his labor force was gradually responding to discipline. In general, a well-organized (given the circumstances) plantation was emerging. This did not imply any real reduction in the volume of his work —indeed, as long as he remained on Andros he put in long and arduous days in activity which ran the gamut of variety from planning roads and uprooting trees to selling corsets in the company store. But it did ease the tension and anxiety which usually prevail in new and strange surroundings.

There is little doubt that, from the very first, Neville established himself as "boss." All plans emanated from him, and he was constantly on top of everything that happened. He commanded his labor force sternly; upbraided Knowles when he had too much to drink, or did anything else which Neville considered less than responsible; used his influence to get Forsyth appointed Resident Justice of Andros; steadfastly resisted the opening of a saloon; and successfully parried the sometimes impractical suggestions of Austen, who, an ocean away, was full of ideas as to how things should be done. He was in no sense heartless, but, feeling keenly the responsibility which rested upon him, he approached his task in a very serious and business-like way, and expected the same response from others. (Both points are illustrated, perhaps, by his beginning of a savings bank which offered two percent interest, and his encouragement to the natives to use it.)

The nature of his position made Neville busy and self-sufficient. Along with the Crusoe-type surroundings on Andros, it also made him lonely. He had no mental companions, and his infrequent encounters with a passing sponge merchant, a mission priest, or his nearest neighbor (an eccentric, red-bearded Scot who scratched futilely on a plot three miles away) could hardly be called social occasions. Nassau did not interest him; it was too formal (socially) and gossipy. He was, in short, "driven in upon himself" (Feiling's words), seeking relief from his labors in reading, letter-writing, language study (especially German), and other equally solitary activities—something not exactly new for him.

Mid-summer, 1892, provided a brief respite. He returned to England for what was to become an annual summer leave. But after two months of "doing nothing," he was not only ready but anxious to return to Andros. Austen accompanied him for a month's visit; then Neville was on his own once more. A letter which Austen wrote to his step-mother shortly afterwards described Neville as "very well and in the best of spirits." Along with his own increased admiration for the "tact and skill" that Neville was showing, he reported the Colonial Secretary's opinion that Neville was "exactly the kind of man we want," in that his example in showing the native whites both what could be done and how to do it was "invaluable." [3]

The two years which followed constitute the "high tide" of the Andros adventure. The Fiber Company's planted acreage gradually increased beyond the 6,000 mark; the number of laborers rose to a maximum 800; and company agents began to operate in other islands. A short visit by Joseph Chamberlain in October, 1893, paved the way for more mechanization (especially a machine to clean sisal leaves for fiber), construction of a railway (accomplished with great effort a year later), more general building, and a questionable debenture issue to raise capital. Neville visited sugar plantations in Cuba to study production techniques, and drove himself relentlessly to improve the efficiency of the Andros enterprise. The Mastic Point plantation seemed on its way to becoming the pride of the Bahamas.

Meanwhile, Neville seemed more comfortably settled in his island surroundings. His house was amply furnished, in part by a flood of presents from sisters and cousins. His vegetable and flower gardens flourished. Two sailing boats and a schooner were now available for both business and pleasure. And perhaps most important to him, he now had his library from Highbury.

His adjustment to the people among whom he worked seemed improved, too. His letters (according to Feiling[4]) revealed a greater inclination than before to observe the good in his employees and others with whom he came in contact. His general understanding of those whose thoughts and ways were vastly different from his own seemed more advanced; and though patience and tolerance towards his subjects did not always prevail in his messages home, his irritabilities did not emerge so much in his actions. He found a congenial friend in the Rev. F. B. Matthews, Rector of Andros; developed a certain attachment to the Knowles family; and took increasing satisfaction from his role as social missionary among the natives (opening a school and serving as an amateur doctor and magistrate, among other things). And his mellowing attitudes reflected in those whom he encountered. The natives sought his aid and expressed their gratitude in simple ways, not the least of which, sometimes to his chagrin, was frequent serenading by tuneless bands. In a letter to Archdeacon Wakefield in February, 1894, Rev. Matthews reported a "most remarkable" change in the demeanor of the people and gave much of the credit to Neville.[5]

But the situation was far from idyllic, especially from the business standpoint. Sisal production was not coming up to expectations. The first hint of this came as early as May, 1893, when Neville wrote his father that "our plant poles in 7 years from time of setting out," thus giving only three years cutting and greatly reducing the profits calculated earlier.[6] But this problem was minor compared with those as yet to come. Nineteen months later (January, 1895) he reported flatly that the plants "certainly are not doing what they ought in many places. . . ." [7] He foresaw at most 300 acres to cut the following summer, and admitted great anxiety about the situation. The awful truth was there, though it was not yet fully grasped: the shallow soil of Andros simply would not grow sisal on so large a scale.

Other problems contributed to Neville's deepening concern for the future of the enterprise. Native laborers could not seem to understand sisal harvesting, often cutting the leaves too short, then allowing cut fibers to be soaked by rain. Mrs. Knowles died, leaving her already worn husband a broken man who was of little aid to Neville. The price of sisal tumbled downward.

But Neville, obstinately hopeful, pressed on. He was not inclined to quit while there was still reason, as he saw it, to hope for success. Though consultation with his father did result in a decision (spring, 1895) to halt land-clearing operations, he continued to buy plants on a large scale and pushed ahead with the construction of a new baling shed and houses for laborers. The shadow of anxiety darkened his summer holiday with his family in the Pyrenees, but he returned to Andros still hopeful that things would improve. Then misfortunes struck in rapid succession: fire destroyed the new baling shed, and with it his first real crop of fiber; New York buyers judged his samples too stiff and short; Knowles' incapacity became complete. All these setbacks might have been overcome, but not in view of the worst calamity of all: the stunted, yellowish sisal plants simply refused to develop. The collapse of the Andros Fiber Company was imminent.

Neville first used the accursed word "failure" in a letter to his father in late February, 1896, and although some months passed before the enterprise was actually liquidated, it had passed the "point of no return." For at least a year, Neville had faced the prospect of failure (perhaps attested by his increasingly frequent black moods) but had refused to acknowledge it openly. One of the two biographers who have seen his personal papers concludes from them that "the truth is probably that Neville went on when he knew himself he should retreat." [8] For at least a year his father, too, was torn between pushing on or calling the whole thing off. But neither had been willing to accept defeat. For Neville it meant bitter disappointment and a keen sense of personal failure. For his father it meant financial calamity (as it ultimately turned out, the loss of £50,000) and the stigma of an unwise venture. Whether a "sharper man" (Neville's term) would have seen ultimate failure earlier, or avoided the venture in the first place is hard to tell—but to shy away from adventure, or to abandon it quickly when the going got rough, was not the Chamberlain way of doing things. And at least one point is clear: the failure of the enterprise did not develop from a lack of effort on the part of its resident director.

The final decision to abandon the plantation was made while Neville was home in the summer of 1896. There was talk about starting again on better land with a smaller project, but it came to nothing. Neville returned to Andros that winter to wind things up. Distressed to find the whole plantation already disintegrating rapidly, he was hardly relieved when it sold, all save land, to a solitary bidder for £560. After making the rounds to say goodbye to his friends, he departed for England in March, 1897.

The Andros adventure "was a great experience, and I know I am much the better and stronger for it," Neville wrote Rev. Matthews that December.[9] An easy passing reflection, it long remained his considered opinion—and biographers have concurred in his view—that Andros made him. More specifically, this experience helped to strengthen elements of his nature already present and forcefully thrust him from youth to manhood. Feiling has summarized this eloquently:

Initiative had become a habit, for with him alone it had rested, and confidence in his own judgment, since there had been no one else to judge. . . . Sensitive and self-dependent, self-respecting and sanguine, he had gone out to Andros, and the same, doubly, he returned. . . . This experience surely drove in deeper the morality of his temperament, of progress dependent on labour, and a duty, indistinguishable from discipline, to his neighbor. . . .

. . . Andros over-sharpened some sides of his virtue, giving him a dislike of anything untidy, over-darkening for him the incompetence of humanity *en masse,* and importing to his energy an unreflective turn, so that a day without incessant action seemed a day wasted.[10]

The son of a prominent statesman, finding life easy and pleasant in the West End of London, was liable to acquire a notion about his own importance which the facts might not warrant. Neville was under no such temptation in Andros. And any young man whose first six years of manhood were spent in managing a project which lost £50,000 for his father could hardly fail to realize that the easier days of youth were past.

In a curious way, Neville's sojourn on Andros was a miniature of his experience in foreign affairs when he was prime minister many years later. He pursued his goal with the same enthusiasm, the same courage and tenacity, the same day-to-day administrative competence—and experienced the same ultimate and complete failure of an enterprise for which, perhaps, success ought not to have been hoped so fervently.

Reluctant to abandon Andros as a failure, not only for his own and his family's sake but also because he was concerned about the natives "falling back into their earlier ways," Neville was nonetheless anxious to get on with something else if a failure it were (so he wrote his father in April, 1896). He must have found the established business atmosphere of Birmingham a pleasant relief upon his return there in 1897.

CHAPTER III

Back in Birmingham

THE BIRMINGHAM TO WHICH NEVILLE RETURNED WAS AN EXPLODING industrial metropolis, vibrant with all the forces of change which characterized the emergence of industrial society at the turn of the century. A rather disorderly place in the 18th century—indeed its atmosphere of "freedom" had made it a refuge for men of genius like James Watt and Joseph Priestley—it had grown rapidly, in the 19th century, into one of the best governed municipalities in England. But the spirit of its wild youth remained. Adventure and experimentation were still widely respected and pursued; political, economic, and social issues, especially as they arose from a rapidly expanding industrial working class and the common needs of these people, were genuinely alive; and local pride engendered by fierce municipal life ran strong. Birmingham was a kind of pioneer city, a place in which liberal politics and nonconformist principles, wielded by an enterprising class of businessmen, was contributing mightily to the demise of the old society and the rise of the new.[1]

Highbury had changed somewhat now that the Chamberlain children were all grown and away from home for lengthy intervals, but it had lost none of its importance and fascination as a gathering place for local and national notables alike. Joseph Chamberlain, now Colonial Secretary, was at the peak of his political career, guiding his Liberal Unionist movement at home, resisting French expansion in the region of the Nile, fighting the Boers in South Africa, testing the idea of a settlement with Germany, and propounding imperial union through tariff reform. As a result, the stream of visitors to Highbury, when Parliament was not sitting, was as illustrious as it was steady; and Neville, now the one permanent resident in the family home, was there to meet them all.

Neville settled gradually into the life of a young, public-spirited businessman—and remained there for the next fourteen years. He did not seem to seek adventure; perhaps Andros had given him enough of that. Nor did he give any indication of political ambition, unless one interprets (and a few writers have) his repeated disclaimers during this period as evidence that the possibility of a political career was never very far from his mind. He may have labored, altogether unconsciously perhaps, in the shadow of his father's dictum that he was destined for a career in business.[2] That he was uncertain about his "mission" (his own word) in life, and somewhat dissatisfied because of that, he stated clearly in a letter of January, 1902, to his friend F. B. Matthews.[3] But the facts of his life at this time suggest that he put his mind to achieving success in business, leaving the future to take care of itself.

With family connections like Neville's, business opportunities were not difficult to find. His uncles, Arthur and Walter Chamberlain, were instrumental in securing several openings for him. The first was a directorship in Elliott's Metal Company at Selly Oak, which employed some 700 or 800 men in the manufacture of copper and brass-work. The second, a far more personal and, it would seem, satisfying venture for Neville, involved the purchase of Hoskins and Son in Upper Trinity Street, Bordesley, a firm whose main business was the manufacture of metal cabin berths for ships. Retaining the old name, Neville formed a private company of which he was chairman. The firm remained small, its maximum employment never exceeding 200, but it was a steady, if modest, financial success.

Neville's undisputed business acumen soon won recognition among his colleagues and associates. While it would be unrealistic not to recognize that his name gave him an early advantage, it would be equally inaccurate to think that his reputation rested on that alone. His administrative zeal and abundant energy were both conspicuous and attractive, as were his awareness of and concern for problems at all levels of production and his clear grasp of the distinction between innovation for the sake of improved operation and innovation for its own sake alone. Though some would not put him in the very first rank of executives, the picture which emerges of his business activity at this point reveals a substantial, consistent, reliable, and conscientious—if, in a sense, monotonously strait-laced and methodical—young man whose counsel was respected and increasingly sought. He became, in time, chairman of Elliott's, and, as his business interests broadened, a director of the internationally-known Birmingham Small Arms Company. The companies with which he associated prospered, their profits rising, in the wake of the Boer War, to such an extent that someone among the anti-Chamberlain faction coined the phrase: "The more the British Empire expands the more the Chamberlains contract." Political patter perhaps, it nonetheless reveals the business success which the Chamberlain family in general, and Neville in particular, was experiencing at the turn of the century. And this was illustrated in another way, too. While father Joseph and brother Austen were inspiring the cartoonists with their characteristic Chamberlain clean-shaven, monocle-adorned faces, over orchid-bedecked lapels, Neville cultivated a mustache and was seen to portray W. S. Gilbert's "serious and solidy, jolly-bank-holiday, stick-and-a-pipe young man."

At Hoskins', to which Neville devoted most of his time (bicycling the two miles from Highbury every day), the gulf between small owner and skilled craftsmen was slight. Close to his men, Neville observed their problems first-hand, and his concern for social action and welfare work, already evident in his Andros days and something of a tradition among the Chamberlain family and Birmingham businessmen, grew. He instituted a compensation scheme for injured men and their dependents, began a pensions program, and early recognized trade union development among his employees. He became, in short, a social reformer with a deep sympathy for the working classes—something which he observed in his father that impressed him very much. Later in his career, when for a variety of reasons he came to be an object of dislike in Labor circles, it was charged that he never really understood the people whose lot he wished to improve. But this should not, if there is truth in it, obscure the fact of his constant and earnest advocacy of social reform in the interest of the workers.

Almost inevitably, given his position in business, his sense of social responsibility, and the opportunities which were his as by hereditary right, Neville was drawn into all kinds of public service. His activities ranged from a resumption of Sunday school work (an outlet for his Darwinism) to finding headquarters and ranges for the Birmingham units of Haldane's new Territorial Force. He was especially active in the Birmingham Chamber of Commerce, his work on the waterways commission, for example, taking him to the Board of Trade as leader of deputations promoting—unsuccessfully, as it turned out—canal construction in the Midlands region. His diary for 1904 makes reference to service on fourteen committees.[4] In all of this, two of his interests are especially noteworthy: Birmingham University and city hospitals.

It was largely through the initiative of Joseph Chamberlain, who became in 1900 its first Chancellor, that Birmingham University grew out of Mason College at the turn of the century. A member of its first Council, Neville was instrumental in canvassing funds and securing the necessary civic support, including an annual grant of tax money, for the institution. In so doing, he had a clear concept of what the University should be. It would not compete with the old and venerable institutions as a place of pure learning; rather, it would emphasize a commingling of applied learning with pure learning, and in this way provide a "wider field of usefulness." This was, no doubt, necessary to secure the support of practical-minded Birmingham businessmen. It also reflected Neville's own approach to knowledge which remained with him throughout his life: theory without application is useless.

The cause of the hospitals was especially close to Neville's heart, and his service in their behalf was long and earnest. Beginning as a regular visitor to the General Hospital, particularly in the casualty ward, about the time it occupied new buildings in Steelhouse Lane (1897), he later served on the board of management and became its chairman in 1906. He seems to have worked closely with staff members at all levels to improve its services, again showing the careful attention to detail which was so characteristic of him. His promotion of the Hospital Saturday Fund raised large sums of money for hospital improvement, some schemes for which he originated himself, partly as a result of an extensive tour of London hospitals. Nor were his efforts limited to the General Hospital. For a time he served the old General Dispensary, then handling 75,000 cases a year, as treasurer; built up a new, though short-lived, Birmingham and District Provident Dispensary; and presided over the Midlands Hospital Conference at the time the National Insurance Act, the general principles of which he supported, became law (1911).

Despite the demands of business and his deep involvement in public service, Neville found time for other kinds of activity. Noteworthy in view of his later Parliamentary career was his membership in the Birmingham and Edgbaston Debating Society. Here, engaging in fortnightly debate on a wide variety of subjects with other young men of his kind, he sharpened his ability to deliver a crushing retort (which he came to do almost as well as his father), and perhaps most important, learned to keep his temper. Though possibly insignificant, it is of passing interest that, during his presidency of the group and on his initiative, the society debated the view that "businessmen make better rulers than lawyers." He also traveled extensively during these years, visiting France (four times), Italy (thrice), Holland, Switzerland,

Algeria, Burma, and India. And he experienced his first serious love affair, which ended in disappointment—the journey to India (winter, 1904) helping him to recapture his "balance."

Meanwhile, Neville drew—or was drawn—closer and closer to politics, both on the local and national level. Though continuing to insist that he had no political ambition, his interests in Birmingham and the circumstances of his father's career and health led almost irresistibly to political involvement. His pursuit of public service brought him into increasing contact with the Birmingham city government and intensified his awareness that to "get things done" sometimes required political action. It was more than once suggested to him that he ought to try for the City Council. In the general election of 1900, he was active on behalf of Unionist candidates in the Midlands—in fact, so much so that the *Birmingham Daily Post* confidently announced that Neville himself intended to stand as a Unionist candidate at the next election. As his father's campaign for tariff reform, which led him to break with the Balfour Government in 1903, developed, Neville was used as an intermediary in the Birmingham region, and in this way became involved in torrid party debate. And after Joseph Chamberlain was incapacitated by a stroke in July, 1906, Neville was drawn still further into the thick of things, serving as a link between Birmingham and Austen in the shadow Cabinet, hotly debating issues in which his father's name was used as a banner, and in general—whether he wanted it that way or not— becoming a new, if somewhat dissonant voice in Liberal Unionist ranks. By 1912 he had advanced to the point of assuming the vice-chairmanship of a committee charged with re-stating the meaning of Unionism, the negative attitude toward Ireland alone no longer satisfying the younger generation. Perhaps all this was a consequence of family tradition, perhaps the result (as he himself said) of his "own incapacity to look on and see other people mismanage things." [5] Whatever the cause, the effect was the same: Neville was slowly edging his way into things political. His life and outlook were broadening much as his father's had done a generation before.

The year 1911 brought significant changes in Neville's private and public life alike: he married and entered the Birmingham city government. While there may be no direct connection between these two important events in his life, it did in time become apparent that the former would have considerable effect upon Neville's service in the latter.

For some years Neville's social life had been confined largely to the family clan, and while he does not seem to have made a special effort to develop it, the shell of bachelorhood had gradually formed around him. It is not surprising then that his marriage grew out of a family connection and a bit of conniving by his half-sister Beatrice. Although Neville had probably met Anne Vere Cole (the niece of Alfred Cole, who in 1907 had married the widow of Neville's uncle, Herbert Chamberlain) at his brother Austen's wedding a few years before, their courtship did not begin until mid-1910. It blossomed following a renewal of family acquaintances at Cannes and, several months later, a dinner and theater party in London, plotted by Beatrice, which brought Neville and Anne together. Thereafter, they saw each other frequently and were married in January, 1911, in the Church of St. Paul's, Knightsbridge, which was bedecked with orchids sent from Highbury for the occasion.

The daughter of a professional soldier, the late Major William Utting Cole (3rd Dragoon Guards), and his Irish wife, Mary de Vere, Anne Cole was quite different from Neville both in background and temperament.[6] Her racy manners and gay humor, which traditionally go with Irish blood, contrasted sharply with Neville's precise and earnest businessman's mien—and all the more so since she was still in her late twenties, while he was now aged forty-two. But family doubts, especially on Anne's side, never troubled the couple themselves, and after a honeymoon in Algeria and Tunisia, they set up their home at Westbourne in Edgbaston. There, in a solid house looking out over the fields to the University, their children Dorothy and Frank were born; indeed, Westbourne remained their Birmingham residence as long as Neville lived.

Assessing a wife's influence upon her husband seems often akin to astrology, and any attempt to measure Anne Chamberlain's influence in specific matters leads quickly onto shaky ground. But it is beyond question that her influence had both a public and a domestic facet. She was an energetic woman with an active mind who remained a close companion to her husband till the end of his life. Throughout his public career, Neville was quick to pay tribute to her for her part in his successes, both great and small. "She has guided me with her counsel; she has warned me off dangerous courses; she had never allowed me to forget the humanity that underlies all politics," he said of her at the height of his political career.[7] How many of his ideas originated with her none can say. But it is clear that theirs was a very happy marriage from which Neville drew peace and strength when the going in public life was rough. And her qualities were such as to lead Sir Charles Petrie to suggest (in 1938): "When the full story of Mr. Chamberlain's rise to power is written it will be surprising if one of his greatest assets does not prove to have been his wife." [8]

Neville's decision to stand for election to the Birmingham City Council had been taken sometime before his marriage. "I rather expect to go on the City Council next autumn," he wrote A. Greenwood on June 5, 1910, "for we have just got a provisional order . . . extending our boundaries so as to make us 'the second city in the Empire,' and if this is confirmed by Parliament I shouldn't like to be outside the administration." [9] His election, once he agreed to come forward as a candidate, was, as the *Birmingham Gazette* (Oct. 11, 1910) put it, "a foregone conclusion for he is extremely popular and his business capacity has already been proved in several directions."

What had persuaded Neville to change his mind and take a step which he had often rejected before? Clearly it was his interest in town planning and the opportunity provided by the proposed creation of a Greater Birmingham. A decade into the 20th century, this booming industrial city had greatly outgrown its effective 19th century municipal government and was splintered into borough councils, urban districts, rural districts, and county councils. Unity of government and administration in this situation was impossible, and the city was suffering extensively from the lack of centralized authority. Public services, for example, were not keeping pace with the city's growing needs, and their increasing deficiency was adversely affecting both the city's development and the citizens' temperament. This led to an official report (1909) recommending the incorporation of the various districts into the city; the initiation of legislation providing for the extension of the city's boundaries; a public inquiry by the Local Government Board (which pronounced in favor of the extension); and, despite some vigorous opposition in Parliament, especially from suburban interests represented there, the passage of the Greater Birmingham Bill in mid-1911.

Throughout the legislative process, Neville had indicated his support for the extension. He attracted considerable attention when, in 1910, he appeared as a witness before the Lords and Commons Committees considering the Greater Birmingham Bill. In voicing eloquently (for him) the absolute need for planning, especially in terms of his horror of slums, his use of statistical data and the simple clarity with which he presented it was unusually persuasive. Indeed, this incursion into public affairs marks another of the many "stages" of Chamberlain's career by which he was gradually casting off his political aversion and setting out on the road of responsibility which was so open to him.

The Greater Birmingham Bill signed into law, Neville came forth as a Liberal Unionist candidate for the All Saints' Ward of West Birmingham in the autumn of 1911. He won election handily as one of three councillors from the ward, and duly occupied his seat on the City Council. This, he insisted shortly thereafter, would certainly mark "the end of my public career." It was, however, only the beginning.

CHAPTER IV

In City Government

ONCE INVOLVED IN—AND FASCINATED BY—MUNICIPAL GOVERNMENT, Neville rose rapidly in positions of authority. Three years as councillor, during which he chaired active committees, were followed by a few months as alderman; and in the summer of 1915 he became, like his father and nine other of his kindred before him, Lord Mayor of Birmingham. In all these positions he was industrious and surprisingly (in view of later stereotypes of him) inventive, and while he inevitably accumulated his share of critics, Birmingham generally seemed pleased to have another Chamberlain showing the way.

It followed logically from the interest that had enticed Neville into city government that his first important activities on the enlarged Council should be as a member of the Town Planning and the Public Health and Housing Committees. That he sought membership on these particular committees might be taken as evidence of his lack of personal political ambition, for they were not regarded, at the time, as of first importance or as offering great political opportunity. Thus demonstrating a genuine public-spiritedness and a real desire to assist in bettering the lot of the workers, Neville also revealed a conviction that health, housing, and planning were but three aspects of a single problem.

The Town Planning Committee was new, although there was an established planning tradition in Birmingham. Opportunities were opened to it by the Town Planning Act of 1909, and under Neville's leadership—he was at once elected chairman—it gave a lead not simply to Birmingham but to the whole country. Refusing to be bound by a strict interpretation of the law, which allowed the development of schemes for unbuilt areas only, Neville and his committee prepared and eventually secured sanction for the first two schemes in the nation for town-planning in built-up areas. These schemes for Harborne and East Birmingham were quickly followed by similar schemes for a half-dozen other regions of the city—some of them very extensive, the plans for Yardley and Stechford, for example, creating or remodeling a hundred streets. Indeed, within a month of Neville's selection as chairman, the committee had resolved to prepare an outline town-plan for the entire city, thus envisaging a renewed and revitalized city center as well as planned suburban development. Birmingham planning provided a model for the nation, the Local Government Board holding up consideration of schemes from other cities until Birmingham's had been reviewed and approved. Coincidentally, the work involved in "selling" these plans to the city and initiating their implementation provided Neville with valuable political training.

Planning was, of course, more of a long-range than an immediate cure for the problem of intolerable housing in some parts of the city, and Neville was one whose inclination was to confront directly each problem at hand before jumping too far ahead to tackle some more distant issue. It was natural, then, for him to take special interest in, and to accept the chairmanship of, an *ad hoc* committee charged with investigating the housing conditions in the poorest sections of the city. Months of inquiry resulted in an interim report recommending: a push on property owners to put their dwellings in more habitable conditions, the corporation stepping in as a last resort if private enterprise failed; municipal ownership of housing estates; planned stages of reconstruction; and a new and separate housing committee to see that these and similar matters, once accepted by the Council, were pursued with vigor.[1] But the submission of this report coincided with the outbreak of war in 1914, and while accepted by the Council, it was laid aside for the duration of the conflict.

Meanwhile, Neville had gotten another taste of real political campaigning when, in 1913, his brother Austen stood for election to Parliament in West Birmingham, their father's old constituency which he was now too ill to retain. Speaking on his behalf, the city councillor sought to influence the minds of his listeners by the logic of his arguments; he did not play upon their emotions. In this he was very effective, and his established popularity was somewhat enviously noted by Austen:

Neville . . . was most warmly received. . . . I chaffingly told him that I was undergoing a new experience. Hitherto, I had been accustomed to be the biggest man in my constituency, but now I found that I was only his little brother. This is half chaff, but it also contains a real truth, for they know and like Neville in a way in which they can only come to know and like me when they have seen a great deal more of me.[2]

Elected alderman in November, 1914, Neville's elevation to the Lord Mayoralty occurred the following summer. His record in social work since joining the Council was certainly a mark in his favor, and, once again, his name was a distinct asset. But perhaps as important as anything in his selection was the restless energy and the business-like manner with which he pursued the work he took up. He was not one to shirk responsibility once he had assumed it, and even his staunchest opponents were prepared to admit that he worked hard and had a way of getting things done. Then, as later, Neville's intellectual integrity seemed to require that a conclusion be followed by positive action; he had little use for reflection divorced from achievement—a fact which, some years later, was a constant potential irritant in his relations with the more reflective Stanley Baldwin. As a councillor, his sheer attendance at Council and committee meetings must have numbered at least 125 sessions annually, and the number of reports and recommendations to which his name was affixed indicated that he met to do more than talk. His record as Lord Mayor did, in time, bear out his deep involvement in varied facets of the city's life. As an *ex officio* member of every committee of the Corporation, he made a habit of attending meetings, and—foreshadowing his performance as prime minister years later—he was intimately associated with almost every aspect of municipal work being carried out under his titular leadership.

It was Neville's ambition as Lord Mayor to pursue "that noble and fascinating ideal, the transference of the working classes from their hideous and depressing surroundings to cleaner, brighter and more wholesome dwellings in the still uncontaminated country which lay within our boundaries." [3] But a wartime mayoralty made achievement of that goal impossible, a fact which undoubtedly contributed to Neville's already keen sense of the futility of war. "Among the many crimes which lay heavy on the head of the German emperor and his advisers," he told the Council, "not the least was that by their wicked ambitions they had stayed the march of progress and had set back for an indefinite period reforms that might have bettered the lot of generations to come." [4]

The war suspended normal life in Birmingham and set the tone of Neville's mayoralty. Much of his work bore direct relationship to the war effort: recruiting and entertaining forces, heading the tribunal for military exemptions, mediating labor disputes which threatened war production, developing schemes for air-raid protection, organizing hospital work and the City Recreation League (to lighten the dreary lives of war workers), curbing liquor consumption in munitions and transport areas, exploring measures (like the municipal distribution of milk) to insure child welfare, and so on and on. In several of these areas his approach was advanced and original, such as his proposal that war pensions be paid from taxation and his scheme for air-raid protection, submitted to the Home Secretary early in 1916, which included almost all of those elements (a zone of observation, preliminary warning, etc.) later deemed essential to air-raid precaution.

There were, of course, other accomplishments connected less directly with the war. Some of them were not unusual; others were indeed unique. His interest in the city's schools, art gallery, and zoo led to modest improvements in each at a time when these concerns did not have high priority. His interest in music, perhaps the "strongest passion of his inner life," [5] led to the formation of a municipal orchestra supported by an annual grant from tax resources. Introducing the idea at a town hall concert in March, 1916, Neville promoted the project to its successful culmination three years later. And this was only the beginning as he saw it; he hoped for a new school of music, an opera house, an orchestra and glee societies for every club and every big works in the city. The city's purchase and operation, in the interest of efficient and economical transportation, of the local motor bus company was largely Neville's doing. Socialistic, some charged; but he cared little, if the new arrangement proved sound.

Undoubtedly among the most outstanding of Neville's accomplishments was the establishment of the Birmingham Municipal Savings Bank. By mid-1915, the British people were being urged to subscribe to the successful prosecution of the war, but a major obstacle lay in the collection of small contributions. Why not, Neville proposed, establish a municipal bank which would both facilitate the investment of small savings in securities issued for the purposes of the war and provide a reserve for the contributors against any bad times which might follow the war? The City Council was easily persuaded, but convincing the Treasury, which saw the proposal as bringing the city into competition with the Exchequer, was a different matter. It was only after an extended series of meetings with the Savings Advisory Committee and Treasury officials, an open press campaign, and a wearing effort at converting Labor leaders (suspicious of any measure that would reveal to employers that workingmen were earning enough actually to save) that the idea progressed to the point of legislation. A bill allowing local authorities to set up municipal banks was introduced in Parliament in mid-1916. But it faltered in the face of stiff opposition from joint stock banks. At once—reacting in a way already characteristic of him—Neville went directly into the enemy's camp, consulted (among others) with Sir Edward Holden, Chairman of the London City and Midland Bank, and Vassar Smith, Chairman of Lloyds, and persuaded them to modify their opposition. A new bill, hedged with reservations (including the limitation of these banks to cities of 250,000 or more), then passed, and the Birmingham Municipal Bank was duly established. Neville's success was especially important in showing the logic and tenacity with which he performed the tasks he set himself, and in demonstrating to many that a stern representative of the capitalist order—as less generous political observers were wont sometimes to picture him—dared to rebel against the spokesmen of big business when this was demanded by public interest.

Nor did the matter end there, for one of the restrictions was that banks established under this act should be closed within three months after the end of the war. Again Neville went to work and was instrumental in securing passage of another bill in 1919 which permitted Birmingham to retain its bank without the hampering restrictions of the earlier act. Meanwhile, the bank had flourished. Although it had started slowly, Neville stimulated the flow of depositors by announcing that those whose names had been on the books a specified time would be eligible for a bonus at the end of the war. The charge of "lottery" was raised, but he responded with the argument that it was a lottery in which nobody lost. And his confidence in the institution did not prove vain. A decade after its founding, it had thirty-five branches throughout the city and a capital of more than seven million pounds. Another decade saw its deposits mount to more than twenty-five million pounds. By then occupying a monumental building, it stood as a unique institution in England, the only municipal bank in the nation.

Although re-elected Lord Mayor in November, 1916, Neville's service in the office ended abruptly a month later when he was suddenly summoned by the Prime Minister to a new post in London which had grown out of the exigencies of war. His mayoralty had lasted just a year and a half, but those months were important ones in his career. He had made a successful debut in politics and seemed to take increasing pleasure in the rough and tumble of political life. Some of the issues with which he had dealt had national as well as local implications; as a result, his own field of vision was broadened and his name became known, in modest ways to be sure, beyond Birmingham.

His general outlook had been further refined, too. Always a social reformer of sorts, he had now advanced to the point where everything seemed to turn on social improvement. Essentially a Radical, like his father, he had developed a kind of utilitarian-socialist approach in his apparent assumption that municipal power must (and always would) be used for "good purposes," such as abolishing slums and building decent homes. He spoke of state socialism (a revolution in the making); discussed capital-labor relations widely; and turned increasingly to the idea of a partnership between masters and men, arguing that, while employers should expect from their men hard work and stable wage conditions, workers should receive a greater share of the wealth produced and a greater voice in the functions of management.[6] "He should have been a Labor man," it was remarked in City Council; and a few years later (1923) Neville did describe himself as a socialist. At the same time, Neville was developing a kind of urban mind. Though some would deny that his vision was parochial, it is nevertheless true that his grasp of the nation's social problems was based almost exclusively on his observations and experiences in Birmingham, so that, in a sense, he came to view all England as a series of Birminghams. This would appear later to trouble his relations with men of other backgrounds and viewpoints.

It may long be argued—and always inconclusively, of course—whether Neville would have emerged as he did had he not come from a rich and powerful family. His abilities were long latent, and even once he had made a mark in Birmingham government, some continued to see him as no more than a "gas and water politician"—an official of small town stature. In all his positions in city government he proved himself a diligent worker and competent administrator; but few had yet perceived in him the makings of a statesman of national stature. Neville was, in short, at age 47, chief citizen of Birmingham and little more.

CHAPTER V

On to London

A CONFERENCE ON MUNICIPAL BORROWING TOOK NEVILLE TO LON-
don in mid-December, 1916. His business completed, he was
boarding a train for Birmingham (December 19) when a messen-
ger from Downing Street summoned him to a meeting with the
Prime Minister. Lloyd George had replaced Herbert Asquith
only a few weeks before, and, anxious to solve a long-developing
manpower problem, had created a new Department of National
Service. Neville was offered the directorship and given ten minutes in which to decide: the Prime Minister wished to announce
the appointment to the House of Commons that evening. "I said
several damns and thought for 2 minutes," Neville wrote a few
days later;[1] then he answered yes.

Suddenly and without forethought Neville had taken a long
jump into the unknown. He knew little personally of the Prime
Minister, and Lloyd George knew just as little of him—except
that he had made a reputation as mayor of Birmingham. (Neville's name had been suggested by Curzon and Milner, at the
prompting of his brother Austen, now Secretary of State for
India, after the Prime Minister's first choice, Edwin Montagu,
had declined the position.) Still worse, perhaps, he knew little of
the office, the nature, authority, and organization of which was
still vague and ill-defined—indeed so much so that some would
later say the whole thing had all the appearances of a whim. But
to refuse public office in time of war is difficult, and Neville was
not the man to do so. Though somewhat dismayed at the thought
of leaving his Birmingham work half-finished, he accepted the
new post with confident assurance: "The outcome of the war may
depend on what I do." [2]

The advent of 1917, then, found Neville in London (his Department was housed at St. Ermin's Hotel) as Director of National Service. He occupied the post for seven months, and his
entire experience was frustrating and bitter. This was due to a
combination of factors revolving around the general circum-

stances in which he labored, the nature of his assignment, and, to a lesser extent, the way in which he approached it.

As Lloyd George explained it to the House of Commons, Neville was "to be in charge of both the military and civil side of universal national service." [3] But that phraseology was deceivingly simple. Up to the end of 1916, the handling of the manpower problem was probably the worst British administrative failure of the war. Various departments (with the Home Office, Board of Trade, Labor Exchanges, War Office, and Admiralty all operating more or less independently) jostled with recruiting officers and a wide range of tribunals for the men available, while cautious politicians, fearful of internal repercussions, stopped short of any measure which might have brought order out of chaos. Indeed, it was this situation which the Department of National Service was supposed to remedy. But the groundwork was weak, and it became quickly apparent that a real definition of the Department's responsibilities would emerge, if at all, only as it pursued its work. Neville began, as he wrote at the time, without "even a scrap of paper appointing me or giving me any idea where my duties begin and end." [4] And a series of interviews with the Prime Minister did not seem to clarify matters much. Such a situation was rich with pitfalls.

There were other problems, too. The new Department was not immediately welcome in the Whitehall family circle, and perhaps not unnaturally, Neville encountered an unsympathetic response from some other ministries. This was especially apparent in his unsuccessful search for qualified civil servants for his staff. Furthermore, it had no seat in the Cabinet and no effective link with Government policy. The director did not sit in Parliament, and the Commons was ill-disposed to sweeping changes in manpower matters when the man who proposed them, and would carry them through, was not answerable to the House. Nor was its basic function settled. By mid-January, the Cabinet had reversed its original plan for the Department to control military recruiting. Yet in the face of all this, the Prime Minister insisted on extensive publicity, expected almost immediate results, and fretted openly when results were not quickly forthcoming.

Most of these problems were not of Neville's making and quite beyond his power to control. Yet he did, in certain ways, contribute to his own difficulties. Failing to secure experienced assistants from other ministries, he developed a staff nucleus composed largely of Birmingham acquaintances. Tactically questionable, this also restricted the Department's vision, for the experience of most of these men was limited to local government. He was disinclined to protest—at least with sufficient vigor—when other departments continued to cut in on responsibilities which appeared to be rightly his. And perhaps most important, he half-awaited a lead from Lloyd George when the Prime Minister, busy beyond capacity with other things, expected a lead from him. All this might be explained in terms of Neville's relative ignorance of the ways of Whitehall, or the inevitable confusion of times of crisis, but the end result was still the same: Neville's first effort in national government got off to a very poor start.

Nevertheless, by early February the Department brought forth a fairly elaborate scheme for combing out volunteers from nonessential occupations to replace men withdrawn from key industries for military duty. Neville traveled to provincial cities to publicize the scheme, and, according to newspaper accounts, was everywhere well-received. He conferred with Members of Parliament and a host of national organization leaders headquartered in London, seeking their cooperation and support. But as weeks passed nothing seemed to change. Publicity for the program may have had certain shortcomings: its posters depicted a pair of hands which appeared to belong to an old man long past productive manual work. More significantly, the voluntary aspect of the scheme retarded its effectiveness and brought Neville in for considerable criticism in the Northcliffe press. Neville, it appears, would gladly have substituted compulsion. In mid-January he had pressed unsuccessfully—he was balked, in deed if not in word, by the War Cabinet—for a cancellation of exemptions from military service, and was apparently prepared to extend the compulsory principle to the industrial area. But this was still unacceptable to the Cabinet, rung round as it was by various pledges earlier extended. So the voluntary principle remained.

In mid-March a dispute with the Ministry of Labor over jurisdictional matters was settled in Whitehall in favor of Labor. Constantly hamstrung in this way, Neville began to recognize impending failure. In June he was still "fighting and scrapping" (his words) with other departments in the hope of acquiring the powers that he felt should have been his at first. Meanwhile, his relations with the Prime Minister, never good, had further declined, especially after Lloyd George changed the Parliamentary Secretary of the Department without saying a word to Neville, and began to listen regularly to his critics without once hearing his side of the story. Although he stayed on until August 8, he was, for some weeks, only awaiting an appropriate time to resign.

An explanation for Neville's failure as Director of National Service may never be agreed upon. His resignation letter charged that he had lacked support. Lloyd George denied it. The nature of the assignment itself is involved. John Dillon, the M.P. for East Mayo, told the Commons on February 27: "If Mr. Chamberlain were an archangel, or if he were Hindenburg and Bismarck, and all the great men of the world rolled into one, his task would be wholly beyond his powers." [5] And this view was shared by many others, including Bonar Law, who became prime minister a few years later. Lloyd George, on the other hand, was more inclined to explain it in terms of the man: "A good municipal executive, perhaps, with sound expert knowledge, but not born for anything higher, possessing neither initiative, power nor imagination." [6] Doubtless there were valid arguments on both sides. Neville's replacement did experience greater success, but in vastly changed circumstances and with markedly increased powers.

Whatever the judgment on this matter, one thing is clear: the effect of the whole experience on Neville. It goes far to explain his enduring estrangement from Lloyd George. There is no doubt, as one writer puts it—and there is wide concurrence with this view—that "the unfairness [as Neville saw it] of the treatment meted out to him by Lloyd George and by the scores of Government officers who deliberately obstructed him burned deeply into his *amour propre*. Men of such single-mindedness and with such a stern personal code as Mr. Chamberlain usually find it hard to forgive in others what they would not forgive in themselves." [7] Neville held "Ll. G., if anyone . . . personally responsible for my misfortunes." [8] In a related sense, this experience helps to explain Neville's gradual turn from a mild Liberal Unionist into a determined Conservative partisan. And most significantly, it appears to have been basic to his decision to stand for Parliament. Not only did he now recognize more keenly than before the difficulties of carrying on administration without being in the House, but he realized anew that to "get things done" there is a distinct advantage in being at the center of things. He may have felt the urge to rehabilitate himself in the public esteem, but it was also the Chamberlain instinct to fight again. And if he needed encouragement to do so, he got it not only from his wife, but also from his sisters Ida and Hilda, who made clear their conviction that Parliament was the "next step" for him.

It is, of course, impossible to construct with assurance the probabilities of Neville's career had his experience as Director of National Service, and especially his relationship with Lloyd George, been different. But it is tempting to think that the sting of failure both inspired him to further effort and precluded his risking in the political struggles of the Coalition Government all chance of attaining a position of leadership later on.

Following his resignation as Director of National Service, Neville turned again to Birmingham affairs. He resumed his work at Hoskins' and Elliott's and rejoined the board at Birmingham Small Arms. He reappeared on the City Council and became deputy mayor—though he resisted the suggestion that he might become Lord Mayor again. He resumed his activity on behalf of a wide range of municipal projects. But there was never any doubt that this would be temporary, if he had his way, for he had already (so he wrote his sister Hilda on August 27) "really and truly . . . made up [his] mind to go into the House. . . ." [9] His political sensitivity aroused, he was not interested merely in settling down to "make money." However, as no Birmingham Unionist M. P. was inclined to retire at once to make room for him, he had no choice but to wait for the next general election.

These months were difficult ones for Neville. He experienced "nausea and revulsion" (his words) over his recent failure, and the darkening war scene did not provide relief. There were periods of depression. "My career is broken," he wrote in his diary in December. "How can a man of nearly 50 entering the House with this stigma upon him, hope to achieve anything?" [10] He was thoroughly shaken by the loss in battle of his cousin Norman, who, while fifteen years his junior, had been a close associate in Birmingham government, his most intimate friend, and a promising Chamberlain standardbearer of the future. Mrs. Chamberlain was seriously ill in the spring of 1918, the children were several times afflicted with childhood diseases, and Neville himself suffered from gout and sciatica.

Never one to waste away in fretting, however, Neville utilized his time pursuing efforts for improving public health and housing, extending workers' benefits, and promoting cooperation between masters and men in industry. Likewise, encouragement of the Municipal Bank, support for a variety of recreation programs (including the Street Boys' Union and the Civic Recreation League), and the establishment at Birmingham University of a course of general education—designed especially to appeal to the workingman—commanded his attention.

There were political activities, too. Agreement was reached in January, 1918, that, at the next general election, Neville should replace the retiring Sir Edward Parkes as Unionist candidate for Central Birmingham. Thereafter, local political organization, eroded by the years of war and political truce, claimed some of his time. And this took on enhanced importance when the Reform Act of 1918 increased the number of Birmingham constituencies from seven to twelve and, by giving the vote to all men of twenty-one and all women over thirty, more than quadrupled the city's electorate. Neville took the lead in reviving the fusion of Conservative and Liberal Unionists which he had initiated in 1914 and, as chairman of the fused Management Committee, accomplished a centralization of organization and finance. As a result, the real direction of Unionist politics in Birmingham came to rest in his hands.

During this time he flirted with the British Workers' League, which to him embodied the true feelings of the Labor movement. Nothing lasting came of this—although one Labor candidate (Eldred Hallas) in Birmingham did receive Unionist endorsement in the election of 1918 and another (Victor Fisher) benefited from Neville's personal support. But it is indicative of the radical thrust in Neville's outlook which was consistent with his earlier views and interests and set him somewhat apart from his more orthodox party colleagues. The same point can be illustrated by his support, in private at least, of federalism as the solution to the Irish problem, even though it might (as he saw it) destroy the Unionist Party. He could not, as he wrote his wife, agree with "the old fogies who can't get away from the old habit of regarding the party as an end in itself, instead of an instrument for attaining ends of national importance." [11]

The long-awaited general election followed by one month the armistice ending the World War. Neville stood in the new constituency of Ladywood, created (as a result of the 1918 reform bill) from parts of the old Central division and West Birmingham, his father's old seat. Comprised of 33,000 electors living primarily in poor areas, the district had benefited from municipal reforms which Neville had earlier espoused. This probably affected the vote, especially since Neville emphasized in his short campaign ample pensions, minimum wages, increased funds for health and welfare, state-supported housing, and other measures of primary interest to workingmen. Equally decisive, perhaps, was his name and reputation and the weakness of his Labor opponent. Although a Labor candidate might have been expected to do well in such a constituency, J. W. Kneeshaw was a pacifist and did not have the endorsement of established Labor men. A third candidate, Mrs. Corbett Ashby, ran on a free-trade ticket which had limited appeal. Neville was duly elected in a very small poll, receiving 9,405 of the 13,529 votes cast. Interestingly, he had received—although he did not use—the famous "coupon" support of Lloyd George and Bonar Law.[12]

Neville was now in his fiftieth year. No other man who became prime minister entered Parliament so late.

CHAPTER VI

Westminster (1919–1924)

THE COALITION PARLIAMENT WHOSE TASK IT WAS TO RESTORE normalcy to the war-exhausted nation and advance toward the new order foretold by wartime rhetoricians convened at Westminster in early February, 1919. Neville was one of 526 members (nearly 400 of them Unionists) who sat behind Lloyd George. In such an array, a new back-bencher might easily have been lost, but Neville never really fit that term as it is normally used. He was an ex-minister with extensive experience in certain aspects of government, and his half-brother Austen was the new Chancellor of the Exchequer. Neither of these facts was an unmixed blessing, for it was possible that his record of 1917 would be held against him and that he would—as indeed he did—differ with his brother on some crucial issues. But they nonetheless, along with his name and his proven capacity for work, set him apart from the beginning.

Delivering his maiden speech on March 12 in support of a rent restrictions amendment, he addressed the Commons on three more occasions, and spoke often in standing committees, during his first six-month session. By his own estimate he "made no sensation," but at the same time judged his contributions well-received. Although direct and lucid in thought and delivery, Neville was not—nor did he ever become—an orator. Yet this did not seem to hurt him much, for as one English historian of the period has put it: "The problems before the country were too serious to serve as catchwords for demagogues; they required treating in a businesslike manner, and here was a man who so regarded them." [1]

Neville made his early mark, at first a modest one, in committee work. Experienced and knowledgeable, not inclined to shy away from the "drudgery of spadework," he was in considerable demand as a committeeman. Some of his assignments reflected his interest in and general sympathy with the social objectives of the Coalition Government. He early became chairman of the Unhealthy Areas Committee, set up by the Ministry of Health, whose task it was to "consider the principles that should be adopted in the clearance of slum areas." He headed a departmental Committee on Canals and Waterways, sat on the Health Advisory Committee, the Colonial Development Committee, the Committee on Licensing, and others—and this in addition to the ordinary committee work associated with specific bills before the Commons. He came to feel himself "the handyman of the House as far as Committees are concerned," and at length (December, 1920) recorded in his diary: "My committees have occupied all my mornings, many afternoons, and frequently part of my nights (in preparation), with the result that I have been able to put in but little time in the House." [2] Committee work is sometimes used by the government in power as a way to contain the energies of those who might otherwise bring inconvenient pressures to bear upon it, with the results produced being less important than the committee's steady activity. Some of the committees on which Neville served were undoubtedly of this kind. But he seems seldom to have viewed his work in this way.

Departmental committees did not, of course, occupy all of Neville's time. Elected to the Unionist committee on reconstruction—which became the accepted forum of back-bench opinion—he was one of a small deputation which, in October, 1919, called Lloyd George to task for his long absences from the House and his well-developed habit of making extra-Parliamentary pronouncements on major policy issues. From this Neville must have derived a certain personal satisfaction. Named vice-chairman of the committee a few months later (he was denied the chairmanship largely because of his junior status), he assumed actual leadership of the group in the absence of an effective chairman. The range of his legislative interests is attested by his ardent labor for the defeat of an Alien Restrictions Bill, his vigorous opposition to the control of electricity by the Ministry of Transport, his efforts in organizing opposition to an anti-dumping bill, and his introduction of a Bastardy Bill (changed later to "Children of Unmarried Persons Bill") designed to provide some protection for the children of unmarried mothers.

To the ills which beset postwar Britain, Neville was prepared to apply radical remedies. He favored the expenditure of vast national funds to construct housing (the individual then to be given every opportunity to buy), and his committee on slums produced a recommendation to empower local authorities to acquire, for purpose of improvement, slum areas at little more than site value compensation to the owners. State ownership of canals seemed to him the best way to waterway improvement—although his committee was for some time limited to an experiment establishing a public trust for the waterways of Trent. Pleased with the miners' considerable victory in the coal strike of 1919, he inclined toward some state control of minerals, with workmen having a voice in the direction of the industry and sharing the profits. He was prepared to suspend tariffs temporarily, to limit profits, and to publish trading accounts. This is not to say that Neville possessed the fiery radicalism characteristic of his father, but neither was he a staid exponent of conservative reaction. He might best be described as "a democrat of the mild bourgeois order," alert to the fact that major problems sometimes require unorthodox solutions. And as the Coalition Government, forced by its very nature everywhere to compromise, became increasingly stalled by matters of pressing national concern, Neville's support for the coalition arrangement, never more than lukewarm, deteriorated.

Once during the life of the postwar coalition Neville received a guarded feeler about joining the Government. In March, 1920, Bonar Law approached him about an Under-Secretaryship, possibly in Health, and indicated that Lloyd George would be glad to have him. Neville declined: "I should be miserable with my head under the Goat's arm again, and am not so enamoured of office that I would sell my peace of mind for it." [3] The sting of 1917 still hurt. A later suggestion by several ministers that Neville might do well as Irish Secretary supposedly met with the Prime Minister's "Oh, I don't like that fellow," and that was that.[4]

While Neville became engrossed in Parliamentary affairs, Birmingham and business were not completely forgotten. Like his father before him, he kept in close touch with municipal matters at home. When in Birmingham, he was constantly occupied with a wide range of activities: visiting constituents, reorganizing party finances, raising money for the university, soothing staff friction at Birmingham Small Arms, discussing amalgamation at Hoskins', and promoting his three major mayoralty ideas (the bank, orchestra, and civic recreation). Somehow, he also found time to serve as chairman of the Chamber of Commerce and to seek diversion from all his other activities in gardening (he was at this moment especially intrigued by azaleas and, as always, orchids) and fishing in the company of his close friend Arthur Wood. Little wonder that he then observed that "life is really not long enough to follow up more than 5 or 6 interests properly." [5]

Thus for a few years Neville was a very active participant in two worlds, Westminster and Birmingham. His interests were that broad. Quickly caught up in national politics, still he found municipal life too much a part of his past to be abandoned lightly. Besides, who could tell which way his fortunes would go? By the end of his first six-month session he was sufficiently sure of his future in Parliament to resign his aldermanic seat in Birmingham. But two years later he still had his doubts about a Parliamentary career, sometimes wishing—especially when circumstances made him feel it a "great handicap to be the son of my father and the brother of my brother"—he were out of the House altogether, yet skeptical whether he would be satisfied if he were. He deliberately postponed buying a home in London, and not until 1922 did he join the Carlton Club, for decades the exclusive organization of Conservative M.P.s. The latter decision was also affected, of course, by the political situation, since none could tell what would become of the party as the Coalition Government encountered increasingly heavy seas.

The year 1922 brought to a close the era of Lloyd George and the Coalition. In the complex political maneuvering which preceded and accompanied that turn of events, Neville played no real part. His dislike of the Prime Minister—a carefully timed holiday which took him away from Birmingham when Lloyd George visited the city to receive honors in 1921 punctuated the fact that their relationship had not mellowed—and his growing disenchantment with the coalition arrangement, in which the tendency to coalesce was much greater at the top than in the lower echelons of party organization, might naturally have led him to join one of the several groups of Unionists (once more beginning to call themselves Conservatives) clamoring against the Coalition. But his loyalty to Austen, who had succeeded to leadership of the House and party, and his conviction that the Labor leaders lacked substance and must not, therefore, be given an opportunity to slip into power, kept him among the public supporters of the Coalition.

During two great times of crisis in the last year of the Coalition, Neville was absent from the country, and thus not involved in the complicated in-fighting. The autumn of 1921, when the Irish question reached the point of explosion, found him visiting Sicily and Rome. In October, 1922, when Lloyd George and Austen decided at length to confront the long-developing party dissidence head-on (in the famous October 19 meeting at the Carlton Club, where the Conservative dissidents carried by a vote of 187 to 87 a motion to fight a general election as a free, independent party, thus killing the Coalition and forcing the resignation of Lloyd George), Neville was in Canada, undertaking an arduous but pleasant tour, busy with public and private talks alike, in which he especially enjoyed the response that his father's memory evoked. Though only a lukewarm Coalitionist, he was "astonished" at what had occurred, and Austen's cabled message that "Arthur was better"—a code term signifying dissolution—sent him sailing for home almost at once.

Surprised, but hardly disappointed (except for Austen's sake) with what had happened, Neville experienced no great difficulty in determining his own attitude. He could not imagine leaving the Unionist Party for Lloyd George; indeed, if Austen were out of the question, he would not hesitate to join the new government, if asked.

A time for decision on the latter point was, in fact, near at hand. Neville had barely arrived in Birmingham when, on October 30, L. S. Amery carried to him from Bonar Law, who had led the dissidents against Lloyd George and assumed responsibility for forming a new government upon the latter's resignation, an invitation to take the office of Postmaster-General. Immediate consultation with Austen revealed that his brother took the idea badly; after all, Bonar Law stood in the way of his becoming prime minister. Neville thought that he could serve well as a link between Austen and Bonar Law, but Austen was unmoved by that. At length, Neville offered to decline the post; their personal relations were more important than politics. But this, he observed, would probably mark the end of his political career, for one could not go on refusing office when he did not differ in principles from the prime minister. That was too much for Austen, who thereupon changed his attitude in favor of his brother's view.[6] But the wound was painful—and it is questionable whether it ever healed completely. Subsequently, Neville took the post in Bonar Law's ministry.

The fall of the Coalition and the ensuing general election brought to an end the first Parliament in which Neville sat. Generally acknowledged to have been less satisfactory than many, in part because the self-sacrifice of the war years was followed by a relapse into party factionalism, it was nonetheless significant in Neville's career. He had certainly not emerged spectacularly, but he had begun to make his way in national politics. Always a keen observer of events around him, Neville learned much about practical politics from four years of close-hand observation of the workings of the Coalition Government. And he developed friendships with a number of men who were closely associated with him in later years, including Edward Wood (later Lord Halifax) and Samuel Hoare.

That there was an element of chance—or at least "special circumstance"—in Neville's elevation to the Postmaster-Generalship is altogether clear. When the Coalition broke up, most of the Conservative members of Lloyd George's Cabinet followed Austen Chamberlain in his attitude of watchful waiting. Bonar Law had to turn to new men, and there was a dearth of talent from which to choose. Furthermore, he especially needed mature personalities who had stayed in the background during the Coalition period, and Neville fit the description exactly. His record of opposition to Lloyd George, a personal rather than a political matter, was now a distinct advantage. It is not likely that, in other circumstances, Neville would have vanished into oblivion, but because of the circumstances which prevailed, he stood out as a potential minister more than he otherwise might have done. It would be easy to draw unwarranted conclusions from such an observation, but it is noteworthy that Neville rose to the front bench in less than five years, something which Lloyd George, Winston Churchill, and Stanley Baldwin—all men of proven ability—could only accomplish in 18, 18, and 14 years respectively.

Neville's satisfaction with the prospect of assuming office must have been shaken momentarily by the fact that, in the general election, his majority in Ladywood (a constituency described as "desperately poor" and teeming with unemployment) was drastically reduced (to 2,443) by a vigorous Labor candidate. But convinced that a weaker candidate would have lost the seat altogether, he concentrated thereafter on a reorganization of his electoral machine.

The first post which Neville held under Bonar Law left him outside the Cabinet, but he was frequently consulted on broader matters having no connection with the Post Office. A potentially formidable colleague for the new Prime Minister, he was also a point of contact with Austen and his followers, a possible second-hand source for Austen's views on foreign affairs, and a knowledgeable adviser on housing, one of the most pressing domestic problems of the time. Indeed, Neville was too valuable to be tucked away in the "comfortable obscurity" (his own term) of the Post Office, and he had barely settled into the job when he emerged as a prime candidate for another post.

Late in January, 1923, Bonar Law told Neville that the vacant Ministry of Health ought to go to him. (Griffith-Boscawen, who held the position, had lost his seat and could not secure another.) Yet this was the only Cabinet vacancy, and the Prime Minister hoped to use it to bring back one of the dissident leaders. While efforts were made to woo Sir Robert Horne, the least critical of the dissidents, into the post, Neville was granted, as a kind of consolation perhaps, the sinecure office of Paymaster General. Then when the efforts to win Horne failed, the Prime Minister turned to Neville. He accepted—but only on his own terms: that he have a free hand over housing, particularly in the matter of rent restriction. Neville thus entered the Cabinet (mid-March, 1923) in an office for which experience and personal interest eminently fitted him.

The Ministry of Health, unlike the Post Office, involved no comfortable obscurity. The problem of housing spawned in part by the war (demobilized soldiers looking to settle down, the deterioration of buildings, the rise in standards of comfort demanded by the younger generation, and so on) still remained acute, and Neville inherited a chaos of rent and housing measures which begged for a semblance of order. To make matters worse, the Cabinet was thoroughly divided on alternative solutions, and the party, shaken by public reaction to Griffith-Boscawen's rent de-restriction idea (as indicated in his loss of a "safe" Conservative seat at Mitcham) was seemingly bent on no action at all. But Neville confronted the issues head-on, and produced in time two bills which, while inevitably compromises, offered some relief in this troublesome area.

His Housing Bill, introduced in late April, aimed to accelerate the construction of houses by offering to both private builders, who should have priority, and local authorities who could submit acceptable plans a subsidy of £6 per house per year (a substantial amount at the time) for twenty years, on houses completed before October, 1925. In subsidiary clauses the government assumed half the cost of slum clearance, extended the power of local authorities to lend money to individuals for house purchase, and supported the work of building societies. For his part, Neville would have been content to see the main burden of construction taken up by the municipalities, but "crusted old Tory" opposition in the Cabinet accounted for the priority provision for private enterprise.

The size of the houses to be subsidized—the bill emphasized the construction of "non-parlor" homes, largely on the assumption that private enterprise would be unwilling to undertake the building of any other type for the working class—drew the most criticism in Parliamentary debate. As sometimes happens, the significant points of debate became engulfed in absurdities, such as what constitutes a parlor or, still worse, who called Sidney Webb "Nannygoat" when he tried to interrupt another speaker. But the bill emerged at length essentially unchanged. It had limitations and was in no sense a cure-all; that was openly acknowledged by Neville. But a stroll through thick underbrush seemed to necessitate the taking of but one step at a time. The Act proved helpful at the very least: within two years schemes for nearly 200,000 houses were approved, a significant figure despite the fact that actual completions ran somewhat under the schemes approved.

Stickier still was the closely related matter of rent restriction. While the Opposition held that new houses must precede any increase in rents, private capital was disinclined to build without increased rents to meet increased construction costs. Neville's second bill, which emerged in June after much Cabinet controversy, provided for a two-year extension of the existing controls, to be followed by a five-year period of decontrol, during which the courts, along with so-called Reference Committees, would safeguard the balance between landlord and tenant. The provision that the court could reduce the rent (with no limits set) on any house not in a reasonable state of repair was barely acceptable in Conservative circles, but the bill nonetheless made it onto the Statute Book by summer recess. Thus Neville's first legislative efforts in the Ministry of Health were successful ones, and the details of his bills, as well as his skill—though not necessarily tact —in persuading his Cabinet colleagues and piloting two such controversial measures through the Commons added to his political stature. At the same time, the drawn-out harangues in Parliament on matters which Neville considered trivial or lacking in good faith, as well as the Labor Party's unrealistic (as he saw it) preoccupation with certain socialist ideas, whether they were practical or not, contributed to the development of negative attitudes toward both which would reappear later in his career.

Meanwhile, Bonar Law had experienced such a physical decline that his return from a forced April holiday was followed almost immediately by his resignation. He was succeeded as prime minister by Stanley Baldwin. In that particular turn of events Neville played no direct role. Although he personally leaned toward Curzon, if there were no chance of Austen's elevation (and there was none), Neville had no reason to regret Baldwin's succession. Confirmed at once as Minister of Health, he got on well with Baldwin, who was in some respects a great deal like him. Both were "bred for business," were in business until middle age, and approached politics as a business-like adventure. Both owed much to transparent honesty, perhaps even simplicity, and saw solutions to the nation's problems in a calm, sensible application of reason through negotiation and conciliation, as a businessman was apt to understand it. Though Baldwin was more graceful, Neville more severe, there was still a close compatibility between them, and Neville had good reason to look toward his future in the Government with confidence. As one consequence of this, he began, in August, 1923, to settle into a permanent home at 37 Eaton Square.

But there was to be no public or personal settling of accounts. Baldwin's succession seemed an opportune time to attempt a reunion with the dissident wing of the party, and a limited reshuffling of Cabinet posts was designed to facilitate this by bringing several members of that group, including Austen, into the Government. Baldwin's approach to Austen, however—made without the use of Neville's services—was clumsy, alienating both the ex-ministers and some of the current Cabinet, so efforts at reunion at that point came to naught. When the conversations ceased, Baldwin was still without a Chancellor of the Exchequer. For a time he tried to carry the load himself, but at length (mid-August) decided that Neville was the man for the post.

The Commons having risen several weeks before, Neville was fishing in Scotland when he received the Prime Minister's summons to the Exchequer. He declined: he had no experience in finance and would be "a fish out of water." But when Baldwin promptly pressed for reconsideration—which Neville indeed expected—he returned to London, talked with Baldwin, and accepted the post. In their interview Neville's objections were aired and other alternatives were considered. But Baldwin brushed these aside and broke him down with well-intentioned flattery: he needed a reliable colleague in Downing Street with whom he could consult readily and confidently, and Neville was his choice. Once more Neville assumed a post proffered him only after others had refused, and any misgivings he may have felt were drowned by calm self-assurance, his willingness to try, and the knowledge that other party "names" approved the appointment. Yet he did acknowledge that his appointment reflected "a certain weakness in the Government" since the Prime Minister felt so strongly that there was no other choice open to him.

Following a rest at Harrogate, Neville moved from Eaton

Square to 11 Downing Street during the first days of October. And a very temporary move it proved to be. Before the year was out, the Conservative Party lost the reins of government, and Neville was, of course, in opposition. These developments revolved primarily around the continuing problem of unemployment and Baldwin's response to it.

When Neville assumed his duties at the Treasury, he found the Prime Minister contemplating protection of the home market, with preference designed to help the Dominions, as one essential weapon in the battle against unemployment. Neville "warmly welcomed" this disposition and personally favored a gradual approach: the immediate initiation of a few extra duties, accompanied by an "educative campaign" toward a more thorough-going policy some months hence. There were prominent Conservatives who opposed the idea; in fact the Cabinet—to the extent that it was informed of the Prime Minister's thinking—was quite divided on the matter. The issue was drawn at the Conservative Party Conference (Plymouth, October 25) when Baldwin declared, in phrases somewhat less than clear (and which Neville had helped him draft), his commitment to Protection. In view of Bonar Law's pledge of no fundamental fiscal change, this seemed to necessitate an early election, an idea with which Baldwin had toyed for some time, against the advice of Neville and others of his colleagues. Consequently, amid continuing controversy over just what Baldwin's remarks at Plymouth had implied, and the wisdom of them whatever they meant, the House of Commons met on November 13. Following debate on a Labor motion of censure on unemployment, it was prorogued three days later. Until the election, held on December 6, Neville had time for scarcely anything save campaigning (with all the "indignities and humiliations" which he loathed) in Ladywood, where the Labor threat continued to grow.

While the election left the Conservatives, with 258 members, still the strongest party, the heart of their program was plainly rejected by the country. As Neville saw it, the new electorate contained "an immense mass of very ignorant voters . . . who could not grasp the idea of better employment and wages as springing from a tariff." [7] Whether his idea of a gradual educative campaign, espoused earlier but rejected because of various political pressures, would have changed things is doubtful; but his judgment on the inadvisability of an immediate election seemed vindicated.

Since Labor now controlled 191 seats in the House, and the

Liberals 158, the composition of the next government was very much in question. Among the numerous solutions propounded, including a variety of coalition arrangements, there seemed much to be said for meeting Parliament in January and taking the verdict of the Commons at the close of the Debate on the Address. That is what eventually happened. Meanwhile, with regard to the likelihood of a Labor-Liberal coalition, Neville's view was clear. Let Labor form a government. They were not strong enough to do much harm but strong enough to be discredited. And let the Liberals bear the odium of installing a Labor government. Some of their number would soon choke on their own election speeches, and when the coalition cracked, the Conservatives would be in an advantageous position. Baldwin and others shared this view, and there was little effort made to forestall this eventuality. The end of the first Baldwin Government duly came in mid-January, 1924, when debate on a Labor motion of no confidence, during which the venerable Liberal leader Herbert Asquith threw his support to Labor—and thereby advanced the demise of the Liberal Party—resulted in Baldwin's expulsion by a 72-vote Labor-Liberal majority.

Thus ended a rather remarkable year for Neville, one in which he had journeyed, with several stopovers along the way, from Coalition back-bencher to Chancellor of the Exchequer. In that period of time he became an important member of Baldwin's team, and his participation in government, or at least in national politics, was firmly set. Cabinet rank brought him into closer contact with foreign affairs. Increasingly restive with British neutrality, he decried the general French attitude toward Germany and urged his chief to respond actively (exactly how is not clear) to France's venture in the Ruhr. He staunchly defended the League of Nations, with particular reference to the Corfu incident; became acquainted first-hand with matters of defense and their relationship to foreign policy; and formulated his own opinions of Curzon and his conduct of the Foreign Office. All in all, it was a year of valuable experience, even for a man in his mid-fifties.

One important by-product of the December election and the ensuing Labor emergence was the opportunity it provided for reuniting the Conservative Party. Although late 1923 saw the first appearance of the "Baldwin must go" refrain—which reappeared intermittently over the next decade or so—and Neville's pre-Christmas diary described the party as "a nest of intrigue," the Labor-Liberal combination in Parliament pressed on the Conservatives anew the need for reunion. Neville was one who set ac-

tively to work on this, spurred in part by the sad lament of his
brother, who had several times written him in discouraged tones,
as on August 30:

> It is an intense regret to me that you and I do not see eye to eye and
> are no longer acting together. . . . Politics are hateful to me since we
> two parted. I shall see this Parliament out, but my position is very diffi-
> cult, and I think it not unlikely that I shall not stand again. The fact
> that you and I both sit for Birmingham makes my position more diffi-
> cult, for whilst I will not argue with you anywhere, Birmingham is the
> last place I would choose for the theatre of our differences—and without
> Birmingham I am nothing.
> Well, fate has so willed it and it's no use kicking against the pricks,
> but it's d—— hard that fate should separate the fortunes of two brothers
> who are to one another as you and I.[8]

For his part, however, Neville was not prepared at this stage and
on this particular point to accept a verdict accorded to fate, and
it is probably not too much to say that the success soon experienced in reuniting the party was primarily his achievement.

Consulting a number and variety of colleagues, Neville gradually convinced the Baldwin group, whose real objection to cooperation with the dissidents centered on the "radicalism" of one of
their leaders, Lord Birkenhead, that it was better to have Birkenhead in than Austen out; and simultaneously persuaded the dissidents that Baldwin was probably around to stay for a while, so
more could be gained by cooperation than stubborn refusal to
accept his leadership. These efforts culminated in a dinner meeting of Baldwin and Austen at Neville's home on February 5.
There, at Neville's prompting, Baldwin told Austen simply that
he had decided to ask him and "his friends" to sit on the front
bench and join in party councils just as if they had been members
of the late Cabinet. Austen frankly accepted the invitation; next
day he and his followers attended a meeting of the shadow Cabinet, at which all went smoothly; and reunion was thus accomplished. Ironically, Neville's efforts helped to bring into the
shadow Cabinet several senior colleagues and ex-Chancellors,
which might have adversely affected his own position and influence. It did not seem to do so significantly, however, and in fact,
freed him to concentrate on the housing debates, where he was
knowledgeable and effective, while leaving finance to those more
experienced in the area.

During the next ten months of opposition, which served as a
kind of tonic for him, Neville was active in both counsel and

debate. His chief Parliamentary encounters were with John Wheatley, the able and militant Scotsman who held the Ministry of Health under Ramsey MacDonald. While some of the bills included in Wheatley's extensive program of housing reform were killed in committee or failed to reach a second reading for lack of time, several others were bitterly contested in the Commons. In early April, Neville tied into the Rent and Mortgage Bill, vigorously objecting to the provision which would have allowed unemployed tenants to live rent-free unless the landlord could prove that, as a result, he would suffer greater hardship than the tenant. He saw no way to confine the principle to housing, and principle aside, deemed the measure simply unworkable. When Asquith and the Liberals also refused to support the clause, the bill was lost.

Wheatley's Housing Act of 1924 was more tedious for Neville, for it involved in essence an extension (increased subsidies over a longer period of time) of his own housing bill of a year before. Disinclined to attack his own creation, Neville nonetheless protested that the increases would set private and municipal builders in competition and inevitably raise building costs, that it would not so much encourage construction as subsidize the rents of a privileged class at the expense of richer and poorer alike. Yet he acknowledged that continuity of policy could be achieved only after certain trial and error, and was in the end so non-partisan that Wheatley was able to term his remarks "generous." The dry statistics of a year later indicated that his prophecy about the effects of the bill was fairly accurate.

Outside of Parliament, Neville was busy with other matters. He prepared for Baldwin the draft of a comprehensive insurance scheme and chaired a committee to elaborate the details. With Leo Amery, he developed in the Conservative Central Office the party's first policy secretariat. His desire to "formulate a policy about everything" prompted his drafting, and publication by the party in June, 1924, of the policy statement *Aims and Principles.* Ladywood, too, claimed much of his time, for the poverty-stricken constituency had become the object of a concentrated Labor campaign. Acknowledging that it seemed almost impossible for him to hold the seat much longer, still he refused to move to the safer confines of Edgbaston until he had fought another general election, which he believed would not be long in coming. His efforts there were frustrating, but there was one saving feature about them: they kept him in Birmingham, where he renewed some of his municipal interests of former years.

When Parliament convened in the autumn, upheaval was in the air. Two issues in particular had caused widespread dissatisfaction: the treaty with Russia, which carried the prospect of a British loan; and the Communist *Workers' Weekly* affair, in which the Government charged editor John Ross Campbell with sedition (for encouraging the forces of the Crown to refuse to bear arms against fellow-workers, British or foreign), then withdrew its charges and stood meekly by while the newspaper boasted that the Government had capitulated to its own backbenchers. Exposed to the general charge of surrender to its extremist wing, and unable to cite any improvement in unemployment in its own defense, the Labor Government was further beset by a still more basic malady: the simple fact that the Liberals had already wearied of the "high adventure"—as MacDonald liked to call the Labor-Liberal combination—and were waiting to call it off at the first opportunity. The end came for the Labor Government on October 8, 1924, when the Conservatives supported a Liberal motion for a select committee of inquiry into the Campbell case, and MacDonald chose to dissolve Parliament.

The resounding Conservative triumph in the election which ensued—aided no doubt by the famous Zinoviev letter[9]—did not reflect in Birmingham. There one seat was lost and every Conservative majority was reduced. Neville, standing in Ladywood against the rowdy but formidable Oswald Mosley, squeezed through, after much suspense, by 77 votes. If it was not the Zinoviev letter which saved him, probably the weather did: it was a fine day except for a downpour in the two hours between the end of the working day and the close of the polls, the time when the socialist vote normally is heaviest.

The Conservative Party, however, had won 413 seats, Labor 151, and the Liberals only 40. In Neville's view, this large majority could be "most dangerous" for "unless we leave our mark as Social Reformers the country will take it out on us hereafter. . . ."[10] That conviction, along with his personal interests and experience, probably influenced his thinking with regard to the role he should play in the second Baldwin Government, about to be established.

CHAPTER VII

Minister of Health (1924–1929)

By the time Baldwin sent for him, Neville had given his own position full consideration. Offered the opportunity to return to the Exchequer, in a Cabinet which placed his brother Austen in the Foreign Office, he chose instead the Ministry of Health. A logical decision in view of the whole pattern of his public life to that point, it gave him the best chance to use his abilities and experience and to pursue his great interest in social improvement. "I ought to be a great Minister of Health, but I am not likely to be more than a second-rate Chancellor," he had already decided.[1] And though tongues might wag in club and pub to the effect that Neville lacked ambition or was out of the running for prime minister, time certainly vindicated his decision.

The Ministry of Health involved a great deal more than the name at first implies. Since its creation in 1919, it had assumed a complex of duties and powers from high-level policy-making to routine inspection and regulation—from authority over housing to control of the phosphoric acid content in raspberry cordial—which involved it intimately with every agency concerned with maintaining daily health and happiness. The responsibilities of the office were frightening, especially in view of postwar British domestic conditions; the demands on the minister's time and talents were little short of killing. But as his "pleasure was in administration" (as his diary noted) and his powers of work seemingly boundless, Neville compiled, with the support of a capable official staff, a record of achievement which stands out prominently in the social history of the inter-war years.

In one sense Neville's real Parliamentary work did not begin until this point in his career. It was typical of him that within a few weeks after taking office he sketched out a far-reaching program of legislation comprised of twenty-five bills to be introduced, according to a definite time schedule, over the next few years. Thereafter, he regularly had six to ten (or even more) bills to pilot through the Commons in each session, and of his original program twenty-one of the bills were eventually enacted. He had earlier said that the Government would rise or fall on its social reforms, and he proceeded to act on that basic assumption.

The Parliamentary session of 1925 was highlighted by two measures in particular: the Widows, Orphans, and Old Age Pensions Act and the Rating and Valuation Bill. The first of these stemmed from his hope to expand health services to something close to "all-in insurance," earlier apparent in the scheme which he had prepared for Baldwin in 1923. Providing pensions of 10 s. a week for widows, 7 s. 6 d. for orphan children, and 10 s. for insured workers and their wives at age 65, the program was to be financed by compulsory contributions from workers and employers alike. In conjunction with existing National Health Insurance and workmen's compensation acts, it rounded out a fairly broad scheme of protection against the major working class risks. Its handling and passage, without extraordinary effort, drew praise for Neville from numerous quarters (including the King and the press) and had one important side-effect: it brought Neville for the first time into close relation with the new Chancellor of the Exchequer, Winston Churchill. The Treasury, of course, controlled the purse-strings of any new program which Health devised, so the need for their heads to work closely together was obvious. They did so over the next few years with surprising success, and while the differences in temperament and outlook which separated the two men in later years were already apparent, they were in the late 1920s an effective combination.

Still more important, in Neville's view, than the Pensions Bill was the Rating and Valuation Act, for it was basic to his housing plans and hopes for local government reform. The bill sought to transfer rating powers to county, district, and borough councils (thus finally eliminating the so-called national overseers provided for in the Statute of 1601); to establish a single basis for valuation; to standardize assessment practices; and to keep rating up-to-date through a re-valuation every five years. Conservative colleagues, particularly the rural element, and Laborites alike found plenty to impugn in the bill, especially those sections relating to what some of the former saw as the "nationalization" of local government and some of the latter interpreted as a limiting of the liberties of English country folk. So the course of debate was arduous and long, extending over a summer adjournment during which a round of flower gardening and Broadlands fishing provided some relief for Neville. In the end, reluctant concessions (including the exclusion of London and separate provisions for agricultural buildings and varying types of industrial machinery) were vital to its passage. But the bill did at length pass—and that is the key point here. Neville carried it almost single-handedly against a wide range of opposition and in the face of gloomy prophecies by his own party's whips about what it would do to the Government and party. His success in so doing, his zeal in debate, and his skill in handling the technical aspects of an extraordinarily difficult measure attracted attention and admiration, even from opponents. And in the longer run, the merit attached to the bill later on was credited to him.

Despite the useful legislation of 1925, the domestic situation in the country, including a deepening trade depression and a developing coal crisis, was not such as to make the Baldwin Government especially popular. But Austen's brilliant success at Locarno helped to even the balance, and Neville, while acknowledging that much would depend on the working out of the pact, took real pleasure in his brother's accomplishment.[2] Austen's ensuing decision to accept a peerage struck Neville at first as out of keeping with the Chamberlain tradition, but amid family consultation he eventually agreed that if one took a title he might as well "go whole hog" (his term) and make it a good one.

The effect of Locarno could not, of course, subdue domestic issues for long, and 1926, the year of the general strike,[3] was a difficult one for the Baldwin Government and Neville alike. The Ministry of Health produced a large number of bills, ranging from smoke abatement measures to wide-sweeping "economy" reforms. In addition, it was intimately involved with other bills not exclusively its own but which had broad implications for Health. Naturally, some of these were enacted with little controversy; others became the subject of long and bitter debate. The so-called Economy Act, which came from Churchill at the Treasury, drew Neville into the direct line of fire for it involved a reduction in the state's contribution to health insurance. To defend the measure in the Commons—which his concern about corruption and waste in the administration of certain programs allowed him to do in good conscience—and yet to protect his own estimates from Churchill's axe was no easy task. It took on additional distaste when Neville quickly became the object of Labor-Liberal charges about "murdering babies" and "plucking feathers from the pillows of sick men." Yet this was mild compared to the partisan acrimony which emerged over the Board of Guardians (Default) Bill, which Neville introduced in July, 1926.

This measure would empower the Minister of Health, in the administration of poor law funds, to appoint commissioners in the place of elected Boards of Guardians wherever such boards had ceased to function properly. It sprang from Neville's conviction that some central direction was necessary to cope with the "open and unabashed corruption" which existed in some places, like West Ham, where relief seemed very little related to the stress of unemployment. This opened up the broader issues of "Popularism": whether relief monies should be used only for the urgent relief of poverty or as a means of advancing social reform. Neville took the former view, George Lansbury and some other Laborites the latter. There resulted harangue of the bitterest sort, in which neither side showed any inclination to turn the other cheek. Labor took this occasion to subject Neville to extensive personal abuse—partly on the grounds that he remained a director at Hoskins', two percent of whose contracts were government-granted—and thereby helped to open a wound which never healed.

The antipathy which Neville so obviously felt for the Labor Party in later years developed gradually over a long period of time. But this episode was decisive in its growth. One biographer who has seen his personal papers notes that from this point on "his letters and diaries begin to fill first with expressions of his exasperation and then of his contempt for them [Labor]." [4] Neville's stiff, Victorian mien made him easy prey for Labor jibes, and few opportunities to torment him were lost. Under increasing abuse of his nature and intentions, he instinctively chose to repay his attackers in kind—and indeed in time took a certain delight in it. The eventual passage of the Guardians Act and the appointment of commissioners in West Ham, Bedwellty, and Chester-le-Street (maintained until the end of the Government) only aggravated the tension. So did Neville's Audit Bill of 1927, which brought forth a charge of "fascism" from his opponents. Nor was his position on the Trade Union Bill of 1927—that compulsory arbitration in the form of a hearing by a tribunal and a joint employer-employee committee should precede the calling of any strike—soothing to Labor.

Neville wrote his sister sometime later of Labor's "gross exaggerations, their dishonesty in slurring over facts that tell against them . . . their utter inability to appreciate a reasonable argument," and the way all of this "embittered his soul." [5] On at least one occasion in 1927, Baldwin had to remind him that Labor M.P.s were gentlemen, for he was too inclined to look on them as dirt. And so it went from that time on. Whatever the merits of specific issues at hand, the antagonism on both sides turned less and less on reason and logic, and a gulf, never thereafter bridged, came to separate Neville from the Labor group.

In retrospect, Neville's aims and those of the majority of the Labor Party were not really dissimilar. But they differed drastically on methods and agents. Neville hoped to accomplish through centralized authority and the expert assistance of the higher civil service what Labor was prepared to do through decentralized local authority and looser methods. For Neville, any state which distributed public money on a very large scale must be punctilious in its methods; on the other hand, Labor's more "generous" approach would hardly have satisfied a first class firm of auditors. As the feud developed, Neville came to think his opponents intellectually insincere, in his opinion one of the gravest of faults. He fought bitterness with bitterness, and no party was more sensitive than Labor when counter-attacked by criticism like that which it dispensed. The battle lines thus drawn, the hostility which came to separate Neville from Labor cannot be appreciated properly except in terms of civil war.

The question of poor law reform, in one guise or another, claimed much of Neville's time and attention—and that of the Cabinet as well—during 1925–1928. But sharp differences among the ministers themselves, as well as the highly aggravated condition of Government-Labor relationships, kept most ideas in the discussion stage. Likewise, the matter of housing, one of his great personal interests and one of the most important concerns of the Ministry of Health, was constantly before him. These years produced nothing spectacular in the area, in part because of Neville's conviction that what the country needed was not new legislation but more effective implementation of acts (including his own of 1924) already on the books. But there were accomplishments. He used his power to reduce subsidies as a means of cutting down building prices, and saw both construction and house purchase rise to unprecedented levels. With the unofficial aid of his sister Ida, who had become a Hampshire County councillor with a special interest in rural housing, he drew up the Housing (Rural Workers) Act of 1926, which provided grants and loans for reconditioning rural homes. Slum clearance moved ahead steadily if unspectacularly.

Administering Public Health Services and National Health Insurance, the Ministry of Health developed, under Neville's leadership, a number of bills which in time assumed an important role in the emerging welfare state. For example, one reform which emitted little political heat but which attracted widespread attention around the country was the establishment of an organized service of professional midwives as a way of attacking the maternity mortality problem. Coincidentally, it also threw some light on the increasingly misunderstood nature of the Minister of Health. Addressing an audience at Leeds, he showed a compassionate awareness of what can happen in a family where young children are left motherless, explaining that his own mother had died in childbirth. There was indeed, though it was not often publicly apparent, an intensely human side in this man who was coming to be regarded by many as a statistical automaton.

His responsibilities required that Neville travel often and widely around the English countryside, and many of his ideas and interests were sharpened by his contact with the numerous "small people" he encountered on these jaunts. His lack of acquaintance with life outside the urban environment, perhaps the largest gap in all his earlier experience, was partially remedied— at least insofar as matters pertaining to the Ministry of Health were concerned. Visiting hospitals and sanataria, inspecting welfare centers and workhouses, touring housing projects and slums —and interspersing all this with luncheons, receptions, and political speeches—he consulted with local authorities, evaluated progress, and assessed the nation's most pressing health needs. Particularly interested in the functioning of local administration, he came to see a pressing need for control and supervision of health services by larger authorities (like county councils) with greater power than most of those which then existed. This idea appeared prominently in the Local Government Act of 1929 for which he, along with Churchill, was responsible.

The Local Government Bill, the most far-reaching of Neville's ventures during this period, was a long and complex document of varied ancestry. Its immediate origin lay in his steady pursuit of poor law reform, which he had pressed upon a reluctant Cabinet for several years. The poor law, and the Boards of Guardians which administered it, had become hopelessly entangled with national health. In addition, a variety of *ad hoc* committees cut across the work of the local councils. A complete reorganization of the whole system seemed essential. As Neville sought to bring his own ideas to the point of action, Churchill introduced derating as a part of the total problem. Thereafter, poor law and derating became integral parts of the same developing bill, and the Ministers of Health and the Treasury once again—though only through long discussion and grudging compromise on both sides

—combined their talents to devise and enact a measure of great significance to the nation's welfare.

As introduced in late November, 1928, the bill abolished all Poor Law Unions (Boards of Guardians), whose powers were transferred to the counties and county boroughs and enlarged to include authority over matters like roads, education, town and country planning, and public health as well as welfare. In short, the counties and county boroughs, often alone, sometimes working with and through newly regrouped urban and rural district councils, became the sole authorities, under the Ministry of Health, for almost all local activities. The derating provisions exempted agricultural land and farm buildings (long subject to special treatment) from the payment of rates, while railways and industrial property rates were reduced by three-quarters. The Treasury was then responsible for making up the money lost by local authorities (estimated at £24 million) and providing additional funds for the new functions assumed by the county units. These monies would be provided in block grants, calculated according to a formula which took into account population, rateable values, and unemployment, and subject to revision every five years, rather than the old percentage grants, which had tended to favor prosperous areas. This roundabout way of subsidizing industry at the expense of the taxpayer and substituting industrial derating for tariffs had been a difficult pill for Neville to swallow during the preparation of the bill. But he had accepted it, in face of Churchill's insistence, for the sake of the larger measure.

The Act made it onto the Statute Book by the spring of 1929 without excessive strain. The wisdom of its major provisions was widely recognized, and in addition, Neville had handled it well. On the second reading of the bill, he spoke for two and one-half hours, carefully explaining the defects of local government which demanded change and, taking Birmingham as an example, describing what efficient local government could mean to the people of any area. He was apparently very effective; when he sat down the House cheered him continuously for several minutes, with Liberal and Labor men joining the others in paying their acknowledgments. Upon final passage of the bill, *The Times* paid glowing tribute to Neville and predicted that the measure would go down as one of the outstanding legislative achievements of the century. A fitting climax to Neville's work at the Ministry of Health, it commanded attention and praise throughout the country, and thrust him closer to the forefront of English political life.

. . .

Aside from his efforts on behalf of health, a few other points concerning Neville's career and outlook at this juncture merit at least passing mention here. Like most ministers, his contact with issues outside his own ministry was only occasional. But his interests were broad and his acquaintance with a variety of matters was constantly expanding.

Economic problems, especially in the form of industrial troubles, constantly bedeviled the Government. In the seemingly endless Cabinet and party discussions on these matters, Neville usually stood on middle ground—and often played a mediating role—between the "die-hard" Conservative element and the Tory-Radical strain. Sympathetic to the plight of the worker, he also believed that society should first help those who helped themselves. Alert to the crying needs of the unemployed, he chafed painfully at the corruption and inefficiency with which social insurance funds were locally administered. His resistance to the general strike of 1926 was based not on unconcern for the miners (and workers generally) but on his conviction that the use of physical power to force the hand of Parliament endangered the very principle of constitutional government. This carried over into discussion of the Trade Disputes Bill of 1927, in connection with which Neville proposed a form of compulsory arbitration which presaged the Industrial Disputes Tribunal at length established in 1940. Committed by family tradition to tariffs, he nevertheless stood by Baldwin's pledge (no general tariff) and accepted derating as a means of "protecting" British industries.

Foreign affairs were less critical during this period than at any other time in the inter-war years, and did not command a great deal of Neville's "official" attention. To the extent that his views were heard, they might again be described as generally moderate. He shared, of course, the satisfaction of Locarno, and noted in passing that Austen had found Mussolini "charming, and excellent to do business with." Whether this influenced his own assessment of the Italian dictator some years later is, however, moot. For a time he seems to have shared the nation's general impatience with France, yet he rebutted charges that Austen was too pro-French with criticism of the prevalent sympathy for Germany. When questions of naval disarmament split the Cabinet, he seems to have stood somewhere between the two extremes, though in time finding the Admiralty's arguments for its own absolute minimum of smaller cruisers "unanswerable." While he had distinct reservations about Egyptian independence and despaired to see

British interests there "going to the devil," he became increasingly doubtful whether the nation could hold on to the area. In Chinese affairs, he stood for decided measures to prevent anarchy in Shanghai—but what these might have been is nowhere clear. He shared his countrymen's deep indignation with Bolshevik propaganda, yet he did not lend strong support to the severence of diplomatic relations in 1927. And as for the League of Nations and the Kellogg-Briand Pact, he saw room for hope but not extreme assurance.

More important at the moment, certainly, was Neville's developing position in relation to Baldwin, the Cabinet, and the Conservative Party. The mind and character of the Prime Minister both intrigued and exasperated him. The two men did not think alike on many issues, and Baldwin's easy-going, apparently lackadaisical nature seemed quite incompatible with Neville's serious, "all-business" demeanor. But whatever their outward differences, they saw life in much the same way, and although Neville was sometimes critical of Baldwin, especially for his lack of leadership, his general attitude showed a deference and loyalty which was constant and firm. He became, as he put it himself, "more and more attached" to Baldwin, and the feeling appeared mutual.

Among his fellow ministers, Neville was closest to Leo Amery (Colonial Secretary), more an old friend than a respected colleague; Cunliffe-Lister (head of the Board of Trade), whose judgment he valued; and Samuel Hoare (Secretary for Air), whose shrewdness he admired. His budding friendship with Edward Wood was momentarily interrupted by the latter's assignment to India, while his warm relationship with Douglass Hogg was cut off by Hogg's promotion to the Lord Chancellorship. Neville's respect for Churchill was very great, but the Chancellor of the Exchequer was too much a maverick and too much a threat to dominate the party for Neville's tastes.

Gradually Neville emerged not so much a power as a steady influence within the party. In July, 1927, Baldwin confided to him, with apparent approval, his view that if anything happened to him (Baldwin), the party would probably select Neville as his successor. Eight months later Neville acknowledged in his diary that he and Hogg were widely talked of as Baldwin's successor. Then Hogg's elevation as Lord Chancellor removed him from the running—a great misfortune, Neville wrote his sister, for he thought Hogg the best man for the position. With regard to his own prospects, his attitude, at least as expressed in his diary, was reminiscent of earlier years: he had "no wish for it; I would not shirk it if I felt it my duty to take it, but I would not lift a finger to get it. . . ." [6] Yet he must have been impressed by an exuberant reception accorded him at the party conference in November, 1928—the first open recognition of his potential future leadership.

An early by-product of Neville's success at the Ministry of Health was the decision that he should leave his Ladywood constituency for the safer fortress of Edgbaston, where elderly Sir Francis Lowe retired to make room for him. He had no real choice; Ladywood was ripe for a Labor thrust, inhabited by poverty-stricken workers to whom Neville had no personal appeal. In Edgbaston he fared well, despite increasing Conservative difficulties throughout much of Birmingham, and it remained his constituency until the end of his career.

The general election of May, 1929, brought the second Baldwin Government to an end. In Birmingham the Conservatives lost four seats (Austen's majority was reduced to 43), and the trend prevailed throughout the country. The general feeling that it was time for a change—which developed, of course, from specific matters such as Baldwin's lack of initiative, the inept timing of certain reforms (like rating), and continued unemployment and trade depression—resulted in Labor's winning 26 seats more than the Conservatives (287 to 261), while the Liberals' 57 seats held the balance. Unwilling to cooperate with the Liberals, Neville still counseled against resignation and recommended "riding for a fall." But Baldwin chose to resign on June 4, and Ramsey MacDonald formed his second Labor Government.

About the future Neville was quite uncertain. He thought it possible for the Labor Government to blunder so badly that within two years the country would be glad to get rid of it. On the other hand, in the same period of time it might be able to convince the people that its failures stemmed mainly from its lack of a clear majority, win a new election, and continue in power for five more years. In that event, he would be 67 when the Conservatives came back, and politics might well have ceased to interest him. There was room for hope: he saw no general conversion to socialism, only discontents (the working classes) showing a desire for change. But only time would tell.

Time indeed had vindicated Neville's decision to take the Ministry of Health. The second Baldwin Government's record of useful social legislation was greater than that of any other inter-war government except for Lloyd George's Coalition, and its solid achievements were in large part his responsibility.[7] He knew his business and supplied a really creative element—perhaps the only one[8]—in an otherwise pedestrian government. What his father had made the Colonial Office some years before, Neville had now made the Ministry of Health: an important and influential post in British Government. His achievement here, as Feiling puts it, "stands out massive and unquestioned, the chapter of his public life least controverted." [9]

During these years Neville began to show for the first time his great competence as an administrator. His industry was, by common consent, astounding. He reveled in figures and reeled them off from memory without the slightest hesitation—and the House of Commons, which has a kind of awe-struck respect, if not admiration, for those so gifted, began to respect him as never before. This reflected in him; he gained confidence in his own powers and his ability to meet attack, and developed in debate a trenchant style reminiscent of his father.

Yet Neville should not be thought of as popular during these years. His manner was dry, his alternating reticence and aggressiveness—frequently explained as a form of shyness—often interpreted as rudeness and resented. But no one questioned his ability, and if party leadership involved more than personality and popularity, it was not surprising that he was marked by his colleagues for higher things.

CHAPTER VIII

Between Ministries (1929–1931)

THE LABOR VICTORY IN 1929 WAS A BLOW TO NEVILLE FOR PERSONAL as well as party reasons. Never very interested in—indeed usually repulsed by—the game of politics, he now faced the prospect of returning to Opposition politicking. Furthermore, Cabinet reconstruction had been much discussed before the election, and it had been determined (insofar as Baldwin determined anything in advance) that Neville should next move to the Colonial Office. This had a twofold appeal: challenging imperial problems awaited solution, and Neville could try his hand in the ministry so closely associated with his father's name. But now that must wait, and meanwhile he must seek other outlets for his momentarily frayed but otherwise unimpaired physical and mental vigor.

To find an appropriate outlet he had to look neither long nor hard. Party problems soon engulfed him and demanded his closest attention for the next several years. For a long time prior to the election, Baldwin's leadership had been subject to a fluctuating wave of criticism within the Conservative Party. The election result, his dull performance in Opposition, and his disinclination to consult his colleagues on vital issues rekindled the critics' zeal, and by October, 1929, Neville found "depression, distrust, and despair" everywhere. He felt bound to alert his leader to these facts of party life, but was embarrassed in so doing, for well he knew that if Baldwin went, the succession would fall to him or Churchill—and he was not certain which alternative he disliked more.

The situation was complicated by Lord Beaverbrook's campaign—the "Crusade" as some came to call it—for "Empire Free Trade" (complete freedom of trade within the Empire but a strong tariff wall around it) as a cure for the country's chronic economic ills.[1] Protection, of course, appealed to a large segment of Conservative opinion, though not necessarily Beaverbrook's scheme for it. Neville saw advantage in holding the party free from limiting pledges while negotiating, within the Empire, treaties which could then be submitted for Parliamentary approval. Along with Baldwin on one occasion and Samuel Hoare on another, he made two attempts at accommodation with Beaverbrook during November. The results were inconclusive, but Neville became convinced that "we should at once begin educating the people to understand that our policy is Empire trade and development, and keep all the emphasis on this. . . ." [2]

In need of a respite, Neville departed England on December 11 for a visit to East Africa. Accompanied by his wife and daughter, and traveling by ship via the Mediterranean and Suez, he now had an opportunity to relax, to think about a new imperial policy, and (once in Kenya) to observe colonial matters first-hand. In many ways an orthodox tour by an ex-minister—with all its inspecting and conferring—it nonetheless allowed him to revel once more in the details of a strange and fascinating land and to fill several diaries with observations on everything from slaves to coffee stems, bittern to business, tsetse flies to trusteeship.

The party situation changed little during Neville's absence, and upon his return in mid-March (1930), he found himself right back in the thick of it. Baldwin had proclaimed safeguarding and imperial preference as the party's policy, while rejecting any tax on food. Later, in attempting to meet Beaverbrook halfway, he had agreed to submit any proposed taxes on food to a referendum of the people. The uncertainty which then prevailed opened the way for Neville to push him toward the formation of a committee (to include Beaverbrook) to consider Empire free trade and the holding of weekly meetings among a small "inner shadow Cabinet" to discuss policy generally. Neither enjoyed spectacular success, but they illustrate Neville's efforts at reconciliation and reconstruction.

His position in the center of things was further enhanced by his assumption of the chairmanship of the party's Research Department, a recently-established agency designed to serve as an information bureau and a long-range research body. Long concerned about the party's crying need for a program, Neville saw that the new department would enable him to influence "the springs of policy." Operating from newly-occupied premises in Old Queen Street, and working through small policy committees (comprised of M.P.s and others)—the most important at the moment being the committee on tariff policy which, under Philip Cunliffe-Lister's direction, produced in time a report of which much use was later made—Neville infused the organization with new energy.

But things were moving quickly, and he soon was called to still another post. Abetted by the vigorous support of Lord Rothermere, his fellow press lord, Beaverbrook's dissatisfaction with Baldwin's lack of interest in Empire free trade broke into the open again. The party became increasingly confused and divided. Failure to achieve any kind of accommodation reflected on J. C. C. Davidson, the party chairman, who was induced to resign. The search for a successor at length pointed to Neville as the one man who could command general confidence. (Loyal to Baldwin, he was also on speaking terms with Beaverbrook.) When Baldwin approached him, he accepted. It was a dangerous thing to do and he knew it. Failure, his own or that of his policy, would mean ruin. But he felt, so he noted in his diary, that he could render a service possible to no one else and did not hesitate.

Neville's idea was to get on with the task of reconstruction quickly, then turn the position over to someone else. Within a short time he was conferring with Beaverbrook again, seeking grounds for a general settlement of differences. Beaverbrook was friendly and apparently willing to accept Neville's terms: cessation of attacks on Baldwin and the party (especially rife in the *Evening Standard*) and discontinuance of efforts to collect campaign funds to support candidates running against official Conservatives, in return for which the Central Office would support Conservatives expressing personal agreement with Beaverbrook, provided they accepted official party policy. But Rothermere balked—though promising full support for the party if Neville replaced Baldwin as leader. Common loyalty and resistance to dictation made Neville reject that suggestion, but he did admit to his sister that the whole party would "heave a sigh of relief" if Baldwin would go. For the moment, however, efforts at conciliation had failed again.

Equally troublesome was the matter of the referendum, which did much to undermine Baldwin's position and authority. By the autumn of 1930, Neville was able to dispose of that. Utilizing the technique of offering policy suggestions in public speeches, assessing party reaction to them, and in that way clarifying issues and determining areas of general agreement, he developed in late summer an "unauthorized program" for the party. Finding his proposal of a free hand in negotiating with the Dominions well-received, he urged Baldwin to issue a policy statement to that effect. An excellent opportunity existed, for at the October opening of the Imperial Conference in London the Labor Government had given no lead whatever, and had reacted coldly to a

Canadian proposal for reciprocal imperial preferences. With Baldwin's consent, Neville then drafted, and issued under Baldwin's name, a declaration that the Conservative Party accepted the principle of imperial preference; it would formulate its own proposals and submit them to the people at the next election for their final assent. This buried the referendum and also strengthened Baldwin's hand. At a subsequent Caxton Hall party meeting (October 30), called at the insistence of the die-hard element, the fiscal policy of the free hand was solidly endorsed (though Beaverbrook dissented) and Baldwin received a healthy vote of confidence (462 to 116). Discontent with Baldwin's leadership had by no means disappeared, but it was momentarily allayed.

In the meantime Neville concentrated on other party matters. He continued to talk intermittently with Beaverbrook, especially about extending the "free hand" to British agriculture. He labored to smooth party division over the status of India, the great question which separated Churchill from his colleagues at the time. The Research Department had to be pressed for more research on quotas and insurance. Official Conservative candidates in by-elections had to be succored in the face of challenges by Beaverbrook "Crusaders." With one eye on the precarious balance by which Labor maintained itself in power with Liberal support, he discussed with a variety of prognosticators a myriad of political "ifs and buts"—including the future of the Liberal Party itself. This activity did not intrigue him; indeed, he found such politics "nauseating," but it was all a part of his job as party chairman.

Most interesting for him since it involved the work of administration, and most important in the long run, was the reorganization he undertook at the Central Office. Taking his cue from a stormy debate at the 1929 party conference, he separated the chairmanship of the party from the chairmanship of the Executive Committee of the National Union. He then set a "General Director" in control of every branch of the Central Office. This set the mood for the implementation of a scheme, devised with the aid of Hoare and others, to enhance the efficiency and also the economy of the party operation. All along the party hierarchy the organizational structure was tightened. Offices and functions were combined or redefined. Ineffective personnel were weeded out; new men with new enthusiasm took their places. The upshot of all this was that Neville developed, not so much as a result of design as almost inevitable occurrence in this transitional moment, a party organization sensitive to his touch. That fact, reinforced by other influences which he wielded in the intervening years, was of significance in connection with the election of 1935, which determined the kind of Parliament Neville had behind him when he eventually became prime minister.

In the first two months of 1931 Neville was again occupied with the acute question of party leadership. He was receiving letters and communications about it from all over the country. Hoare reported that the feeling in the House could not be worse. The party die-hards were up in arms at Baldwin's apparently uninformed reply to Churchill's India speech. Neville himself, loyal beyond question, was sorely tried by his leader's eccentricities and inconsistencies, his lack of consideration and concern. But he was loathe to act when his action might result in his own elevation to Baldwin's place.

The breaking point came at the end of February, when Sir Robert Topping, General Director of the Central Office, laid before Neville a memorandum detailing the widespread dissatisfaction with Baldwin and the "definite feeling" that he was not strong enough to carry the party to victory. So serious was the situation in his view that he would not shrink from placing his impressions before Baldwin himself. Consultation among the party's senior figures resulted in agreement that the memorandum must be shown to Baldwin, and Neville arranged for a slightly edited version to be sent to him at once. Seeing Baldwin on March 1, Neville found him apparently resolved to retire, as most of the senior figures consulted had agreed he must do. But during the next few days—for a variety of reasons and motives— the redoubtable Baldwin changed his mind and determined not to go. Indeed, he came to resent the notion that his colleagues wished him out, and to feel that Neville should have offered him more support. Nor was his attitude improved when Austen asked him bluntly on March 11 when he intended to release Neville from the Central Office so as to utilize once more his front-bench debating talent. While the question was posed without Neville's approval, Baldwin could hardly fail to reach his own conclusions. Neville himself allowed that it was "pretty plain" what Austen —concerned from the beginning about what the party chairmanship might do to Neville's chances of becoming leader—had in mind.

His position with Baldwin thus compromised, and inclined to think Austen right ("though not on the ground he put forward"), Neville chose to resign from the Central Office. Personal embarrassment was counterbalanced by his knowledge that the reorganization of the office, one of his major objectives in the first place, was now complete. In addition, conversations with Beaverbrook had made progress following the early March defeat of his "Crusader" candidate in the crucial St. George's by-election. In the last few days before his resignation became effective, Neville produced a truce with Beaverbrook which stood to be of substantial aid to Baldwin. Relations between leader and out-going chairman were severely strained for several weeks, but a frank conversation on March 24 cleared up a basic misunderstanding, their grievances were allayed, apologies made, and mutual confidence—of a sort—restored.

Free for a time to garden and fish, Neville was not out of things for long. He soon recovered, if indeed he had lost, second position in the party. Back in the role of Baldwin's closest associate, he emerged the undisputed heir apparent. His return to the Commons coincided with the onslaught of financial crisis (including a severe drain on gold), and as that danger to the nation forced a quick abandonment of partisan maneuvering on all sides, his advice and assistance were much in demand. The way was opened for the espousal of two favorite themes, the tariff and economy in government. Just before Parliament rose for the summer, he explained his thinking on the financial situation: the return of prosperity would ultimately depend on tariffs and special trade arrangements within the Empire. While these were being worked out, drastic economy, involving sacrifices by all, was essential. The ensuing months provided ample opportunity to pursue this scheme.

By the end of July, Prime Minister MacDonald had made soundings about the formation of a National government to meet the emergency. So Neville was not surprised when recalled to London (August 11) from a Perthshire holiday to participate in discussions about necessary economic measures. In the conferences which followed among Government officials, representatives of the Conservative and Liberal Parties, and the Bank of England, Neville was the chief Conservative spokesman. After a brief initial appearance, Baldwin had acknowledged that crises of this kind were not his forte and departed, leaving everything to Neville (who then asked Samuel Hoare to join him).

Convinced that the basic problem was to restore foreign confidence in British credit, and that only a drastic cut in national expenditure would achieve the desired effect, Neville argued vigorously for greater economies than those proposed by Chancellor

Snowden for the Labor Government. Unemployment benefits in particular, he averred, must be adjusted downward in an effort to bring planned economies more into line with expected deficits. Neither MacDonald nor Snowden resisted the point, but both faltered in the face of opposition from colleagues within the Labor movement. At length Neville bluntly posed what he saw to be the alternative to greater economy: the anticipated crash would come and the Government would be turned out immediately when the House reassembled. It was the Prime Minister's duty, as he saw it, to avoid a crash, and the Conservatives stood ready to support him in that, "either with his present or a reconstructed government." [3] Herbert Samuel spoke similarly for the Liberals, and MacDonald, painfully aware of what this would do to his Government and party, was won over. He would assert his own views and tell his colleagues who could not support him to go where they liked.

As Neville expected—and anticipated with a certain relish— eight Labor ministers refused to accept the dole cut. With the Cabinet irreparably split, MacDonald at once advised the King to see the three party leaders. Government change was certain, though what form it would take was not yet clear. MacDonald seemed inclined at first to eliminate himself from the next Cabinet. But on August 24—influenced perhaps by Neville's gentlemanly arguments that he might still command great support in the country and respect abroad, and that a three-party government would be stronger than a two-party combination—he undertook to form a National government for the one purpose (as a Downing Street statement declared) of meeting the national emergency.

The new Cabinet of ten (four Laborites, four Conservatives, and two Liberals), in which Neville returned to the Ministry of Health, was constructed amid dispute and sore feelings. Nevertheless, it moved ahead quickly with the task at hand. Further economies (ranging from reductions in unemployment benefits to cuts in ministers' salaries) were prescribed, new taxes were imposed, and the budget was balanced. But this did not arrest impending crisis. Demonstrations by teachers, sailors, and the unemployed followed. Foreign confidence was shaken anew. The pound continued to falter and, on September 21, Britain abandoned the gold standard. The strained Cabinet was soon confronted with the fundamental questions of whether it should hold together and, if so, under what conditions.

On these points Neville's thinking was clear. Since emergency

measures had failed, the Government could work effectively only
with public approval. It must, therefore, go to the country as a
National government led by MacDonald—and on a program of
the full tariff and a free hand, which seemed to him the only way
to redress the increasingly adverse balance of trade. In this he had
the unanimous support of the Conservative Business Committee.
But not unexpectedly, some Labor men and Liberals balked at
the full tariff. Indeed, agreement on a program proved impossible
to achieve, and it was decided at length (October 5) to follow a
rather extraordinary procedure: to go to the country as a united
government, one section of which would advocate tariffs while
the other would only declare an open mind on the matter. The
leaders would make concurrent appeals in terms palatable to
their own followers.

The tactic proved surprisingly successful, perhaps because the
real nature of the emergency was everywhere recognized. The
election of October 27, 1931, resulted in the return of 558 supporters of the National Government (471 Conservatives, 68 Liberals, and 52 Laborites). All the Labor ex-ministers who had recently refused to follow MacDonald were ousted, and the more
than 200 Conservative gains from Labor, duplicated in the municipal elections as well, revealed significant change in the mind of
the country.

In Birmingham, where the Conservatives won all twelve Parliamentary seats and Labor was completely shut out of the City
Council, Neville had keynoted the campaign. While recognizing
that no single remedy could cure the crisis, and holding himself
ready to examine every proposal, he declared the tariff indispensable. The major subject of his father's last great political campaign was very much in his mind.

Resounding electoral victory did not diminish the problems of
Cabinet formation, especially in view of the drastically altered
relative strength of the three parties. MacDonald eventually put
together a Cabinet of eleven Conservatives, five Liberals, and
four Labor men. As for Neville's position, the King apparently
thought he should return to the Ministry of Health, where he had
been so effective. Baldwin suggested him for the Foreign Office.
But MacDonald placed him at the Treasury—an outcome decided perhaps by the election itself. There the burden would be
heavy, but Neville faced 1932 as "the year of opportunity." As he
wrote to a friend in early January: "To be given the chance of
directing such great forces where I am convinced they should be

applied, is such a privilege as one had no right to hope for; and I intend to make the most of it." [4] With a committee of Conservative ministers, which he formed, and a Research Department of his own creation behind him, he soon began translating these words into action.

CHAPTER IX

Chancellor of the Exchequer (1932–1935)

THE NATIONAL GOVERNMENT HAD BEEN BORN OF IMPENDING FINAN-cial ruin. The nation's financial salvation was its most immediate and pressing concern. The Exchequer was, therefore—poten-tially, if not in fact—the key position in the state. Its task was awesome. As one respected (though admittedly pro-Chamberlain) English historian has put it: "Never since the younger Pitt was called upon to put the national finances in order after the disas-ters of the Wars of American Independence had a Chancellor shouldered such a burden." [1] But Neville was undaunted by it all, and by his confident control of the Treasury in the months and years which followed, he contributed to his nation's eco-nomic well-being, added to his personal reputation, and moved still closer to the center of English political life.

Fiscal revolution in the form of Protection was his first order of business. The Abnormal Importations Act gave the Board of Trade a free hand to levy emergency duties (up to 100 percent) on manufactured goods, thus providing immediate protection against dumping. Quickly formulated as a result of the work done earlier by the Conservative Research Department, it was also quickly enacted—and with surprisingly generous provisions —when Neville, in overcoming stiff opposition from two of his colleagues, induced the Cabinet to agree to the general principle and permit a subsequent "filling in of the blanks" (the setting of specific rates) as need dictated. It was followed by a Horticultural Imports Act, placing duties on certain vegetables, fruit, and flow-ers—"luxuries" at the moment, even Liberals had to admit. But these measures were only a prelude to a permanent tariff policy, toward which Neville uncompromisingly pushed. The road was short but exceedingly rough. His Cabinet Committee was torn by dissent; Snowden, Samuel, and others threatened to resign when MacDonald came down on Neville's side. But the day was saved when Lord Hailsham, Secretary of State for War, intervened with a proposal (a limited version of which Neville had suggested to MacDonald a short time before) allowing the dissentients to voice their objections and still remain in the Government. With this curious "agreement to differ," a tactic not unlike that which preceded the election appeal of the previous October, the way was opened for "the great day" of Neville's life.

He laid before the Commons on February 4, 1932, a tariff scheme calling in the main for a 10 percent duty on all goods except those on a specifically exempted list, plus a superstructure of additional duties to be levied by the Treasury upon the advice of an independent tariff board. (Dominion goods were exempted pending the forthcoming Ottawa Conference.) It was a memorable, and in the end emotional, occasion. His reasoned presentation of the bill was climaxed by a reference to his father's earnest but futile efforts for tariff reform, and ended with these words:

I believe he would have found consolation for the bitterness of his disappointment if he could have foreseen that these proposals, which are the direct and legitimate descendants of his own conception, would be laid before the House of Commons, which he loved, in the presence of one, and by the lips of the other, of the two immediate successors to his name and blood.[2]

Amid the cheers of the House, Austen went to the Treasury bench to grasp his brother's hand. Next day congratulations poured in from all manner of men. The century of free trade was at an end, the tariff campaign of the last generation was over. Joseph Chamberlain's cherished dream was fulfilled—ironically, by the son set aside from politics and put to an accountant's desk. From this accomplishment Neville derived the keenest satisfaction.

There was, however, little time to rest on laurels. Development of his first Budget followed, with the end result an austere program in no way reflecting the soft mood of the Aberdeenshire Dee where Neville had gone to think it out. There was no relief from taxes; that might lead to a premature relaxation of the efforts which were beginning to produce a revival of public confidence. Drastic economies were necessary before the normal expenditure of revenue could be balanced; therefore, drastic economies there would be. Aside from revenue matters, the Budget sought to borrow up to £150 million to establish an Exchequer exchange equalization account to protect the country from perilous fluctuations in currency caused by speculative activities. And though more an outgrowth than an actual part of the Budget, Neville moved, two months later (June, 1932), to reduce debt charges by converting the interest rate on the £2 billion war loan from 5 to 3½ percent. This was later considered by some as one of his more substantial financial achievements.

Matters of international finance also claimed his attention for, after many a dispatch and communiqué, the powers had agreed to meet in conference at Lausanne to discuss reparations. It was Neville's hope to get both reparations and war debts cancelled, although the pre-Lausanne reservations of other nations provided little ground for optimism. Nor did the conference itself, convened in mid-June with MacDonald in the chair, achieve that end. Although Neville opened with a flat appeal for cancellation, several weeks of disagreeable wrangling resulted in something less: mainly a German lump sum to France in place of continued annual payments. An additional Anglo-French-Italian-Belgian agreement to withhold ratification of Lausanne until they had reached a settlement with their own creditors appeared to reflect Neville's contention that America should not refuse to play her part in a world settlement. But that was as far as they got with war debts.

Disappointing as Lausanne was to Neville, it was not without personal significance for him. It provided a prolonged and intense experience in international negotiation—especially since MacDonald, bothered by headaches and unable to understand French, relied heavily upon him to carry the British view. He established close rapport with Herriot, the French Premier; indeed, the final sum which Germany was to pay and the wording of the political declaration which followed were hammered out by the two of them. He got on reasonably well with the Germans, although he found some of them, especially von Papen, "incredibly stupid." At the same time, he was quite unfavorably impressed by the general inability of "the foreigner" to get down to business without long and needless (as he saw it) preliminary sparring.

Barely rested from Lausanne, Neville departed on July 13, as part of a strong British delegation, for Ottawa, where imperial economic questions awaited discussion. The special interests of Britain and the various Dominions did not always coincide, and five weeks of tense negotiation preceded the reaching of even tenuous understanding. Neville reported that he had never worked so hard in his life, and hoped that he would never have to go through such an experience again. He had hoped to begin the conference with a series of general resolutions to which all could agree and against which all specific propositions could be tested.

But when his draft resolutions were quickly brushed aside, the conference devolved into a free-for-all in which there was little order or sense of direction—an outcome abetted by the inclination of the conference chairman, Prime Minister Richard Bennett of Canada, to act more as head of the Canadian delegation than general chairman.

In the end, agreements were severally negotiated between Britain and the Dominions in which ideas largely of Neville's devising were prominent. They involved reciprocal preferential arrangements with a view, ultimately, to a descending scale of duties which would place British traders on the same level as Dominion producers, and an approach to the agricultural problem (where prices had tumbled disastrously) through voluntary restriction of Dominion production rather than a British restriction on imports. But it had not been easy. Several times the conference had teetered on the verge of collapse. And several times the British delegation was torn to the point of threatened resignations. On one occasion Neville felt it necessary to say flatly to certain of his British colleagues that if the conference broke down over a British refusal to put a duty on foreign meat, as Australia was demanding, he would have to "fade out." Compromise and good will at length prevailed, but—despite Neville's opinion that the only real disappointment was the failure to get a better set of general resolutions—it was not a confident, contented British delegation which sailed for home in late August.

Nor was it a satisfied Cabinet that received them. Snowden, Samuel, and Sinclair, free-traders all, had expressed extreme displeasure at the first news of the Ottawa Agreements. Prime Minister MacDonald had at first dissuaded them from precipitate action, but his argument that Britain's strong position in the world was due largely to her "present political combination" was not sufficient to hold them indefinitely. On September 28, accompanied by a half dozen minor ministers, they resigned. Thereafter, precious little National flavor remained in the Government. Neville observed all this with pleasure. Those who remained would be more homogeneous now, and might move toward "that fused Party under a national name" which he regarded as both certain and desirable.

It had been a strenuous summer for Neville. The pressure of work had taxed him severely, the international conferences coming, as they did, upon the heels of his worst attack of gout in years. But such involvement in the nation's life had its own rewards, and there had been other compensations as well, including

honors bestowed upon him by his native city for "services ren-
dered." Having contemplated retirement from politics in May,
the idea had disappeared along with his physical affliction, and he
was ready to go on again. Indeed, if anything, his interests broadened and his pace quickened—and many who have written about
this period of English history have seen in him the one dynamic
element in the last MacDonald Government. This may reflect in
part the shortcomings of his colleagues; it also stemmed from his
role as Chancellor of the Exchequer and chairman of his party's
thinking-machine (the Conservative Research Department), and
from his temperament. He could not, by his own admission, contemplate a problem without trying to find a solution to it.

His Budget of 1933, like the five other budgets which he introduced as Chancellor, was altogether orthodox. Beyond raising the
exchange equalization fund to £350 million and lowering the
beer duty, his positive proposals were few. He fought tenaciously
against growing agitation for a deliberately unbalanced budget,
which would, it was argued by some eminent economists (including J. M. Keynes) and journalists, give a psychological lift to the
economy, and introduced a strictly balanced document. He resisted cuts in the income tax, proposed by others (again including
sections of the press) for their psychological effect, and thus in-
curred considerable disfavor. He refused to borrow in order to
reduce taxation. But what his Budget lacked in imagination, it
seemed to make up in a thorough understanding of fundamental
economics and hard common sense. His view that the nation's
condition warranted steady, time-tested methods, not wild experimentation, had many supporters; and while he remained open to
the charge of "too orthodox," his control of the Treasury was not
seriously questioned. Gradual recovery, which Neville later attributed to tariffs, conversion operations, cheap money, balanced
budgets, remission of taxation, and the spirit of confidence which
grew out of all these things, slowly eased the pressure and increased his confidence in his own methods. Whether his policies
were indeed responsible for recovery remains somewhat in question,[3] but there is little doubt that Neville saw them so.

Budget-making did not make Neville popular; a tax-gatherer
can hardly ever be that. It did, however, demonstrate his efficiency and reveal the mastery which he had over his subject. In
this he resembled his father and also Bonar Law, whose capacity
for recalling statistics was almost uncanny. It won for him the
esteem of older officials inside the Treasury and the respect, if not
the admiration, of colleagues who found themselves befuddled by

certain of the intricacies of depression-era finance. His tidy mind became, in the circumstances of the time, an impressive attribute, and in matters of finance he definitely remained in control.

There were, of course, periodic challenges. Late 1934, for example, brought Neville into conflict again with his old adversary Lloyd George, who propounded an English version of the "New Deal," to include a vast program of public works for the purpose of providing employment. Some of Neville's Cabinet colleagues were impressed—to the point of suggesting Lloyd George's return to the National Government. But Neville demurred, not so much on personal grounds (so he said, although he later made it clear he would not serve with Lloyd George) but because he felt that English experience showed such a policy to be thoroughly impractical.[4] At length he won his point, and the unemployment problem was further attacked through the Unemployment Assistance Board, a statutory (six-member) commission which removed, in principle at least, unemployment assistance from troublesome local control and party politics and made it a national government concern. Significantly, this agency, like much of the Unemployment Act of 1934, was largely of Neville's devising.

Aspects of international finance remained troublesome to Neville during these months. He found the American position (since Lausanne) on Britain's repayment of war debts unreasonable (in part because of her refusal to allow debts to be paid in goods and services) and inequitable in relation to the treatment accorded other countries. Though reluctant at first to consider non-payment, when the point of a choice between full payment or default was reached in 1934, he came down firmly on the side of default. Earlier, as leader of the British delegation to the World Economic Conference held in London in the summer of 1933, he had been annoyed by America's unwillingness to consider a lump sum settlement along the lines of the Lausanne model, irked by the cavalier (as he saw it) American attitude toward dollar depreciation, and frustrated by the failure of the conference to arrive at any broad international agreement concerning financial stabilization, which he saw as the only solution to the world's economic ills. He had worked hard to avert the conference's failure. Tirelessly expounding his country's view that economic equilibrium could be recovered only by means of raising prices (cost reduction would bring "intolerable suffering"), he had also detailed basic elements in British policy: national determination on the issue of public works; careful distinctions between market quotas assuring remunerative price levels and those arbitrarily protective; tariff reduction through bilateral treaties; general abandonment of export and shipping subsidies. Among the great powers, however, there was no agreement on stabilized exchanges or the matter of tariffs, and Neville had reluctantly transferred his hope for positive accomplishment to special interest or regional groupings. But even his efforts to promote special arrangements with the Dominions through an elaboration of the Ottawa resolves met with little response beyond a provision for continuous Commonwealth consultation on monetary policy. So the success which Neville experienced at home—in the sense of promoting his own "solutions" to economic problems—had no international counterpart. And while the conference did allow him to expand his international contacts, its sad demise did little to strengthen his confidence in the viability of such unwieldy gatherings.

Aside from finance, or only tangential to it, Neville's interests ranged wide. Often his ideas were the accepted bases of action by his colleagues. Within the party at this time he probably initiated policy more than any other man. (Churchill referred to him as the "packhorse" of the Government, and Harold Macmillan later called him the "mayor of the palace.") London transport and metropolitan police measures, iron and steel modernization, petroleum and housing acts, and a score of other Government interests and acts all reflected a measure of his influence.

Not all of his ideas were accepted, of course. His scheme for a reform of the House of Lords (which would have cut down on hereditary peers in favor of life peers) was pigeonholed as "too thorny" to touch at the time. His proposal for the establishment of a Department of Housing, aimed in part at demonstrating the Government's earnestness about slum clearance, failed to inspire the Prime Minister. His "limited liability plan," which envisioned the upholding of a mutual guarantee among a group of nations by a kind of international police force, was blocked by the Chiefs of Staff. Neville did not always take defeat gracefully, and his responses to failure were often tinged with irritation and impatience.

The limited liability scheme marked Neville's growing interest in foreign affairs. With actual foreign policy-making he was still only occasionally concerned, but passing months brought increasing involvement. The general ineffectiveness of John Simon, the Foreign Secretary, opened the way for this. His hesitating and irresolute attitudes were a spur to action for a colleague like Neville, who could not contemplate a problem without trying to solve it.

The collapse of the World Disarmament Conference in mid-June, 1933, following hard upon the Nazi take-over in Germany, prompted a reassessment of the European scene and a decision to release departments from the operating principle that no major war need be envisaged for ten years. That obviously implied a possible realignment in the expenditure of Exchequer funds. As for the conference itself, Neville was inclined to the view that it had tried to do too much at once. Consequently, he proposed to Simon disarmament by stages, an approach that was much discussed—though unfortunately with little success—the following year.

Though hopeful for disarmament, Neville held in early 1934 that Britain was "giving too much attention to the details of disarmament, and not enough to security." [5] It was in this context that he worked out his scheme for the limited liability force, which embraced the basic concept of collective security. Neville was not at this stage, as he was indeed a few years later, adverse to the collective approach to security. The Saar imbroglio of later 1934 seemed to him a "heaven-sent opportunity" for Britain to lead in the establishment of a truly international force to maintain order in the region until its fate was decided by plebiscite. It was at length his idea, not Simon's suggestion of an Anglo-Italian force, which was accepted by the Cabinet and advanced through the League.

The Nazi-engineered murder of Austrian Chancellor Engelbert Dollfuss in July, 1934, horrified Neville and increased his loathing (his terms) of Nazism. He had earlier begun to insist that Germany was the enemy to watch, and all his later lack of perception in this regard notwithstanding, he was at *this* point in time considerably ahead of many of his colleagues. The ensuing Italian movement of troops had his full support: "It's the only thing Germans understand." What did not satisfy him was that "we do not shape our foreign policy accordingly." [6]

He had at least two things in mind: a more vigorous effort to clarify Britain's position on a number of international matters, and greater attention to the requirements of defense. Deeming it impossible for Britain effectively to divide her forces in the event of conflict between Europe and the Far East, and seeing Germany as the primary threat, Neville pushed for a non-aggression pact with Japan (to include assurances on the integrity of China). But inquiries made of the Japanese offered little hope. A unilateral declaration that the integrity of the Low Countries was a vital British interest which she would defend by all the means in her power greatly appealed to him—but not to his colleagues. Likewise, his urging that Anthony Eden should visit Moscow coincident with Simon's scheduled visit to Berlin—a notable position in view of his later attitude toward Russia—got little support in the Cabinet. Significantly, he saw that Britain "should not be too stiff with France, or too insistent upon her discarding weapons which she may think essential for her safety." [7]

The German cancellation of Simon's invitation to Berlin (March, 1935) sprang mainly from the British Government's publication of a White Paper relating to defense which contained a sizable increase in military Estimates. A fierce denunciation of the document by the Labor and Liberal Parties, largely on doctrinal grounds, ensued; but Neville rose quickly to its support. Indeed, the White Paper reflected to a considerable extent his own thinking on rearmament and defense. Two years before, he had concluded that "common prudence" necessitated a strengthening of British defenses. While as Chancellor he deplored the prospect of diverting millions of pounds to rearmament, he saw the resolute remedying of defense deficiencies as the only alternative to his limited liability plan. Early 1934 brought the establishment of a Defense Requirements Committee (composed of the permanent advisers of the service chiefs), whose proposals were channeled to a Cabinet committee. There Neville became the moving spirit—to the point where he came to feel, with some justification, that he had practically taken charge of the defense requirements of the country. He scaled the estimated five-year expenditures of the DRC downward from £76 million to £50 million, but rearranged it so as greatly to increase the strength of the home air force. Air defense against Germany he saw as *the* preeminent need, and the Cabinet's eventual decision for an acceleration of air power owed much to him. In short, Neville played an active role, perhaps as active as anyone, in promoting British rearmament during these uncertain years. Of course, the temper of the nation was such that rearmament was not a popular cause, so no one made it a crusading issue.

From late 1933 on, the MacDonald Government was exposed to increasing criticism on a number of fronts. The Foreign Office was especially vulnerable, for the uncertain efforts of Simon had captured the imagination of no one. There was widespread talk of a change there as 1934 wore on, and much of it centered on

Neville. When Chief Whip David Margesson, supported by a group of ministers, at length (late 1934) warned MacDonald bluntly of Simon's liability, he added that both the House and the country would like to see Neville in the post. The idea was not new. Over the preceding six years Churchill, Baldwin, and Halifax had all suggested Neville for the Foreign Office, and MacDonald acknowledged in 1933 that he could think of no one better suited to succeed Simon. But the Prime Minister felt him indispensable at the Exchequer.

Margesson's remonstrances brought the idea into the open, and while Neville may have been momentarily tempted by it, his general reaction was negative. He noted in his diary, somewhat speciously, that the Foreign Office was too expensive; he could not afford it. He would not welcome the journeys to Geneva, and perhaps more to the point, he would "loathe and detest" the social ceremonies associated with the post. Further, he did not want to risk the charge that, seeing budgetary difficulties ahead, he had moved to abandon the Exchequer while there was yet time.[8] With Neville pride was an important thing, and it is likely that his reasons may be accepted in ascending order of importance. Within a week he had decided that he would not change to the Foreign Office during that Parliament, and there the matter rested.

The question of Neville's transferral to the Foreign Office was just one aspect of overdue Cabinet reconstruction, which was much discussed during the last year of MacDonald's leadership. The Prime Minister frequently hinted at retirement, and as criticism welled up against both Government measures (especially those pertaining to unemployment assistance) and the lack of them, a change became only a question of time. In the spring of 1935, Neville himself judged MacDonald ill and worn, Baldwin tired and unwilling to apply his mind to problems. Earlier he had taken a certain delight in finding new policies for each of his colleagues in turn. But delight was gradually replaced by irritation and frustration; he came to feel, somewhat justifiably, that he was carrying the Government on *his* back. So with a characteristic commingling of impatience and loyalty, he prodded his colleagues toward the needed change. It finally occurred in June, 1935, when MacDonald stepped down in favor of Baldwin. In Neville's view, it might well have come earlier.

Coincident with the change at the top, Simon was replaced at the Foreign Office by Samuel Hoare. A long-time friend of Neville, with whom (by his own testimony[9]) he had a great deal in common, Hoare had received Neville's support for the post. Neville remained at the Exchequer, from which spot his influence in the Government continued to expand. A rather stern and forbidding figure for all who did not know him well, he was at times concerned, as he admitted to his sisters, with the view that he was over-cautious, humdrum, commonplace, and unenterprising. But he quickly reassured himself that the charge was groundless. Otherwise, he could not have accomplished what he had during his first three years at the Treasury.

CHAPTER X

"Heir Apparent" (*1935–1937*)

ALTHOUGH THREE MONTHS BEFORE, NEVILLE HAD CONSIDERED BALD-
win tired and unwilling to grapple with problems, he nonetheless
welcomed the change in leadership. Even if the past provided
little ground for optimism, there was still the opportunity to in-
troduce policy changes necessary to meet increasingly ominous international developments. Most troublesome at the moment was
Italy's campaign of aggression in Abyssinia—a problem which
was to harass the British (and others) for many months. Rum-
blings from Germany, especially the March, 1935, announcement
of her intention to rearm (the first formal repudiation of a clause
of the Treaty of Versailles) was an additional cause for alarm.
That event had prompted an Anglo-French-Italian meeting at
Stresa in April, but the moral condemnation of Germany's action
which resulted did little to clarify matters—particularly when
two months later the British appeared to condone German rearmament by negotiating a naval treaty with Germany in Berlin.[1] The uncertainty, confusion, and general flaccidity which
were to characterize British foreign policy in the latter half of the
1930s were already painfully apparent.

The confusion reached down to—indeed many have argued
that it sprang from—the British people. The so-called Peace Bal-
lot sponsored by the League of Nations Union in June, 1935, emphasized the already obvious fact that Britain stood for peace.
But it had a significant element of uncertainty in it. While a vast
majority of the more than ten million people canvassed indicated
a willingness to push collective security to the point of economic
sanctions, only two-thirds of them were prepared to use force, and
a crushing majority stood for an "all-around reduction of armaments." The question of what would happen should economic
sanctions lead to hostilities was thus ignored. Neville termed the
whole thing "terribly mischievous"; it only enhanced existing
confusion and undercut the case for rearmament set forth, however modestly, in the White Paper of three months before. That
those who championed the League of Nations, and the covenant

of force it seemed to imply, were also those most opposed to armaments was for Neville a contradiction most difficult to accept.

The place that British rearmament occupied in Neville's thinking is perhaps best illustrated in his attitude toward a national
election in the autumn of 1935. Given the state of Europe and the
confusion in Britain, there were good reasons for electing a
House which Baldwin could call his own. That was abundantly
clear by the time Parliament rose in August. The Conservative
Central Office worked on the assumption that the election would
turn on unemployment. Busy with a variety of plans for public
works to bolster distressed areas, Neville might easily have accepted that assumption. Instead, he insisted from the start that
defense was the central issue, both in terms of national interest
and party advantage. Alarmed by Italy's action in Abyssinia,
fearful lest the Nazis find the temptation to demand territory too
great to resist, and aware that Labor intended (on the basis of
rearmament plans) to charge the Conservative Party with war-
mongering, he advocated the "bold course" of openly appealing
to the country on a defense program.[2]

This course did not in the end prevail. After weeks of uncertainty, it emerged that Baldwin, prompted perhaps by Horace
Wilson, chief industrial adviser, was more inclined to go to the
country on the grounds that (as Neville put it) "we were in for a
long and anxious period in foreign affairs in which it was essential that we should have a stable Government with the authority
of the nation behind it." [3] Neville bent to this approach, but in
his speeches in over a dozen constituencies and in the party manifesto which he was largely responsible for drafting, references to
rearmament and defense stuck out prominently. In consequence,
he was subjected to violent abuse by the Labor Party as the campaign progressed, the terms "scare-monger," "fire-eater," and
"militarist" being among the milder ones applied to him. If there
is any truth in the charge, later made by the Government's opponents, that during the campaign the question of rearmament was
subverted to the point of deceit, the basis for this does not lie
with Chamberlain.

Other issues were not, of course, forgotten. In Birmingham,
Glasgow, London, Cardiff, and Stoke, Neville spoke of houses
built, taxes remitted, and new plans to increase employment. The
cause of the League, whose first function he saw as the prevention
of war, received firm support. The dangers of socialist administration, as he saw them, were outlined in full. Often, however, he

returned to the central theme: "Our policy is defense without defiance; their policy is defiance without defense."

Whatever the issues on which the voters judged, the election resulted in a surprisingly large 250-seat majority for the National Government. (Neville held Edgbaston by more than 21,000 votes, while Birmingham again returned all twelve Government supporters.) Very little Cabinet reconstruction followed, Duff Cooper's move to the War Office constituting the most notable change. In Neville's view the Cabinet was weak, particularly in the House of Commons. It was an unfortunate condition, for a very stern test was now at hand: Abyssinia.

Since December, 1934, aggressive Italian action in Abyssinia had been a thorn in the flesh of the League and its individual members. Acknowledging the economic and population factors, as well as prestige motives, in Italy's action, Neville still found it "barbarous" and felt it necessary to convince Mussolini that he must abandon the use of force. Determined Anglo-French measures seemed to hold the best prospect. But in any case the League must act; its fate was at stake. As Neville put it in early July: "If the League were demonstrated to be incapable of effective intervention to stop this war, it would be practically impossible to maintain the fiction that its existence was justified at all." [4] Nor did his viewpoint quickly change. Some weeks later it was still the same: "If members of the League from fear of consequences were to say they would stand idly by . . . notice would have to go out to the rest of the world each is to be for himself, and the devil take the hindmost." [5]

Hoare's address to the League Assembly on September 11 advanced—at least in words—the cause of resolute collective action. It probably bore the marks of Neville's influence, for Hoare had consulted him (on the eve of his departure for an infrequent holiday) in its preparation. But strong words were one thing, strong action another. The French, obsessed with cajoling Italy in an effort to keep her apart from Germany—they had reached an "understanding," the so-called Laval-Mussolini Agreements, some months before—were disinclined to do anything more than stall. Indeed, most Englishmen were only (in Vansittart's famous phrase) "eager to kill Musso with their mouths." [6]

The Italian invasion of Abyssinia in early October spurred the League to develop, and in mid-November to approve, a policy of economic sanctions against Italy. Neville's attitude toward sanctions is not entirely clear, perhaps because his thinking on the issue was subject to change, perhaps because he saw in them at different times a variety of purposes: to intimidate the aggressor, to promote conciliation, and to strengthen the League. He seems early (August, 1935) to have doubted their value, in part because of German and American absence from the League. And at least one colleague found him later on "frankly cynical": the League must be "tried out" mainly for domestic political reasons.[7] But he apparently came to believe that sanctions *might* work, both in halting Italy and, consequently, in deterring Germany. In fact, by late November he was taking a lead in advocating the extension of sanctions to include oil, believing that otherwise the plan "would crumble, the League would lose its coherence and our whole policy would be destroyed." [8] He was willing, however, to hold up a decision on oil pending further contact with France.

An early December conversation between the British Foreign Secretary (who was merely passing through Paris on his way to Switzerland) and his French counterpart resulted in the infamous Hoare-Laval plan. It proposed to settle the Abyssinian tangle by giving two-thirds of Abyssinia to Italy, in return for which the Abyssinians would acquire a corridor to the sea through British Somaliland. Premature leakage of the plan not only created a great outpouring of public indignation in Britain; it also took the Cabinet entirely by surprise and confronted it with the unpleasant alternatives of accepting responsibility for the plan or throwing over the Foreign Secretary. Though jarred and perplexed by Hoare's misjudgment, Neville was one of those who chose to stand behind his colleague and friend. He deplored the effect on the Government's position: ". . . Nothing could be worse. . . . Our whole prestige in foreign affairs at home and abroad has tumbled to pieces. . . ." [9] But he termed the clamor for Hoare's resignation "absurd," resisted using the Foreign Secretary as a scapegoat (once the Cabinet, amid tense dissatisfaction, had agreed to accept responsibility for the plan), and at length proposed that Hoare offer to resign, leaving acceptance or rejection to hinge on the course of debate in the Commons. His suggestion was not accepted by his colleagues. Hoare was forced to step down without delay, and Anthony Eden succeeded him. Thus the case was closed, but among its numerous side-effects were these: Neville was severely stung by the abuse leveled at Hoare, especially by Labor. Aside from the merits of the plan, which were admittedly debatable, the Foreign Secretary was, after all, exploring "the possibilities of the League." Neville was also strengthened in the view that force alone was the ultimate sanction of the League, and unless it could be wielded with real effectiveness, it was best not to wield it at all.

Impressed by the obvious lesson in the Abyssinian affair, Neville looked again toward the nation's military requirements. He set about drafting, after long committee consultation, a second White Paper on rearmament. Published in early March, it called for a modernization and modest enlargement of the army and navy, an increase in planes both for home and imperial defense, and expansion of the country's capacity to produce war goods (to be accomplished by increased orders and financial aid to companies not normally engaged in the manufacture of munitions). With several colleagues, he pressed for a full inquiry into the whole structure of defense. This resulted (early March, 1936) in the establishment of a Ministry for the Co-ordination of Defense. Baldwin thought that Neville should take the post—a reflection perhaps of his initiative and leadership in this area. But Neville declined, his instinct, the advice of those he consulted (including Austen), and his reluctance to leave the Treasury in someone else's hands[10] weighing against the move. Others were considered, including Churchill and Hoare, whom Neville favored at first even though public opinion might be against him. The nod eventually went to Thomas Inskip, the Attorney-General, as the safest man. He would, as Neville put it, "excite no enthusiasm," but neither would he enmesh the Government in "fresh perplexities."

The choice of one whose name involved no risk reflected the Cabinet's response to events of the previous weekend: Germany's military occupation of the Rhineland. While time was spent in talk of avoiding the repudiation of Locarno, and awaiting a reaction from the distraught and hesitating French, there was never a question of real retaliatory action. When the Locarno powers, followed by the League Council, gathered in London, Neville and his colleagues were unanimous against any notion of using military force. A half-hearted French suggestion of sanctions was quickly brushed aside. "Public opinion here would not support us in sanctions of any kind," Neville told Pierre-Etienne Flandin, the French Foreign Minister, on March 12.[11] In this he appeared to convey a widely-held conviction. No wonder; the impending failure of Italian sanctions was clear to all who looked.

Negotiation among the Locarno powers eventually came to naught—though resolutions on future procedures were not in short supply. Britain remained impaled on the "contradiction which had become [her] sustenance." [12] By treaty she was guarantor, by temperament mediator. Eden talked of hard alternatives should conciliation fail; he also spoke of Britain's motive as "the appeasement of Europe." In all of this Neville was deeply entwined. Encouraged that the Commons debate, from which strong words had emerged, would strengthen Britain's hand in dealing with the Germans, he had also refuted Flandin's view that a firm Anglo-French position would force Germany to yield without war as an unreliable estimate of a "mad dictator's" reactions.

The apparent ineptness of both the League and its individual members in relation to the events of preceding months led Neville to hard thinking about foreign affairs. Late in April he recorded some general ideas in his diary. Collective security, as then understood, had failed, largely because it depended on the individual action of League members whose capacities and interests differed widely. Consequently, the idea that the League could use force should be at least temporarily abandoned—though the League should remain as a "moral force and focus." In its place, he favored "some kind of international police force." Pending the formation of such a force, peace might be promoted through a series of regional pacts registered and approved by the League. This might make it easier for Germany to return to the League and open the way for Halifax, Lord Privy Seal, to visit Hitler.[13] The approach to European affairs which he was later to pursue as prime minister was now in process of development.

Translated so as to pertain directly to Italy and Abyssinia, this meant that in Neville's view the League was beaten. The time was not yet right to admit it, but it was beaten all the same. He said so in a startling speech to the 1900 Club on June 10—the much-quoted address in which he termed continuation of sanctions "the very mid-summer of madness." The episode is notable in several ways: it demonstrates Neville's accurate diagnosis of the weaknesses of the League and reflects his thinking that it was silly to prolong sanctions which had been designed to prevent the Abyssinian war when the war was now in fact over—especially since prolongation would increase the risk of provoking a broader struggle. It shows his expanding initiative in foreign affairs, for by his own explanation, he presented his ideas without first consulting Eden (who was bound to resist them) so as to give the party and country a lead, a sign that the Government was not drifting without a policy. Further, it illustrates a developing *modus operandi*—at best irregular procedures, at worst behind-the-back tactics—which Neville would utilize increasingly in the future. Since only days before, Eden had assured the Commons that no change was contemplated in the Government's position on sanctions, ethical considerations might well have suggested to Neville a somewhat different course of action.

In the weeks which followed the mid-summer outbreak of civil war in Spain, the British Government quickly and surely embraced the policy of non-intervention to which it clung tenaciously until the end of that brutal conflict three years later. While Neville's role in the policy's acceptance is moot, he doubtless shared the view of colleagues that neutrality was the only viable response. Also like them, he was ready in early August to grasp a formal agreement on such a policy when the French, with British encouragement, proposed it. As with his early view of Italian sanctions, he appeared to believe that a policy once adopted was best fully applied. Consequently, he pressed for strict adherence, frowned upon all efforts to accord belligerent rights to either side, and pushed for legislation barring British ships from carrying war materials to Spanish ports. For a time this stand was highly popular. When it became less so later on, Neville was very little moved.

While the course of international affairs became ever more distracting, a variety of domestic matters also laid claim to some of Neville's time. In addition to his key position at the Exchequer, his broad interest in many areas of Cabinet responsibility, and his natural inclination toward work, Neville's personal work-load was further increased by the fact that he was coming to be recognized everywhere as Baldwin's heir apparent. In the process of gradual development for some time, this fact was enhanced during 1936 by his occasional assumption of the role of "acting P. M." and by increasing talk of Baldwin's retirement. As a result, Neville was drawn into a number of issues and problems which sprang not so much from his official responsibilities as from his impending leadership. Throughout the year he suffered from genuine overwork, his troubles compounded by another severe and lingering attack of gout. But he was able to get away for fishing weekends and occasionally to indulge his lifelong interests in nature study and music. So he was more than content with his lot, and wrote his sister in the autumn that, although almost every day brought a volume of work sufficient to keep him out of bed until the "small hours," he would not now willingly change his position for any other.

The Budget of 1936 caused him little difficulty. In reviewing his stewardship since 1931, he saw the introduction of the tariff and the establishment of cheap money as the "two main pillars" of his policy. They had worked to eliminate an adverse balance of trade, added millions to revenue without greatly affecting commodity prices, helped to reduce unemployment, and greatly boosted individual deposits in savings banks. They were not, therefore, subject to major change. Increased defense spending, of course, demanded new revenue. To meet this Neville proposed a series of measures to deal with tax avoidance, the appropriation of excess money from the Road Fund, a moderate increase in the income tax, and an increase in the duty on tea. Looking ahead, he saw the need to meet future defense expenditures by loan. Such sacrifices involved disappointment for all, but, he declared in response to the Opposition's charge that this was a war budget, "no man hesitates to set his fire-fighting appliances in readiness when already he can feel the heat of the flames on his face." [14] In retrospect, neither side came close to realizing just how hot those flames would be.

More troublesome at the time were intra-party clashes, often present in any government, but now particularly sharp and defiant of resolution. They sprang from a variety of sources, perhaps the most important among them being the daily scrutiny of Government activity by powerful elements outside the Cabinet and the absence of clear-cut alternative policies. Whether defense efforts were yet sufficient to meet the growing European danger was the subject of hot debate—Neville and Austen once coming to verbal blows over what Neville saw as "panicky" proposals on armaments. Similarly, the attitude to be adopted toward the League and its future caused party colleagues to bristle at each other intermittently. Still more intense was the question of how to deal with the "special areas," enclaves of mass unemployment which grated on the national conscience. Disagreement on ends was slight, but disagreement on means was great—and growing. Some of these issues continued to tear and divide the party for years thereafter, and Neville's time and efforts were increasingly consumed by them.

Cabinet change might have been one result of such disputes. But the changes which occurred were minor and piecemeal. Hoare went to the Admiralty, W. S. Morrison (Chamberlain's financial secretary at the Treasury) took over Agriculture, and Leslie Hore-Belisha became Minister of Transport—in moves effected mainly by Neville. But none of the "powers" (Churchill, for example) was taken in, nor were any "bright young men" involved. The old-man character, which the Government retained until 1940, was already apparent and clearly set.

Perhaps the most tedious domestic issue in which Neville was involved in 1936 was the abdication crisis which grew out of the new King Edward VIII's apparent intention to wed an American divorcée. Baldwin was, of course, responsible for handling—masterfully, some would say—the negotiations with the King. Neville was one to whom he turned for advice and, as it turned out, staunch support if such were needed in warding off all danger to the throne. Perturbed by the King's slow response to Baldwin's first private warning in late October, Neville favored sternly advising him to reorder his private life (which meant ending his association with Mrs. Simpson) or face the resignation of the Cabinet. To the King's eventual suggestion of a morganatic marriage, Neville was at once opposed. He had no doubt it would only be a prelude to making Mrs. Simpson queen with full rights. With Dominion and Opposition backing, the Cabinet then (December 2) rejected such a solution. While truth and fiction, fanned by the press, swirled together in wide confusion, Neville saw the alternatives as being very simple: abdication and marriage, or complete renunciation of the marriage. And the King should be pressed to make up his mind quickly, for the drawn-out affair was "holding up business and employment" and "paralyzing" foreign policy. Though approaching his task somewhat more moderately, it was along these lines that Baldwin acted, and the King proceeded to make his choice.

Neville was relieved, for he had "felt all through that we should never be safe with this K[ing]." [15] Nor did his attitude mellow toward the end. To the suggestion of Walter Monckton, the King's personal adviser, that special legislation, coincident with the Abdication Bill, make Mrs. Simpson's divorce final at once, he reacted coolly. It might smack of a deal. The idea at length collapsed. Throughout the whole affair Neville's austere standards, his instinct against procrastination, and his insistence that even a king must face reality made him a less-than-ideal counsellor. At the same time he helped to provide a demand for decision and support for the throne which allowed the least possible diminution of respect for an institution which Englishmen regard so highly.

After a short holiday in France, Neville returned to the last session of Parliament under Baldwin's leadership. His own assumption of command was now firmly fixed. The Conservative Party Conference at Margate, October, 1936, had acknowledged him as leader-designate, and by the end of the year, Baldwin's resignation had been set for the following May. The five months which preceded his take-over were difficult ones. His burdens in government were heavy, the Parliament was full of controversy, and his brother Austen died suddenly in March.

By 1937 considerations of Budget and Defense were closely entwined. Still another Defense White Paper, on which Neville again did most of the work, expanded the plans laid down a year before—with special emphasis on the air force and navy[16]—and envisaged a five-year expenditure of £1500 million. A modest document in terms of later needs, it nevertheless represented a sharp increase in defense appropriations and reflected the impact of the Abyssinian and Rhineland affairs. To meet such expenditures, Neville introduced (February, 1937) legislation authorizing the Government to borrow £400 million. When his Budget was announced in early April, it proposed to increase the income tax and, to everyone's surprise, to levy a new graduated tax (which he called the N. D. C.: National Defense Contribution) upon the growth of business profits.

The latter provision raised a howl of protest. The stock exchange slumped, business organizations screamed, and many Conservatives writhed at what seemed to be a socialist measure. A promise to control excessive profiteering by contractors involved with the nation's expanding defense program had been part of the Government's election manifesto in 1935. Neville now saw that this might be accomplished by a measure which would raise revenue at the same time. So he stuck to his guns through more than a month of vicious controversy—coming to feel it "the bravest thing" he had ever done in public life, for by it he risked the premiership. He had, however, embarked upon this difficult course (taxing profits was one thing, taxing their rate of expansion something else indeed) without taking wide counsel. His defenders were few, and in the end he was forced to settle for a straight 5 percent tax on business profits—which itself would probably have been intolerable to business had not the N. D. C. scare preceded it.

Other matters kept Neville busy during the spring. The thorny problem of the "special areas" was met by his proposal to extend the Act of 1934 for five years, modestly enlarge the commissioners' powers, and increase the Exchequer block grants by £5 million. It was all "pretty thin" he admitted in private; but he defended it vigorously in the belief that a quick and all-embracing remedy was impossible to find. The Coronation brought a number of important persons to London, and Neville spoke with many of them: Foreign Minister Beck of Poland, Premier Hodza of Czechoslovakia, Foreign Minister Delbos of France, and War Minister Marshal von Blomberg of Germany. An Imperial Conference, held in conjunction with the Coronation, studied and endorsed a general approach to foreign policy with which Neville's name would eventually become synonymous: appeasement.

Austen's death in March weighed heavily on Neville for a time. Though often at odds on political issues, the brothers had always held a deep respect and affection for each other—within a family setting where ties were unusually strong. As he thought of his father and brother, and his own impending leadership, Neville could not help but wonder whether "Fate" had some dark secret in store for him, "to carry out her ironies to the end." Indeed in a sense she had. But it was to take a very different form from any he might have imagined then.

PART II

PART II

CHAPTER XI

Prime Minister: The First Months

CHAMBERLAIN'S ELEVATION TO THE PRIME MINISTERSHIP IN LATE May, 1937, was not a sudden or spectacular occurrence. It was, in a sense, a bureaucratic formality, an internal affair of the Conservative Party long in process of development. Supporters and opponents alike pretty much expected him to pick up where Baldwin had left off, perhaps infuse the administration with a higher standard of efficiency, but hardly attain any special prominence in the galaxy of English prime ministers. Indeed Chamberlain himself seems to have had no illusions about any particular "call to greatness." Leadership had come to him, so he himself insisted, without his having raised a finger to obtain it; and his ready acceptance of the role was due at least as much to a sense of duty and service common to men of his class and generation, and perhaps a vague notion about fulfilling a family promise which ought to have fallen to his father or brother, as anything else. But as time would quickly show, the Chamberlain era would not be simply a continuation of the Baldwin years. The new Prime Minister turned out to be a very different person from his predecessor, and the conditions in which he labored were ones of abnormal, vast, and continuing turmoil in European affairs. It is one of the ironies of history that a man so suited to deal with pressing domestic issues should need to devote his efforts almost entirely to international problems in a situation of constant crisis.

Perhaps the major factor in Chamberlain's approach to the prime ministership, as compared with Baldwin's conduct of the office, was his readiness—no, eagerness—to provide a lead on almost every question. His immense power of industry, his instinct for order, and his insistence that plain language be followed by firm action had long been in evidence; and the fact that he was now in his later sixties had in no way diminished these qualities. Chairman of almost all the Cabinet committees that really mattered, he was thoroughly familiar with a wide range of government activities, and worked incessantly not only at keeping abreast of but maintaining an active role in the developments in each. He took great interest in the individual problems of each of his ministers—although his regard for their collective views was another matter. A model middle class businessman—capable, efficient, diligent, upright—he believed in planning ahead. Not surprisingly, one of the first tasks he assigned his department ministers was that of developing two-year programs in their respective areas of responsibility.

Diligence and industry did not, of course, always mean imagination, and in the matter of Cabinet-making Chamberlain was extremely cautious. He made no changes of substance until they were forced upon him, and those effected under such circumstances opened no new or refreshing vistas. Although some of his colleagues possessed executive ability, they were, with few exceptions, men who shared his views or submitted quietly to his leadership. There was no one second-in-command, as he had been to Baldwin. There was no successor-apparent, which probably helps to explain the almost unnatural loyalty shown to him by his ministers. Chamberlain stood out above his Cabinet colleagues, and in this sense there is truth in the charge that his was something of a one-man government. Certainly he consulted some of his colleagues frequently, but there is little evidence that they greatly influenced policy. For positive decision he looked to himself.

This situation, in development for quite some time, was enhanced by Chamberlain's solitary nature. While in private life, within a small circle of close friends and family, he seemed to have a warm and human side, in public he appeared cold and unsympathetic. Even in the Commons, he was aloof and somewhat magisterial. Having long been alienated—to the point of detestation—from the Opposition (Labor) group, he was also barely known by his own back-benchers. He seldom if ever visited the smoking room and was not easily approachable in the Lobby. He had little contact with the younger men in the party, whom he was inclined to regard as a disappointing lot. His lack of humor, self-consciousness, combative intelligence (which often showed in sharp and castigating speech), his general attachment to things Victorian, even his formal dress, contributed to the gulf which separated him from all but his closest colleagues. He was, in short, a man whose efficiency, drive, and high sense of responsibility and public duty commanded real respect; but he was not a man with personal appeal to whom fellow politicians became sentimentally attached. Aware of his personal shortcomings, perhaps to a surprising degree, he could not, of course, significantly alter his character and personality at his stage in life—even had he wanted to do so.

Despite his "conservative" nature, there is some question as to whether Chamberlain was ever temperamentally Conservative, whether he ever really escaped from his Liberal Unionist traditions. Though open, perhaps, to the charge that he lacked vital understanding of the people whose lot he desired to improve, he retained the old Liberal ardor in his approach to social and political problems, and his interest in social progress remained keen. The first months of his prime ministership saw further, if modest, advances on this front. The "black coat" Insurance Act, a comprehensive Factory Act, and his own Physical Training and Recreation Act went through their last stages. A new Housing Act was planned to further the clearance of slums, a Criminal Justice Bill reflected a change in public sentiment on the very meaning of crime and punishment. A Coal Bill nationalized royalties. A White Paper on milk recalled one of Chamberlain's earlier Birmingham interests, as did a campaign to encourage wider use of national health services. And Chamberlain seriously contemplated—so those who have seen his papers attest[1]—both a vast scheme for "a central authority to act at once as an information bureau, with special regard to the location of industry, and as a central planning body for the country as a whole," and further reform of local government.

Among the other delicate, if not explosive, matters with which Chamberlain early busied himself were these: trade (especially with America and the Dominions), Palestine, and Ireland. Continued economic recovery in America and the Dominions seemed in 1937 to demand a relaxation of the quantitative restrictions established by Britain at Ottawa in 1931. Though England had less to gain than the others by such a relaxation, Chamberlain moved gradually toward it, and the eventual outcome was trade treaties with the United States and Canada (November, 1938) which not only mutually reduced duties, but had by that time potentially significant overtones of an identity of political interests. In Palestine the need to reconcile Britain's wartime pledges to both Jews and Arabs still defied solution, while the atrocities committed by each side against the other, the influx of refugees, and industrialization problems heightened the tension in the much-beleaguered British mandate. Not content with Dominion status, Ireland had moved to sever all her ties with Britain. But weighty problems of economics and defense remained. With

Prime Minister Eamon De Valera, Chamberlain confronted these directly, and through a series of conversations the two produced a specific agreement on trade, treaty ports, and land annuities (April, 1938), as well as general good will which did much to soothe the sensitive feelings on both sides of the Irish Sea.

Long aware of the pressing need to quicken the pace of rearmament, Chamberlain's interest and activity in that area did not diminish once he became prime minister. And while hindsight once again forces acknowledgment that far too little was done, it is nonetheless true that much of what was accomplished was owing to his efforts. By 1937 he was speaking of a £1500 million expenditure over the next few years, whereas two years earlier he had thought in terms of £120 million. Very doubtful that the next war, if it came, would be anything like the last, he now believed that British resources would be most profitably employed in the air and on the sea, not in building up armies. This view was not without its critics, especially in the Army itself, but it reflected in the air and naval construction emphasized in the White Papers of 1937 and 1938. The establishment of an Air Ministry and Air Staff under Lord Swinton were important steps in this direction. The Army was not by-passed entirely. Leslie Hore-Belisha was sent to the War Office with express instructions to effect "drastic changes"—which meant, among other things, the passing of authority to younger men, bringing the Army commands into closer touch with the War Office, and reducing the obstacles to recruitment. So it was not so much the Prime Minister's grasp of the problem which was deficient, as some have held; it was his (and the nation's) inability to make speedier progress toward his goal which stands in question. The extent to which this rested on Britain's relative technological decline after the World War is still a matter of some debate. More pertinent, perhaps, was the lingering conception that rearmament must not— no matter how broadly and urgently viewed—be pursued in such a way as to interfere with the normal operations of British industry. Behind this there lurked the fact that few Englishmen were yet prepared to believe that the nation must now prepare for all-out war; defense was still generally understood in terms of minimal deterrent protection and nothing more. Thus it was in their unreadiness to make an *emergency* commitment to rearmament, to undertake the task confronting them on a veritable crash basis, that Chamberlain and Britain fell short.

This inevitably influenced Chamberlain's foreign policy, for he was thoroughly convinced by now—if ever he had thought it otherwise—that policy must depend on power. And foreign policy had quickly become his primary concern and greatest challenge.

Appeasement. The word is synonymous with the name of Neville Chamberlain, and rightly so, for the "appeasement of Europe" was fundamental to his whole approach to foreign policy. This is not to say that the idea of appeasement was original with Chamberlain, that it had no precedent in international relations, or that the appeasement policy of the 1930s was wholly his creation. But he was the one democratic statesman who sought to develop appeasement into a systematic approach to foreign policy, and who was, from mid-1937 onward, its principal architect and primary exponent.

The term "appeasement," a respectable word used by a wide range of British policy-makers midway through the 1930s, had never been clearly defined. Indeed, it defied precise definition, in part because it involved a psychological reaction against the shortcomings of Versailles. It was "an affair of the heart, intuitive, not taught; a strong emotion, not an academic speculation." [2] The term generally was taken to mean the reduction of international tension by the methodical removal of the principal causes of friction among nations. More specifically, to Chamberlain and his associates it meant, in practice if not in theory, the making of timely concessions to disgruntled powers—who may have been disgruntled for good reasons—in the hope that this would alleviate their grievances, reduce their tendency toward aggressive action, and open the way to lasting international peace and harmony.

The motives, experiences, and feelings which converted a variety of Englishmen to appeasement—at least temporarily—were certainly complex. Some very general in nature, others quite specific, they ranged from a natural revulsion against war and the impact of world-wide depression on European political life to the military weakness of Britain, fear of Bolshevism, and the potent notion that Germany was only agitating for a long overdue revision of Versailles. Chamberlain's commitment to appeasement must be seen in terms of two broad factors: his assessment of the European situation in late 1937, and certain deep impulses and/or traits of his nature. While unavoidably open to a variety of interpretations, these factors, in combination, come close to explaining all. And attempts—of which there have been many—to seek an explanation of his views in terms of deep-seated psychological instability, blind class prejudice, a child-like ignorance of foreign affairs, and other similarly vague and nebulous notions are often misleading or genuinely inaccurate.[3]

There was nothing simple or reassuring about the international situation which Chamberlain faced. Germany was momentarily quiescent, but menacing. Italy had been on a rampage, to the great discomfiture of most of Europe, for several years. The tragic confusion which was the Spanish Civil War, complicated by ideological chaos and the intervention of Italy, Germany, and Russia, threatened to blow open at any moment, with European-wide repercussions which none could gauge. France was so distraught with domestic ills, and political paralysis which accompanied her affliction, as to appear quite incapable of resolute external action. Nor was there any real basis for bringing the United States into European calculations. President Roosevelt spoke in October, 1937, of a "quarantine" on states infected by lawlessness, but it remained to be seen both how and whether sentiments of this kind would be translated into something more than words. Casting a still deeper shadow over this already gloomy picture was the apparent inability of the League of Nations to fulfill, momentarily at least, the chief function for which it had been created. Its dismal failure in the Abyssinian affair left little room for optimism, and Chamberlain said frankly that his estimate of its power and potential had changed considerably since 1935. As for Britain's own power, her plans for rearmament notwithstanding, a broad chasm still yawned between blueprint and product. In the face of all this, it was not surprising that Chamberlain would say: ". . . In the absence of any powerful ally, and until our armaments are completed, we must adjust our foreign policy to our circumstances, and even bear with patience and good humor actions which we would like to treat in a very different fashion." [4]

But there was more to it than that. Chamberlain abhorred war —a view undoubtedly shared by an overwhelming majority of his countrymen, who by this time had reached a stage of moral and social development where war had come to be widely regarded as a barbarity incompatible with civilized life. He recoiled from its waste of human and material resources, and saw any concept of its inevitability as morally indefensible. He could not condone its use save for "a cause that transcends all the human values." It followed from this that the avoidance of war was one of the highest ambitions of statesmanship, and to placate or appease an adversary was a fundamental purpose of diplomacy because it was a necessary condition of the civilized order which it was the purpose of that diplomacy to preserve and develop.[5] What finer achievement could there be for a statesman than to allay the suspicion and fear poisoning the life of Europe? And this could be done only by positive action. Nothing could be gained by allowing Britain and France on one hand, Germany and Italy on the other, to go on "glowering at one another across the frontier, allowing the feeling . . . to become more and more embittered, until at last the barriers are broken down and the conflict begins which many think would mark the end of civilization." [6] Some effort must be made to promote an understanding of one another's aims and objects. A division of European nations along ideological lines must be avoided at all costs, Chamberlain reasoned, and Britain, by her very aloofness from the rest of Europe, might have "some special part" to play as conciliator and mediator. Russia was excluded from his thinking; it was Versailles, not Brest-Litovsk, that demanded rectification, and Russia did not appear to him to be of potential assistance in solving these particular problems. She remained, in a way, outside of Europe.

In Chamberlain's view, an understanding could be reached only through direct discussion. He was optimistic about what could be achieved in this way. The notion that Hitler and Mussolini were too inhuman to approach was rejected as "quite erroneous." While it was the "human side" which made them dangerous, it was that side on which they could be approached with the greatest hope for success.

Much has been written about Chamberlain's "businessman's approach." This is proper, for it is undeniable that his thinking was conditioned by his long years of business experience. Just as the best way to settle business disputes was through quiet and orderly discussion, compromise, and conciliation, so it was with disputes among nations. To Chamberlain, the idea appeared so reasonable that he could not believe that even Hitler would repudiate it. In this he made a major miscalculation. Unable or unwilling—which is more accurate will never be entirely certain —to believe that the ruler of a state so close to Britain could have such an utterly different outlook on life from his own as to be determined to have war for its own sake, Chamberlain took at face value Hitler's repeated declarations that his territorial aims were limited to securing the application of the principle of self-determination (which, the Führer once reminded him, was not a German "invention"). He assumed that Hitler's ambitions were limited to obtaining for Germany an overdue measure of justice.

Indicative of Chamberlain's thinking is a portion of a Guildhall speech he made in early November, 1937:

For any Government deliberately to deny to their people what must be their plainest and simplest right [to live in peace and happiness as opposed to the nightmare of war] would be to betray their trust, and to call down upon their heads the condemnation of all mankind.

I do not believe that such a Government anywhere exists among civilized peoples. I am convinced that the aim of every statesman worthy of the name, to whatever country he belongs, must be the happiness of the people for whom and to whom he is responsible, and in that faith I am sure that a way can and will be found to free the world from the curse of armaments and the fears that give rise to them, and to open up a happier and a wiser future for mankind. . . .[7]

Consequently, it followed that disputes arising within this limited field could be solved by the common-sense, give-and-take methods by which two businessmen would iron out complications in the dealings between their respective firms.

The situation, as Chamberlain saw it, demanded personal action. He was all the more bent on this because the old-established machinery of the Foreign Office did not seem to move quickly enough for the crisis threatening Europe. Contacts established through the normal channels of diplomacy seemed to have a habit of "running into the sand." The time had come for the Prime Minister to deal directly with those who controlled foreign policy in other countries. This led him to employ special emissaries, to maintain close relations with the German and Italian ambassadors in London through confidants, and most important, to develop at 10 Downing Street what appeared to be his own little Foreign Office. Headed by Sir Horace Wilson, the civil service chief whose administrative talents had been helpful to Chamberlain earlier in the Ministry of Health and the Treasury, this office assumed responsibility for keeping Chamberlain informed (and humored), for making and maintaining the contacts he wanted, and for promulgating—if not sometimes actually helping to shape—Chamberlain's ideas on foreign affairs.[8] Its usurpation of the function of policy-making and its constant interference with the details of diplomatic procedure caused, quite naturally, both resentment in the regular Foreign Office and a serious lack of coordination in the administration of foreign affairs. In his zeal for action, Chamberlain thus initiated what became in time —and still remains—one of the most highly questionable and widely-criticized aspects of his policy formulation and execution.

Although concerned about the belligerent and aggressive attitudes of both Germany and Italy, Chamberlain's first thought was to "get on terms with the Germans." In that event, he would not "care a rap for Musso." [9] Thus it was only as his first approaches to Germany failed to elicit a favorable response that Italy loomed larger in his calculations and Chamberlain came to think in terms of weakening the Axis by wooing Italy from it.

Shortly after Chamberlain became Prime Minister, an invitation was extended to Baron von Neurath, the German Foreign Minister, to visit London in June. He first accepted, then declined on a pretext found in Spain. During the next several months the major contacts made were those of Nevile Henderson, the newly-appointed British ambassador in Berlin, a career diplomat of pro-German sentiments who had been assigned to his new post with the express purpose of conveying English good will to Germany and smoothing the way for better Anglo-German relations—and who indeed, as time elapsed, was often ahead of Chamberlain in his efforts to cajole the Germans. But these were not encouraging, Nazi officials (Göring in particular) posing two basic alternatives: an Anglo-German division of world power, with Germany paramount in Europe, Britain overseas; or a Germany forced by lack of cooperation to plan the destruction of Britain. It was not until November, when Lord Halifax, Lord President of the Council (and Master of the Middleton Foxhounds) was invited by Hermann Göring, head of the *Luftwaffe* (and Chief Huntsman of the Reich), to an international hunting exhibition in Berlin that a really good opportunity for sounding German leaders arose.

Chamberlain was anxious for Halifax to go. Here was an excellent chance to establish personal contacts, and the private and unofficial nature of the visit would preclude exaggerated hope or excessive apprehension. Foreign Minister Anthony Eden and the Foreign Office had their reservations—especially after it became clear that if Halifax wished to see Hitler, he would have to seek him out in Berchtesgaden, thus giving the impression that the whole idea was of British origin.[10] Then, too, the British press had caught hold of the news and was inclined to make a big thing of it. But Chamberlain's mind was set on the potential value of the Halifax visit; it was entirely compatible with his policy of "getting together" with the dictators. So Halifax went to Berlin—and Berchtesgaden—during the third week of November.

The visit failed to produce any tangible result, save that of re-emphasizing the wide gulf which separated Britain and Germany.[11] But Halifax returned content that Germany was not about to do anything rash. Chamberlain was satisfied. "The German visit was from my point of view a great success," he wrote his sister a few days later, "because it achieved its object, that of creating an atmosphere in which it is possible to discuss with Germany the practical questions involved in a European settlement." He saw "a fair basis for discussion" in certain of the points which Hitler had raised (colonies, the League, disarmament), though acknowledging that they bristled with difficulties. Nor was there any reason why Britain should not give Germany, in return for assurances that force would not be used against Austria and Czechoslovakia, her own assurance that she would not resort to force to prevent the changes Germany sought, provided they could be obtained by peaceful means.[12]

Consultation with the French (Premier Chautemps, Foreign Minister Delbos, and Under-Secretary Leger came to London in late November) found them anxious to pursue negotiation. So Chamberlain, with Eden and Halifax, explored with them some questions to be raised, positions to be taken, and approaches to be made. Examination of the colonial question as part of a general settlement was one of the points agreed upon—though Eden was unconvinced about the need for haste in this.

Subsequent contacts with Germany, however, produced no positive response. Nazi leaders appeared uninterested, even hostile. It was this which prompted Chamberlain to turn toward Italy, an alternative course of action he had contemplated for quite some time. This brought him into open conflict with his Foreign Secretary. A Cabinet crisis ensued, and in fighting it through to an outcome he was willing to accept, Chamberlain demonstrated an unremitting commitment to appeasement, an earnest confidence in his own judgment, and a stern determination to pursue a solution to European troubles in his own way.

CHAPTER XII

The Pursuit of Appeasement: Phase I

BY EARLY 1938 THERE WERE, IN CHAMBERLAIN'S VIEW, COMPELLING reasons for beginning conversations with Italy. Not only were Anglo-Italian relations deteriorating, but the Rome-Berlin Axis appeared to be tightening. Italy had joined the Anti-Comintern Pact, which Germany had earlier arranged with Japan, and had resigned her membership in the League of Nations, laying the blame for this on Britain's evasion of promised conversations. On the latter point Chamberlain was especially sensitive for a July, 1937, exchange of letters with Mussolini (about which Eden, the Foreign Secretary, was not only not consulted but purposely by-passed because he might object) had proclaimed a mutual readiness to discuss all points of difference between the two nations. That nothing had happened in the meantime was due in part to the unresolved question of the League's attitude toward Abyssinia, Italy's blatant boasting about her share in Franco's victories, and the strong side-effects of the Nyon Conference.[1] But these difficulties notwithstanding, Chamberlain saw deadlock developing and hoped to avoid it by making a new initiative. His general attitude, so apparent in the year that followed, had been outlined graphically a few months before in his speech to the Cordwainers' Company:

When I served as a member of the Birmingham City Council, I learned one lesson which I have never forgotten, and that is that in this imperfect world a man cannot have everything his own way, and that those who get things done are those who are ready to work with and for others, and who are prepared to give something in return. There is always some common measure of agreement if only we will look for it, and there is but little satisfaction in standing out for the last item of a programme on which we have set our hearts if, by so doing, we are going to miss the opportunity of obtaining anything at all.[2]

The Prime Minister's views on the urgency of conversations with Italy were not shared by his Foreign Secretary. This was soon to result in tension between them, culminating in a crisis

which opened the question of appeasement to national consideration in an abrupt and pointed way. Though willing to accept the
idea of Italian talks in principle—and thus reluctant to raise
strenuous objections as the idea moved through its early stages—
Eden was convinced of the need for more tangible proof of Italian good will before actually undertaking negotiations. After all,
Italian propaganda against Britain was still rife, and Italy was
providing extensive support for the Nationalist cause in Spain in
open defiance of the agreement on non-intervention. As the issue
intensified over a period of several months, Eden came to believe
that his chief was displaying immoderate haste in approaching
Mussolini, whereas Chamberlain felt that the Foreign Secretary
was obstructing his efforts to open discussions. The divergence of
opinion between the two men was for a time (to put a different
twist on an old expression) more real than apparent. Loath to
create a ruckus in the circumstances of the time, or to aggravate a
problem by surfacing it prematurely, each was inclined to sup-
press his displeasure with the other's point of view. Mid-February,
1938, however, brought them to a crossroads, and the split between them emerged with force and shocking suddenness. But it
had been building for quite some time.

Other factors figured prominently in the background of the
budding Chamberlain-Eden controversy. The temperament and
outlook, indeed the general political philosophy, of the two men
differed. Chamberlain considered himself more practical than
Eden and, despite his stern personal morality, was disinclined to
allow moral or ethical considerations to stand in the way of his
dedication to the one great cause of peace. He was imbued with a
sense of personal mission which the more professionally-oriented
Eden did not share. While the Foreign Secretary had won his
reputation at Geneva and was a devoted adherent of the French
Entente, the Prime Minister did not wish to be bound by arrangements from Britain's past. Chamberlain was now less inclined to fear the Nazi peril, to feel alarm at the weakness of
British armaments, or to turn pessimistic about the impact of this
weakness on British foreign policy. He was often intent upon acting, when in Eden's view the best course would have been to wait.
And he was strongly inclined to act on the basis of his own judgment alone, or at least without extensive consultation with those
whom Eden considered most competent to give advice. So despite
their friendly personal relations, their ability to speak the same
language while meaning different things, and the polite assurances which they exchanged during the early months of their as-

sociation in Chamberlain's Cabinet, there was a fundamental difference between them which could not be long subdued.

Chamberlain's handling, in Eden's absence, of a mid-January message from President Franklin D. Roosevelt might have caused a break had it not been surrounded by the President's appeal for secrecy. When Roosevelt proposed to issue a world appeal for law and order as a prelude to calling a conference in Washington to consider the underlying causes of international tension, Eden was vacationing in southern France. So Chamberlain acted alone, sending what amounted to a negative response to Washington. His diary reveals that he found the plan "fantastic and likely to excite the derision of Germany and Italy" [3]; his official reply noted "a risk of this proposal cutting across our efforts here." [4] There was a need to act quickly, for Roosevelt had requested a reply within four days. But Chamberlain replied within twenty-four hours. There was perhaps some danger, in view of the need for secrecy, in telephoning Eden. But Chamberlain consulted only Sir Horace Wilson and Sir Alexander Cadogan, the Permanent Under-Secretary, and acted against the advice of the latter as well as that of Sir Ronald Lindsay, the British ambassador in Washington. He saw the American proposal in the context of his own plans to approach the dictators and was determined that nothing should obstruct those hoped-for conversations. In this his vision of potentiality was narrow.

Called back to London by dismayed officials at the Foreign Office, Eden was "outraged" (his word) at the way this opportunity had been handled, and immediately telegraphed Washington, attempting to minimize the effects of the Prime Minister's chilling reply. When Chamberlain received him at Chequers next morning (Sunday, January 16), they were seriously at odds. Beyond the fact of mutual resentment, Chamberlain believed the President's proposal vague and certain to fail; the dictators would pay no heed and only use this line-up of the democracies as a pretext for a break. Eden preferred to risk that result rather than the loss of American good will—to which he attached considerably more importance than the Prime Minister; even if the proposal failed, Britain would gain immeasurably from this American initiative in Europe. When the conversation turned to Italy, deadlock was complete. Insisting that there was now an excellent chance of coming to terms with Italy about the future of the Mediterranean, Chamberlain was not prepared to brook Eden's opposition to the *de jure* recognition of the Italian conquest of Abyssinia. It was at length agreed to lay these issues before their

Cabinet colleagues. Four stormy meetings of the Foreign Affairs Committee of the Cabinet[5] produced a rather significant modification in Chamberlain's views. A cordial explanatory message "welcoming" the President's initiative was sent to Washington on January 20, and agreement was reached that *de jure* recognition would be offered only as a factor in general appeasement.[6] But Roosevelt's guarded bid to modify American isolation from the affairs of Europe—the potentialities of which were great, the possibilities quite uncertain—had already been discouraged. And between Chamberlain and Eden a gulf had opened which soon would prove unbridgeable.

Anxious to get the talks with Italy moving, Chamberlain found in early February an unexpected, and in some ways unfortunate, point of contact. His sister-in-law Ivy Chamberlain (Sir Austen's widow), a long-time acquaintance of Mussolini and other prominent Italians, had, while vacationing in Rome, conversed at length about the British desire for better relations with Italy. Through her, Chamberlain's sentiments were relayed—apparently more by coincidence than by design—to high-placed Italians. Word came back of strong Italian distrust and dislike of Eden, though Mussolini stated a desire for early agreement covering all points in dispute between the two countries. Distressed by this kind of unofficial diplomacy, both because it placed him in a difficult position and fed Mussolini's hope that he could by-pass or disregard the British Foreign Secretary, Eden complained to Chamberlain. The Prime Minister, however, saw no real harm in such contacts, and this divergence in method added weight to the policy differences now dividing the two men.

Meanwhile, a series of meetings between Eden and Count Dino Grandi, the Italian ambassador in London, had resolved nothing. Eden proceeded cautiously, insisting upon revision of certain Italian attitudes and policies (especially with regard to propaganda and Spain) as a prelude to negotiations. Impatient at this, Grandi sought to see Chamberlain along with Eden. Eden resisted for a time, but as Chamberlain learned of Grandi's desire, he too pressed the Foreign Secretary to arrange a meeting. Argumentative exchanges passed between them on this issue for almost two weeks.

Hitler's Berchtesgaden bullying of Kurt von Schuschnigg, the Austrian Chancellor, on February 12 helped to bring matters to a head. The German demand for three Nazi ministers in the Austrian Cabinet surprised Italy as much as it did Britain. Fearing that *anschluss* would change the whole situation so as to make

Italian rapprochement with London appear to be a journey to Canossa under German pressure, Count Ciano, the Italian Foreign Minister, instructed Grandi to press quickly for a full and final agreement with Britain. Grandi then attempted to arrange a meeting directly with Chamberlain—apparently utilizing intermediaries to make the contact.[7] Against the advice of Eden, who believed that Britain now occupied a particularly favorable diplomatic position and who wished to continue his talks with Grandi at their earlier pace, Chamberlain insisted upon meeting the Italian ambassador. Impressed by another message from Lady Chamberlain, in which she reported Ciano's plea that "time is everything," he recorded his determination—and his broader thinking—in his diary:

> To intimate now that this was not the moment for conversations would be to convince Mussolini that he must consider talks with us off, and act accordingly. . . . Italian public opinion would be raised to a white heat against us. There might indeed be some overt act of hostility, and in any case the dictatorships would be driven closer together, the last shred of Austrian independence would be lost, the Balkan countries would feel compelled to turn towards their powerful neighbours, Czechoslovakia would be swallowed, France would either have to submit to German domination or fight, in which case we should almost certainly be drawn in. I could not face the responsibility for allowing such a series of catastrophes.[8]

Consequently, he had decided to stand firm, so his diary declared, even if it meant losing his Foreign Secretary.

The first Chamberlain-Eden-Grandi encounter occurred at 10 Downing Street on the morning of February 18. It was a tense and trying session. Chamberlain went far beyond the demands of diplomatic nicety in agreeing with the charges levied against the British by Grandi and in accepting the positions put forward by the Italian ambassador. Indeed, he seems openly to have encouraged Grandi's exaggerated claims in an effort to demonstrate to Eden the error in his views and to emphasize the need for getting on immediately with conversations. Eden's protests were dismissed by the Prime Minister with an air of irritation and impatience.[9]

When Grandi withdrew, to return again that afternoon, the Chamberlain-Eden conflict broke with fury. Unable to refrain from reproaches (as he put it in his diary), Chamberlain charged Eden with missing one opportunity after another of advancing towards peace. Now he wanted to throw away what was probably the last chance. But Chamberlain would not permit it. Grandi must be told that conversations should begin at once. Eden flatly objected; he did not trust Mussolini. The Prime Minister replied that he did, and interpreted Eden's position to mean that it was no longer a question of when to begin talks, but whether they should ever begin at all. Though obviously chagrined, Chamberlain at length agreed to place the issue before the Cabinet the following day. That was the message relayed to Grandi when Chamberlain and Eden gloomily confronted him at 3 P.M.

At the Cabinet meeting next day, Chamberlain likened Italy to a hysterical woman. Thwarted by Britain in her assault on Abyssinia and resentful because of it, she had more recently experienced at least a partial return of composure and was gradually becoming more amenable to reason. Events in Austria had sobered her, and there now existed one of those rare opportunities which appear at intervals and do not recur. Eden's rebuttal centered on his deep distrust of Italian motives. As their colleagues spoke, it was clearly evident that Chamberlain carried a strong majority, especially the older members, with him. Few seemed to know what benefits negotiations with Italy could bring, but there appeared to be a feeling that any positive step, however fruitless, would be worthwhile. Three hours of discussion culminated in Chamberlain's firm proposal to go ahead. It was then that Eden revealed his intention to resign. A few moments of stunned silence followed, then a few expressions of concern and dismay. Quickly, however, the Prime Minister made it clear that he could not accept another decision on Italy.

The remainder of that day, and the next, were spent in efforts to induce Eden to change his mind. In this Chamberlain was not a prime mover. It was more an exercise by Cabinet colleagues to plumb the nature and adjust to the shock of the Chamberlain-Eden row.[10] For his part, the Prime Minister had concluded—and he so informed Eden when they conversed alone at noon the following day (February 20)—that it was in the national interest for them to part. The two agreed that the difference between them was vital and unbridgeable, and in this sense Lord Halifax was right when he wrote some years later that the Chamberlain-Eden parting was inevitable.

There was at least one embarrassing moment for Chamberlain during his private conversation with Eden. His revelation of Italian acceptance of the British formula for the withdrawal of volunteers from Spain—which had earlier been urged upon Grandi as a way to strengthen the British case for opening conversations with Italy—was met by Eden's surprised retort that no such word had come through the Foreign Office. Clear it was that Chamberlain's unofficial diplomacy had been at work again. Later, recording in his diary what he withheld from his Foreign Secretary, the Prime Minister wrote that the message had been carried by Sir Horace Wilson, who probably (though he was not sure) got it from Joseph Ball, an official at the Conservative Party Office and an intermediary of some standing at the Italian embassy.

Eden's resignation touched off an acrid and lengthy debate in the House of Commons. Indignantly denying the charge of Viscount Cranborne, Under-Secretary of State who resigned with Eden, that Britain had surrendered to blackmail, Chamberlain argued again that a rebuff to the Italian desire for immediate conversations would confirm their suspicion that Britain did not want conversations at all, but was rather engaged in a "Machiavellian design" to lull the Italians into inactivity while Britain completed her rearmament. The Prime Minister was "never . . . more completely convinced of the rightness of any course that I have had to take than I am today. . . ." [11] Some members were not convinced, however. The Labor and Liberal leaders (Clement Attlee and Sir Archibald Sinclair) denounced this "abject surrender to the dictators," a theme which several of their followers then developed in different ways. Harold Nicolson, National Labor member, labeled Chamberlain's scheme "a splendid bit of give-and-take: we give and they take," while Lloyd George pronounced the Prime Minister "only fit for a stained glass window." Dissatisfied Conservatives—both dissidents, like Churchill, and regulars (P. V. Emrys-Evans, J. R. Cartland, and A. C. Crossley among them)—condemned the surrender of right to expediency and warned that Britain must take a very different line from Chamberlain's if she were to maintain her liberty and respect in the world. In consequence of this, Chamberlain had to fight a Labor motion of no-confidence, on which fifty Government supporters abstained from voting, before his opening of negotiations with Italy was vindicated by the Commons.[12]

British press reaction to the proposed Anglo-Italian conversations and Eden's resignation generally followed party lines. Chamberlain's initiative received support in most Conservative journals as a move toward peace and the easing of international tension. Labor and Liberal organs denounced it and the general policy it implied—the Labor *Daily Herald,* the Liberal *Manchester Guardian,* and the Liberal *News Chronicle,* among others, assuming positions from which they did not diverge in the year and a half ahead: relentless, vigorous, and ofttimes constructive criticism of Chamberlain and his policies. The independent press, while showing skepticism, took up a wait-and-see position.[13] This episode was instrumental in bringing the question of appeasement to the forefront of the public mind, and from this point onward Chamberlain's policy became a matter of open and increasingly heated debate. And stubbornly confident though he was, the Prime Minister was not oblivious to what was said in the nation's press.

Eden's departure was a blow to Chamberlain in the sense that he was a bright young man of high political promise, blameless reputation, and great popularity. He was a distinct asset in a generally colorless Cabinet and could not, in that regard at least, be easily replaced. On the other hand, the Prime Minister now had an opportunity to place in the Foreign Office a man completely attuned to his own way of thinking—not a yes-man necessarily, but one whose personal qualities and general sympathy for Chamberlain's policy would greatly reduce internal strains in the conduct of foreign affairs. He found him in Lord Halifax, a friend and colleague of long standing, whose prestige and experience made him appear to Chamberlain, and to many others as well, the logical man for the post.

The appointment of Halifax had at least one significant procedural implication for Chamberlain. With the Foreign Secretary in the House of Lords, the Prime Minister would now be deeply involved in the day-to-day details of foreign affairs in the House of Commons, called upon to answer scores of questions, and forced to bear the brunt of Opposition attacks. Temperamentally, he was not the kind of man to bear the latter well, and the effect was hardly beneficial. It underlined the differences between his own ideas and those of his opponents, stimulated his combative aptitude, and led him frequently to interpret criticism of his policy in highly personal terms—thus making him still more combative and inclined to believe uncritically in the superiority of his own judgment. This may have occurred in any case, but it is tempting at least to ponder whether some shielding from the daily wrangles that embittered almost every discussion of foreign affairs might have tempered certain of Chamberlain's attitudes. On the other hand, the arrangement appears never to have bothered him to a point where he deplored it. Finding Halifax an unusually compatible colleague, he was quite content to carry the burden in the Commons in return for a "steady, unruffled Foreign Secretary who never causes me any worry."

· · ·

Anglo-Italian conversations began in Rome on March 8. Lord
Perth, the British ambassador, and Count Ciano had barely set
their agenda, however, when Germany delivered a rude shock to
all of Europe in the form of the annexation of Austria. Momentarily, Chamberlain's attention was diverted in that direction.

Sudden though the *Anschluss* was, there had been indications
that trouble was brewing. The full significance of Hitler's mid-
February demands on Chancellor Schuschnigg had gradually appeared as nothing less than the end of Austria's independence.
But of this portentous event few in Britain seemed to think or
care. Within the Government there was general acceptance of the
view that a closer union of Germany and Austria, in one form or
another, was next to inevitable. Some time before the event occurred, the British had washed their hands of Austria.[14] Chamberlain was pressed in the Commons on March 2 to endorse a declaration of the French Foreign Minister, Yvon Delbos, that the
independence of Austria was an essential element of European
peace. Entirely unmoved, he thought it too early to estimate the
effect of arrangements between Austria and Germany and wished
the matter "left alone for the present." And left alone it was till
the news of the German march arrived. Then when the British
protested, it was the "use of coercion, backed by force" which
drew their fire, *not* the fact of Austria's absorption by Germany.

It was this use of force which Chamberlain found disquieting—
so much so that he momentarily entertained conclusions that he
desperately wished to avoid. "It is perfectly evident . . . now,"
he wrote his sister, March 13, "that force is the only argument
Germany understands. . . . Heaven knows, I don't want to get
back to alliances but if Germany continues to behave as she has
done lately, she may drive us to it." As for the immediate future,
"we must abandon conversations with Germany, we must show
our determination not to be bullied by announcing some increase
or acceleration in rearmament, and we must quietly and steadily
pursue our conversations with Italy." Then, as if to resist being
drawn too far away from his overall hopes and aspirations, he
added: "If we can avoid another violent coup in Czechoslovakia,
which ought to be feasible, it may be possible for Europe to settle
down again, and some day for us to start peace talks again with
the Germans." [15]

If Chamberlain felt some personal pique, and well he might, it
could have stemmed from the circumstances in which he heard
the news of Germany's action. Hosting a farewell luncheon in

Downing Street for Joachim von Ribbentrop, who was departing London after a time as German ambassador there, he was not only stymied by Ribbentrop's protestations of ignorance and surprise but apparently delayed in making telephone contacts by irksome small talk which the ambassador insisted upon pursuing. This was at most, however, only a sidelight of the larger affair.

The Prime Minister's explanation of the Government's position in the House of Commons on March 14 reflected accurately the attitude toward *anschluss* which it had adopted before the event occurred. While Germany's methods called for "severest condemnation" and could not fail to prejudice the hope of removing misunderstandings between nations, Britain was under no commitment to act on behalf of Austria. She was pledged to consultation with France and Italy, and the pledge had been fully discharged. The French had addressed a protest to Germany; the Italians had made no reply. Then came the key pronouncement: "Nothing could have arrested this action by Germany unless we and others with us had been prepared to use force to prevent it." And almost as an afterthought he added that Britain's defense program was "flexible"; a fresh review would be made to see what further steps it might be necessary to take.[16]

Few could dispute the contention that only force would have halted Germany. But the Opposition, and a few Conservatives as well, were clearly disturbed that Chamberlain could let it go at that—especially in view of the now precarious position of Czechoslovakia. In the debate which followed, the need to foster collective security and return to the principles and policy of the League of Nations was urged from all sides of the House. Labor members (Attlee, F. J. Bellenger, R. T. Fletcher, A. V. Alexander, and J. C. Ede) who insisted upon the absolute necessity of such a course drew strong support from Sinclair, Liberal Geoffrey Mander, Liberal Nationalist E. L. Granville, Communist William Gallacher, and Conservatives Vyvyan Adams and the Duchess of Atholl, all of whom openly stated or apparently assumed that it was Britain's duty to form the backbone of a coalition of powers (to include France, Russia, and possibly the United States) that could forestall an impending succession of aggressions. In the midst of this, Churchill made his eloquent—and famous—appeal for a "grand alliance": a number of states assembled around Britain and France in a solemn treaty against aggression, their staff arrangements concerted and their purpose sustained by the moral sense of the world. But Chamberlain was not impressed. Long since, he had come to believe the League entirely ineffectual. The cry for collective security quickly became—and long remained—for him only a meaningless shibboleth with which his critics could attack his plan for appeasement. As for the grand alliance, he told his sister a few days later that the idea had occurred to him long before Churchill had mentioned it. He had even talked about it to Halifax and submitted it to the Chiefs of Staff and Foreign Office experts. On paper a very attractive idea, its attraction vanished the moment one began to examine its practicability. "You have only to look at the map," he explained, "to see that nothing that France or we could do could possibly save Czechoslovakia from being overrun by the Germans, if they wanted to do it." Consequently, he had already "abandoned any idea of giving guarantees to Czechoslovakia, or the French in connection with her obligations to that country." [17] And there the matter rested.

There were other pressures, during the days which followed, for the urgent development of some scheme of protection against a growing German menace. Alarmed by the *Anschluss*, the Russians made on March 17 a muted bid to "commence immediately together with other States . . . the discussion of practical measures called for by the present circumstances." [18] But this was coolly received in London. The Government's distrust of Soviet motives (whether justified or not will long be argued), its very low estimate of Russian military potential, and Chamberlain's great reluctance to let anything cut across his hopes and efforts for appeasement combined to kill that weak initiative while still in infancy. A system of collective security, such as the Churchillian plan for mutual defense, gained solid support in sections of the press.[19] The respected *Manchester Guardian* (March 15, 18), for example, adjudging Chamberlain's policy incompatible with both national interests and the cause of democracy, believed the Government could confer a "great service on humanity" by setting out honestly to rebuild a collective system. And the Commons debate of March 24 saw "Red Riding Hood" Chamberlain severely criticized for his negative attitude, the Opposition leaders charging him with "amazing credulity" in believing that he could pursue successful conversations with dictators who had so blatantly demonstrated their belief in force even while the Prime Minister was negotiating with them. Others saw him attempting (in Churchill's words) "to bridge a 12-foot stream with an 8-foot plank," and, in support of a revitalized peace front based on the rule of law, demanded in turn "less attitude and more policy"; "action, not drift."

Chamberlain had been on the latter occasion unusually vague and negative. His address to the House left wholly uncertain the essential issues involved in the new situation in Europe. It clarified what Britain would not do, but little more. Proclaiming his belief in the League (as an instrument for preserving peace) profoundly shaken, the Prime Minister also quickly dismissed the Soviet proposal as premature; it envisaged "a concerting of action against an eventuality which has not yet arisen." On the vital question of Czechoslovakia, he could make no commitment—although he did at length admit, in very guarded phraseology, the probability of Britain's becoming involved should France go to war in honoring her obligations to the Czechs. The fundamental basis of British policy, as he described it, was "the maintenance and preservation of peace and the establishment of a sense of confidence that peace will, in fact, be maintained." [20] This was, of course, far more an aim than a policy—a distinction which Chamberlain had difficulty making.

While acknowledging that conversations with Germany must be momentarily postponed, Chamberlain was deeply concerned lest for any reason Germany should get the impression that Britain was less than gracious, understanding, even sympathetic. The depth of his concern is illustrated by the watchful eye he kept on the relations of British corporations with German business. When one firm (Lewis's) broke off its contacts with German buyers in protest against the *Anschluss,* the head of the company was summoned to Downing Street, told of the Prime Minister's strong disapproval, and reprimanded for interfering in this manner in the foreign policy of the country.

So Chamberlain was not prepared to think in terms of resisting Germany. What had occurred in Austria was not so much deplored as the method in which it had occurred. And the Eden crisis had amply demonstrated that Chamberlain was not inclined to let matters of method take precedence over the basic principles involved in an issue. Certainly, in his mind, it was insufficient grounds on which to discard or alter the new approach in which he had come to hope so fervently. Appeasement was still an untested idea, and he could not think of abandoning it without a thorough trial.

CHAPTER XIII

The Pursuit of Appeasement: Phase II

THE SITUATION IN CZECHOSLOVAKIA, WHICH GRADUALLY THREAT-
ened to engulf Europe in war, was Chamberlain's major concern
during the long, hard summer of 1938. The potential German
threat to Czechoslovakia was apparent immediately after the *Anschluss;* however, some weeks passed before the real nature of the
threat, and any willingness on the part of the Chamberlain Government to consider it openly, appeared. In the meantime, the
British conversations with Italy were making apparent progress,
and the issue of the Spanish Civil War was increasingly bedevil-
ing the Prime Minister.

The Perth-Ciano talks begun on March 8 continued for nearly
six weeks. Of the eleven points which constituted the agenda,[1]
the questions of Spain and Abyssinia proved to be most acute, a
fact reflected in the terms of the Anglo-Italian Agreement signed
on April 16. Covering a wide range of interest conflicts between
the two countries, and including an Italian disclaimer of territorial or economic ambitions in Spain, Italian acceptance of the
British scheme for evacuating "volunteers." from Spain, and a
British promise to raise at Geneva the recognition of Italian
Abyssinia, the agreement would take effect only after the implementation of the latter two provisions. Chamberlain had earlier
rejected the view that some positive Italian act in the form of a
withdrawal of troops from Spain ought to precede the opening of
negotiations. Now, however, he was prepared to insist that the
agreement remain in suspense until "a settlement of the Spanish
question" (as it came to be called) was reached. This may be
taken to suggest that, anxious to talk as he was, the surrender of
basic points without significant compensation was not a foregone
conclusion. It is equally possible that this reflects a kind of lesson
Chamberlain had learned from the controversy surrounding the
Eden crisis, the blistering criticism to which the Opposition in
Parliament and the press had subjected him,[2] and/or the misgivings of the Foreign Office about the whole transaction. The latter's coolness was graphically described by Chamberlain himself:

"You should have seen the draft [of the agreement] put up to me by the F.O.; it would have frozen a Polar bear." [3]

When Chamberlain moved approval of the agreement in the House of Commons, May 2, he was highly optimistic about its potential. Explaining that his Government meant to remove the danger spots of Europe one by one, and that the agreement had already effected "a radical change" in Anglo-Italian relations, he asserted flatly: "The clouds of mistrust and suspicion have been cleared away." Clement Attlee, the Labor Party leader, interrupted to demand a definition of "a settlement" in Spain. This the Prime Minister refused to give; "at this stage it would be wrong to try to define the circumstances in which one could say that a settlement had been arrived at." Attlee stormed back that to request approval for a treaty whose implementation depended on a settlement in Spain, without indicating what would constitute a settlement, was "ridiculous." But Chamberlain was unperturbed. Ignoring Attlee, he went on to proclaim that the world had received the agreement with an "almost universal chorus of praise" and to declare that "for Italy and ourselves this Agreement marks the beginning of a new Era." [4]

The attack then launched against Chamberlain and his policy, mainly but not entirely by the Labor Party, was bitter in the extreme. He was blasted as an "admirer of the Mussolini regime with all its tyranny, murders, and assassinations" and pictured as a fool for taking Mussolini at his word. He was charged with "abject, dishonorable, cowardly surrender" and chided for his superb success in always restraining the victims of aggression. Attlee termed his refusal to define for the House a settlement in Spain "contempt . . . absolutely unparalleled." But this vigorous censure went for naught. When the House divided, Chamberlain's motion prevailed by more than 200 votes. Commenting on this later, the Prime Minister noted: "It is in our willingness to face realities, which we cannot change, and to make the best of them, that the difference lies between this side and the other side of the House." [5] The Abyssinian conquest was an accomplished fact. Spain might now be eliminated as a menace to European peace— a loose definition of "a settlement" which Chamberlain had not yet enunciated but had clearly come to accept in his own mind. And there was now a chance, or so it seemed, to detach Mussolini from his German connection. These were the considerations, for better or for worse, which molded Chamberlain's thinking.

In keeping with its assessment of reality, the British Government raised the Abyssinian issue at Geneva during the second week in May. No formal decision was taken, but at the close of protracted discussion, the chairman of the Council observed that "a great majority of the members . . . considered that it lay with the divers members of the League to decide on their attitude individually in the light of their own situation and obligations." [6] The effect was clear: Britain had freed herself (and all the other members of the League) to recognize Italian sovereignty over Abyssinia whenever she chose, and this with reference only to what was expedient. This was the subject of considerable controversy in the British press. Though argued on many grounds, the issue was simple. It was the age-old query as to whether the end justifies the means. Chamberlain and his Government voted "yes," a fact clearly reflected in Halifax's address to the League Council. There he had argued, somewhat illogically, that the greatest end which the League existed to serve was peace, and assuming that the course he espoused would serve that end, it involved no question of principle. Where the ideal of devotion to some high purpose conflicted with a practical victory for peace, the latter, he insisted, was the stronger claim.

Even so, the way was not yet open to the implementation of the Anglo-Italian Agreement. Speaking at Genoa on May 14, the Duce was downright hostile toward the British, and his attitude was sufficient to hinder a settlement of the Spanish problem with any degree of speed. While Ciano insisted in early June that Italy had met her obligations, the British were not satisfied about Spain. Chamberlain was momentarily stung—to the point of formal protest—by Mussolini's lack of gratitude, and the Government felt compelled to proceed cautiously, so a note of June 20 explained, in consideration of British public opinion. Not only had Chamberlain encountered serious opposition in working to bring about the agreement with Italy, but the recent bombing of British ships had produced an especially unfavorable reaction. In fact, Britain could no longer consider as a settlement in Spain Italy's acceptance of the British plan in the Non-Intervention Committee, but would insist on one of three alternatives: execution of the plan, unilateral withdrawal of Italian volunteers, or the arrangement of an armistice. These the Italians flatly rejected.

The bombing of British ships in Spanish ports had long been a festering sore in Britain. By June, scarcely a day passed without a report of damage suffered by some ship flying the British flag in Spanish waters, and the situation had Chamberlain and the Cabinet "almost distracted" and "frankly up against it"—so Cadogan informed the American ambassador, Joseph Kennedy. The British people were beginning to feel their Government "not courageous" and feared that the nation's prestige was rapidly diminishing.[7] This lent weight to the longstanding demand of Labor that the belligerent rights of the Republican Government be recognized and the "farce" and "sham" of non-intervention abandoned.

On this issue there was never a question in Chamberlain's mind. Committed from the beginning to non-intervention as the only way to prevent the Spanish Civil War from spreading to the rest of Europe, he stuck firmly to his position despite all the vicissitudes of that tragic affair. Immediately after the *Anschluss,* he had termed the fact that war was still confined to Spain a "remarkable tribute" to the policy of non-intervention. Defining the Government's position in the Commons on June 14, he explained that "retaliatory action of various kinds" had been considered, but he was "not prepared to embark upon such measures which, apart from their inherent disadvantages," could "not be counted upon to achieve their object." [8] And he added, in correspondence with his sisters, they might lead to war with Italy and Germany, and "in any case would cut right across my policy of general appeasement." [9] Early July found him, according to Joseph Kennedy, "inwardly very sore" that he had to take "all this nonsense" from Mussolini, but as the Prime Minister had bluntly phrased it: "My job is to try to keep England out of war if I possibly can; therefore, I am doing a lot of things that are difficult for me to do." [10] In sum, he still preferred to withstand charges of cowardice and incompetence (constantly forthcoming from the Opposition in Parliament and now from British shipping interests as well), and to tolerate the bombardment of British ships in the fighting zone, than to take a position which might mean involvement in war. The issues at stake were by no means great enough for that.

Chamberlain's unyielding position had repercussions on the British political scene. Few issues of the inter-war period excited the Labor and Liberal Parties, attuned as they were to domestic issues and highly sensitive to the cause of the socialist-leaning Spanish republic, like the question of British policy toward Spain. Chamberlain's adamant stand was instrumental in converting their feelings of strong dislike for him to the bitterest personal animosity. The Prime Minister, for his part, was increasingly galled by the inconsistency, indeed hypocrisy, in Labor's constant harping for sterner action while refusing to budge from its traditional opposition to rearmament. From this point on, there was little but open conflict between the Prime Minister and the official Opposition.

So British policy toward Spain did not change. But in these circumstances it was difficult for Chamberlain to talk of putting the agreement with Italy into effect. He continued to hope that Mussolini's attitude would mellow and that he would exert some pressure in Spain to bring about a settlement. Meanwhile, his attention was distracted by another and even greater problem, the German threat to Czechoslovakia.

In the wake of the *Anschluss,* Chamberlain had envisaged Britain's obligations to Czechoslovakia as those of one member of the League of Nations to another, and nothing more. Apparently taking Germany's peaceful assurances to Czechoslovakia at face value, and confronted in any case with warnings against war from his military advisers, he encouraged the Czech Government to work diligently toward a settlement of questions relating to the position of its disaffected German minority of three-and-a-half million. There the matter rested until the Sudeten German Party —which, through financial subsidization and other pressures from Germany had become little more than a Nazi instrument for use against the Czech Government—convened a Congress in Carlsbad late in April. The pretense that the party sought autonomy was all but discarded in favor of union with Germany. Its demand to control the Sudetenland "in accordance with the ideology of the German people" and its insistence upon a complete revision of Czechoslovak foreign policy suggested differences with the Czech Government far more extensive than those at first imagined in Britain. And this conclusion was sealed when, in the wake of the Czech refusal to negotiate on these terms, the Germans, both in the Sudetenland and Germany proper, engineered a fresh outburst of abuse against Czechoslovakia, the former primarily by demonstrations, the latter by grossly exaggerated press reports.[11] It was then that Chamberlain invited Edouard Daladier and Georges Bonnet, the French Premier and Foreign Minister (who had taken office less than three weeks before) to London on April 27 to discuss the situation.

Those conversations found the British basing their "spirit of realism" on the military situation: Germany could not be prevented from overrunning Czechoslovakia if she chose to do so. Further, it was very doubtful whether, even after a victorious war, the Czech state could be re-established on its existing basis. It was therefore essential for the Czechs to reach agreement with their German minority, and Britain and France should use all their influence to that end.

Daladier was prepared to pressure the Czechs, but favored a clear declaration that Britain and France would not permit the destruction of Czechoslovakia. This struck Chamberlain as unwarranted bluff. If war resulted after such a declaration had been issued, Czechoslovakia could not be saved. The Czech army was no doubt good, but the *Anschluss* permitted Germany to turn her fortifications. The organization and efficiency of the German army was apparent in its Austrian operations. To issue a declaration such as Daladier had in mind would constitute "casting the die"—deciding that the opportune moment had come to tell Germany that Britain and France would no longer "tolerate her continued progress in Europe," and that, from the military point of view, the time had come "to declare war on Germany with the object of bringing about her defeat." Conceding that he shared Daladier's emotions, that it "made his blood boil to see Germany . . . increasing her domination over free peoples," Chamberlain labeled "such sentimental considerations" dangerous. He and the French would be gambling with men, not money, and he could not enter lightly into a conflict which would mean frightful results for "innumerable families, men, women and children, of our own race." In fact, public opinion in Britain would not permit him to take such a gamble on war or peace, and it was no use for his or any government "to go beyond its public opinion with the possible effect of bringing destruction to brave people." He was not convinced that Hitler really desired to destroy Czechoslovakia (in some form), but if he did, Britain and France—and outside support could not be expected—were not sufficiently powerful to assure victory. So it was finally decided that there should be simultaneous approaches to Berlin and Prague, the former by the British alone, the latter by the French and British jointly.[12]

The sometimes guarded language of diplomatic by-play should not obscure the essence of Chamberlain's evolving attitude: the stakes in Czechoslovakia were not sufficiently high to warrant the horrors of war. It was not simply that the Czechoslovak state in its existing form *could* not be defended; rather, in bluntest terms, it *should* not be defended. It was right that Czechoslovakia should make significant concessions to German demands. At least vaguely familiar with the minorities problem, and reasoning that, should Germany overrun Czechoslovakia the Czech state would have to await the end of ensuing war to be re-established, Chamberlain found it but a short step to the view that re-establishment would take a different form from that which then existed. The way for such a view had been effectively opened during the week of the *Anschluss* by a dispatch from Sir Basil Newton, the respected (and at least mildly pro-Czech) British minister in Prague, who held that the status quo in Czechoslovakia could not be perpetuated even after a victorious war, that Czechoslovakia's position was not "permanently tenable," and that "it would be no kindness in the long run to try to maintain her in it." [13] From this it followed, in Chamberlain's mind, that war for the sake of preserving something that would not be preserved in the peace which ensued would be indeed most foolish and futile. This opinion did not dawn upon him suddenly; it emerged gradually from his thinking about the problem. Consequently, it is almost impossible to define the point at which his commitment to the view became certain. But surely it was set in his mind by late April.

That Chamberlain's concept of appropriate Czech concessions included the cession of the Sudetenland to Germany emerged from his "off the record" interview of May 10 with American and Canadian journalists at Cliveden (Lady Astor's country estate where government officials often—though Chamberlain seldom—retired on weekends to discuss political affairs in semi-privacy[14]). Long suspect because of the circumstances in which it appeared, and also because Chamberlain carefully evaded later questions about the whole affair, the account of Joseph Driscoll which appeared in the New York *Herald Tribune,* May 15, was apparently correct in tenor if not in detail. It reported the British convinced that Czechoslovakia could not survive in its present form and that frontier revision was advisable. Whether the episode involved any calculation by the Prime Minister, in the sense of launching a trial balloon, is still unanswered for lack of conclusive evidence. But in any case, the point concerning Czechoslovakia remains the same.

If Chamberlain was thus already prepared to accept the cession of the Sudetenland to Germany, another question follows. Why did the British not advise the Czechs to give way to Hitler and make the best terms they could while there was yet time? The answer seems to lie in one or more of the following factors: the conciliatory attitude of Konrad Henlein, Sudeten German chief, during a May 12-14 visit to London revived the hope that Czechoslovakia could be peacefully reconstructed into a federal state; the Prime Minister did not want to risk this potentially unpopular (however realistic) solution by offering it prematurely; Chamberlain did not wish to encourage German aggressiveness by over-anticipating German demands and playing his hand too quickly. Though bent on settlement by concession, he was also determined to resist a solution dictated by force.

The so-called May crisis nearly forced Chamberlain to abandon the idea of settlement by concession, at least momentarily. When a suddenly deteriorating situation in the Sudetenland, accompanied by rumors of German troop movements, made it appear on May 20–21 that another lightning German *coup* was impending, Britain staidly warned the Germans (indeed on two occasions) against precipitate action.[15] The scanty evidence available points to Halifax, acting alone, as the author of these warnings,[16] though Chamberlain wrote his sister Ida a week later that he did not doubt that Germany had made all preparations for a *coup* and decided that the risks were too great after receiving the British warnings. (The extent to which the latter observation was tempered by the widespread approbation which the Government's warnings had received in the British press and elsewhere is unknown.) In any case, the incident showed him "how utterly untrustworthy and dishonest the German Government is. . . ." [17]

Yet, Chamberlain soon resumed his efforts to placate Germany. Even before the May crisis had passed, he explained to the House of Commons, May 23, that Germany fully shared Britain's desire to see the Czech-Sudeten German negotiations succeed, and reported a message from the German Foreign Minister welcoming British efforts to promote a settlement by negotiation. His latter point was a novel interpretation of what Ribbentrop had actually said: that Britain should exercise pressure in Prague, "where strong language was needed." [18]

Bilateral Czech-Sudeten German negotiations sputtered along from early June to mid-July. Then they collapsed altogether, leaving an entirely unresolved and highly explosive situation in their wake. At that point the Sudeten German question ceased to be a matter of Czech internal politics and became the object of European *haute politique*. The British, of course, had no legal commitment (outside of their obligations to the League) to become further involved in this dangerous dispute. But the precedent of policy already initiated, the Prime Minister's longstanding aim of removing trouble spots in order to assure the continuation of peace, and his hope of settling the Czechoslovak problem in such a way as to advance the general appeasement of Germany made it certain that further British involvement there would be.

Chamberlain's belief in the requisite nature of a Czechoslovak settlement, now that matters had gone this far, is reflected in his response to Captain Fritz Wiedemann, Hitler's personal adjutant, who journeyed to London in mid-July, on Hitler's initiative, to propose a visit by "some important German personage" (probably Göring) to discuss Anglo-German relations and if possible, to arrive at a "comprehensive agreement." Only Halifax (with Chamberlain's approval) spoke with Wiedemann. He held the present moment of tension over Czechoslovakia "not propitious" for what Wiedemann proposed—though it would be different if a settlement were reached there, or even if Germany would promise not to use force in resolving the Czechoslovak issue. A follow-up message from the Foreign Office suggested an Anglo-German undertaking to cooperate in promoting a peaceful settlement in Czechoslovakia. That was hardly useful to Hitler, and there the contact ended. The appeasement of Germany was still his goal, and Chamberlain was prepared to demand great sacrifice from the Czechs to attain it. But he was not yet ready to abandon Czechoslovakia entirely.

Meanwhile, in fact, he had decided to pursue a long-contemplated idea of mediation. Having pressed the reluctant Czechs for approval—they were not happy about a move which seemed to put their government on the same level as its discontented subjects—he announced in the Commons, July 26, that Lord Runciman, Lord President of the Council, would proceed to Prague as mediator.[19] Chamberlain carefully explained that Runciman would act in a personal capacity, not as a representative of the British Government. He would be a conciliator, hearing all the facts and arguments and suggesting expedients and modifications in the demands of both parties. Though perhaps intended in part to meet the criticism and allay the fears of Parliamentary skeptics (who were making known their fear of a "deal" that would weaken Britain's position or the translation of appeasement to mean unreasonable concessions to aggressor powers who had already shown themselves unappeasable), this explication of Chamberlain's appears to be one which he honestly believed. Sir Samuel Hoare later testified: "Perhaps none of us fully realized at the time that the [Runciman] Mission . . . inevitably dragged us more deeply into the forefront of the struggle between Germans and Slavs." Chamberlain saw it as a logical incident in his plan of taking every possible step to avoid war and promote conciliation, and did not suspect that a highly respected English liberal, who had never confronted the passions of continental nationalism, might have little influence upon an inflammable controversy that had already ignited.[20] But Runciman's presence in Prague did commit the British more deeply. In view of Chamberlain's (and the Government's) sentiments, he could neither pose as an impartial observer nor divorce himself from his British connection.

The occasion for Chamberlain's announcement of the Runciman mission was the last debate on foreign policy in the House of Commons until October 3. During the Parliamentary session which was closing (February-July, 1938) there had been twenty-four major debates on foreign affairs and 1400 related questions for the Prime Minister and the Under-Secretary to answer. These unusually high figures reveal both the interest and anxiety which Chamberlain's policy had aroused and the constant stress under which the Prime Minister labored. But there was no hint of fatigue or strain in what he had to say. He was optimistic, feeling the atmosphere "lighter" throughout the continent. If a peaceful solution could be found to the Czech question, he would "feel that the way was open again for a further effort for general appeasement." [21]

Unfortunately, the course of events in central Europe did not bear out his optimism. During the month of August, against a background of German troop movements and modest British efforts to restrain both Hitler and the Czechs, Runciman achieved almost nothing. Four plans for settlement were developed and rejected. The Czechs were willing to grant everything short of what would endanger the security and integrity of the republic; the Sudeten Germans (and Hitler) were unwilling to accept anything short of what Prague would never grant. In early September the conversations were broken off again.[22] Runciman at length (September 2) informed both London and Berlin that, if the parties refused to agree, he could have ready a plan to press upon them by about September 15. But this went far beyond the original purpose of his mission and was, in any event, too late.

As the crisis deepened amid bloody civil disturbances in the Sudetenland and sensational atrocity stories in German newspapers, there developed in Britain a distinct sentiment against surrender. The famous *Times* leader of September 7, which suggested the secession of the Sudeten fringe from Czechoslovakia, provoked a "volley of abuse" (the term of editor Geoffrey Dawson, a confidant and sometimes a mouthpiece and/or "ideas man" of Chamberlain) from many other newspapers of all political hues. The Foreign Office went "up through the roof" and promptly denied that *The Times'* suggestion represented in any way the Government's view. Chamberlain met with the principal Cabinet ministers and Foreign Office officials on September 9, and agreed to send a strongly-worded warning to Hitler, making it plain that Britain would stand by France in the event of war. The message was never delivered, however, for when it reached Berlin the British ambassador, Sir Nevile Henderson, implored the Government not to insist that he deliver it; it would have an effect opposite to that desired. His request was granted.

Chamberlain's momentary flirtation with a stiffer attitude toward Germany may have owed its existence in part to late August and early September warnings about Hitler's true intentions which came to him through several behind-the-scenes contacts with respected members of an alleged anti-Nazi fronde. Their primary message was that only an unambiguous British declaration of her intention to resist the use of force in Czechoslovakia would deter Hitler from persisting in the course on which he now seemed bent. But there was little concrete data on which the British could base crucial decisions, the message itself coming from a cabal of undisclosed composition and unknown strength, a group whose capacity to act was uncertain then and in fact remains so yet.[23] Though apparently tempted for a time, Chamberlain was not inclined for long to put much stock in what they had to say.

Though the other view was constantly before him, Chamberlain was, in fact, not at all convinced of the advisability of strong action, and his reservations were strengthened by a book he was reading at that moment. He explained to his sister on September 11:

I fully realize that, if eventually things go wrong and the aggression takes place, there will be many . . . who will say that the British government must bear the responsibility, and that if only they had had the courage to tell Hitler now that, if he used force, we should at once declare war, that would have stopped him. . . . But I am satisfied that we should be wrong to allow . . . the decision as to peace or war, to pass out of our hands into those of the ruler of another country, and a lunatic at that. I have been fortified in this view by reading a very interesting book on the foreign policy of Canning. [24] . . . Over and over again Canning lays it down that you should never menace unless you are in a position to carry out your threats, and . . . we are certainly not in a position in which our military advisers would feel happy in undertaking to begin hostilities if we were not forced to do so.[25]

The extent to which Chamberlain's attitude and actions, as the Czech crisis moved to a climax, were dictated by British military weakness has long been—and will surely continue to be—vigorously debated. However, there is no doubt that, in addition to his horror of war and his unshakable belief that it should be contemplated only as an absolutely final resort, the nation's military condition weighed heavily on his mind. In the spring of 1938, the Chiefs of Staff had advised Chamberlain that war with Germany over Czechoslovakia must be avoided, *no matter what the cost,* until the British rearmament program began to bear "substantial fruit." [26] While the tempo of rearmament had picked up modestly during the summer, it was still exceedingly doubtful whether the substantial fruit required by the Chiefs of Staff had yet been produced and assembled.

The important thing here is to recognize that Chamberlain did not weigh the issue of peace or war on the basis of military power alone. Certainly other considerations were important. Both Hitler and the Sudeten Germans had made tremendous political capital with the demand for self-determination, a principle in the establishment of which British statesmen had had a considerable hand. Seeing the issue on its own merits—for he was not yet willing or able to think in terms of a larger German threat to central Europe, which was, of course, in retrospect his greatest shortcoming—Chamberlain believed, rightly or wrongly, that the country simply would not follow him had he tried to lead it into war to prevent a minority from obtaining autonomy or even choosing to pass under another government. "If we have to fight," he had poignantly said, "it must be on larger issues than that." It must be on something "irresistible," like the apparent attempt of one nation "to dominate the world by fear of its force." [27] He did not yet believe this to be the case with Germany. Thus his passion for peace and his optimistic estimate of the essentially peaceful nature of all men were at the same time his greatest personal strength and his greatest political weakness.

There was also a question of France. Chamberlain was well aware of the division in the ranks of the French Government and the great gulf which yawned between robust public pronouncements—based perhaps as much on the hypnotic assumption that Britain would act in her stead as anything else—and irresolute private utterances. And his suspicions were wholly confirmed when, on the night of September 13, France abandoned all initiative to Britain, Daladier in effect begging Chamberlain to do something to avoid a situation where France might have to live up to her obligations to Czechoslovakia. While a question remains concerning the extent to which evasive British replies to earlier French questions about the defense of Czechoslovakia contributed to Daladier's attitude, the French abdication of initiative certainly left Chamberlain with a decidedly reduced potential for maneuver.

Dominion sentiment was another factor that could not be ignored. The Dominions were extremely cool toward the prospect of war over Czechoslovakia, and Chamberlain was keenly aware of this. How much effect it had on his thinking is impossible to measure. There are some who deem Dominion sentiment significant; there are others who believe it was utilized only as needed to provide reinforcement for the course on which the Prime Minister had already determined. But he acknowledged its weight in the Commons and elsewhere in such a way as to suggest that he truly considered it important.[28]

In view of all these factors, Chamberlain was still determined to find a way out. He had earlier "racked his brains" (his term) to devise some means of averting catastrophe, and had thought of one, so he wrote his sister on September 3, "so unconventional and daring that it rather took Halifax's breath away." [29] Henderson had encouraged him to save it as a last expedient, so he had laid it aside till the proper moment arrived. It did not take long for the moment to come. Hitler's venomed speech to the Nazi Party Congress at Nuremberg on September 12,[30] the violence in the Sudetenland which followed, and Runciman's failure to get negotiations reopened persuaded him to employ his last idea. He would go to Germany to see Hitler at once.

Acting alone, Chamberlain telegraphed Hitler on the evening of September 13, proposing to "come over" at once to seek a peaceful solution to the Czech problem and requesting a meeting time and place. Next morning he informed the Cabinet of what he had done and received unanimous, indeed enthusiastic, approval. Hitler's reply of late afternoon was favorable, so the Prime Minister, who after the May crisis had pronounced the German Government "utterly untrustworthy and dishonest," prepared to pursue appeasement into Hitler's lair.

If Chamberlain's action was risky, he recognized it, later comparing himself to a man obliged to play poker with a gangster, and without any cards in his hand. But risk meant nothing to him, for as he confided to a colleague before departing London, he would never forgive himself if war broke out before he had exhausted every expedient to avert it. So whatever fears harassed him in the hectic days which followed, second thoughts about the approach to which he was now committed were not among them.

If Chamberlain's action had a dramatic quality about it, he certainly intended it that way. He had kept the idea to himself in order to ensure its full effect at the final moment. And he admitted to his sister that an offer from Hitler to come to London—which seems but fleetingly to have crossed the Führer's mind—would not have suited him at all: "It would have deprived my coup of much of its dramatic force." [31]

The Prime Minister had his wish. The announcement of his flight to Germany caught the sporting instincts of the British people. The press greeted it with universal approval—though quite significantly, much of its initial support rested on the assumption that Chamberlain would now have an opportunity to impress upon Hitler Britain's determination to resist excessive German demands or a violent solution of the Czech crisis.[32] Widely acclaimed abroad as well as at home, Chamberlain must have felt a twinge of satisfaction as he boarded the plane, September 15, for the first long flight of his life.

CHAPTER XIV

Berchtesgaden, Godesberg, Munich

CHAMBERLAIN'S THREE SEPTEMBER JOURNEYS TO GERMANY TO confer with Hitler are synonymous with appeasement and comprise the most familiar episodes of his entire career. Already described by many hands, sometimes in great detail,[1] they need be reconstructed here mainly to elaborate the Prime Minister's general state of mind and the nature of his thinking on specific issues involved in the Czech crisis as it reached its final stages.

Accompanied by Sir Horace Wilson and William Strang (head of the Central Department of the Foreign Office), Chamberlain departed London in early morning, September 15, and flew to Munich, where he was greeted by German Foreign Office officials. Transferring—amid large and cheering German crowds, which impressed him greatly—to Hitler's special train, he then proceeded to Berchtesgaden in the scenic Bavarian Alps. Hitler received him, shyly and coolly, at his mountain retreat (the Berghof) some distance above the town. Following tea, the two adjourned to a starkly-furnished private room, accompanied only by Hitler's interpreter, Paul Schmidt. It was Chamberlain's wish that they should speak alone.[2]

In pursuit of his larger objective of improving Anglo-German relations, Chamberlain first proposed a frank discussion of a general character, leaving the problem of Czechoslovakia to the next day. Hitler would have none of that, however, and insisted upon confronting the Czech issue directly. From that point on, Chamberlain was largely at the mercy of Hitler's invective. For a time the Führer rambled over Germany's peaceful relations with her neighbors, interrupted only occasionally by the Prime Minister for the sake of clarifying a point or two. Then, switching to a higher key, he poured out his indignation against the Czechs and demanded the incorporation of the Sudeten Germans into the Reich. Spotting a modest opening, Chamberlain asked bluntly whether that was all the Führer wanted; and reacting to a generally affirmative reply, the Prime Minister began to speak of the practical difficulties connected with secession. These Hitler dismissed as academic and, shifting into highest gear, threatened to move into Czechoslovakia to settle the issue at once. Taken aback —and now warming temperamentally to his task—Chamberlain asked indignantly why, then, he had been allowed to waste his time in flying all the way from Britain. Hitler got the point. Quieting down somewhat, he said that if the British were prepared to accept the idea of secession (self-determination), he would discuss the procedure. Chamberlain's personal feeling was that he did not "care two hoots whether the Sudetens were in the Reich or out of it," but he could not commit his Government without consultation. He proposed, therefore, to return to London to take counsel with his colleagues and to visit Hitler again within a few days. The Führer agreed, offering to meet Chamberlain near Cologne and promising, at Chamberlain's urging, not to march into Czechoslovakia unless some outrageous incident forced his hand. The Prime Minister then departed confident that Hitler would keep his word.[3]

Back in London, Chamberlain first reported to the Inner Cabinet (an impromptu and unofficial body comprised of Halifax, Simon, Hoare, and official advisers Wilson and Cadogan, which had sprung into being a week before and met almost continuously during the weeks which followed), consulted the full Cabinet, September 17, and conferred with Daladier and Bonnet, who flew over from Paris on September 18. From beginning to end, the acceptance of self-determination was for him a settled issue. Convinced that his visit to Hitler had stopped an impending German invasion of Czechoslovakia, he was equally convinced that only the transference of the Sudetenland would assure the continuance of peace. Runciman, now home from Prague, fully shared this view, but there was enough resistance in the Cabinet (from a minority led by Halifax and Duff Cooper) to force postponement of a decision until the visit of the French. In those sessions, where peace, not Czechoslovakia, was the central concern, Chamberlain's efforts to get Daladier to commit himself first—and Daladier's efforts to avoid committing himself—would be almost comical were it not for the gravity of the situation. French reluctance to speak up surely confirmed Chamberlain's earlier impression about their indecision and unreliability and forced him, in effect, to corner them into accepting his view of "reality." [4]

The outcome was never seriously in doubt. The so-called Anglo-French Plan developed for submission to the Czechs embodied the concessions to Hitler which Chamberlain deemed essential. It involved the cession to Germany of all areas in Czechoslovakia containing over 50 percent Germans. There was opposition to this in the Cabinet, but it was subdued by the lack of an acceptable alternative. Chamberlain himself realized that he would be charged with the rape of Czechoslovakia. But the only alternative was war, and he could see "no rhyme or reason in fighting for a cause which, if I went to war for it, I would have to settle after it was over in about the same way I suggest settling it now." [5]

While the press argued the merits of the case and a deputation of Labor leaders protested to Chamberlain and Halifax, the Czechs pondered their plight and determined to reject the Anglo-French proposal. They were promptly warned by both London and Paris that to do so would be to court isolation and forfeit all Anglo-French support and concern. The language of the notes was diplomatically polite, but the meaning was painfully clear. The Czechs thought again—and again—and at length gave in. So the way was clear for Chamberlain, now armed with a concession of far-reaching proportions, to see Hitler again.

The second meeting had been arranged for Godesberg on the Rhine, a short distance south of Cologne. Chamberlain set out on the morning of September 22 with an air of confidence. He would now be able to meet Hitler's central demand, the Czech problem would be solved, and (as he told assembled newsmen at Heston airport) the way would hopefully be opened for European peace. The warm reception given him by throngs of German people at Cologne and Godesberg, and the splendid accommodations provided in the famous Petersberg Hotel (atop a knoll on the east side of the Rhine) did nothing to dampen his spirits. So with real expectancy he ferried across the river, shortly after lunch, to meet with Hitler at the Hotel Dreesen.

Had he paused to think it over carefully, Chamberlain might have been less than certain about the kind of man he would encounter at Godesberg, for his post-Berchtesgaden estimate of Hitler was anything but clear. To his Cabinet colleagues, he had pictured a tragicomic Charlie Chaplin type, but to Labor leaders and others he had spoken of being greatly impressed by Hitler. Amid his adverse reactions to the Führer there lurked a keen sense of satisfaction that Hitler had thought him "a man"—a point which some have used to demonstrate Chamberlain's personal vanity. Terming Hitler at one stage "the commonest little dog" he had ever seen, he remarked to a colleague at Heston, September 22, that he was off to see the "wild beast" again. This last estimate proved to be the best—for Godesberg at least—and Chamberlain was not long in discovering it.

Withdrawing (through ceremony in the lobby which would have done honor to the court of a Roman emperor) to a second-floor conference room, Chamberlain and Hitler sat down to talk again. This time the Prime Minister took with him Ivone Kirkpatrick, an official from the embassy in Berlin. Following the conversation in Berchtesgaden, the Germans had adamantly refused to provide the British with a copy of Schmidt's record of the meeting. Consequently, Chamberlain was forced to rely on his memory throughout all the discussions with his Cabinet and the French ministers. Kirkpatrick would now keep a British record of the conversation.[6]

In opening the discussion, Chamberlain recapitulated the situation after Berchtesgaden, described the essence of the Anglo-French proposals, and turned expectantly to Hitler, who brusquely replied that all that was no longer of any use. Chamberlain was surprised, chagrined—"profoundly shocked," as he later put it—and, slowly recovering from his amazement, he sought an explanation from Hitler. It was offered in terms of new Hungarian and Polish demands on Czechoslovakia and the need for an immediate German military occupation of the Sudeten districts. Chamberlain protested to no avail, and a period of ill-tempered floundering followed. At length Hitler agreed to look at the proposals which Chamberlain carried with him, but argument waxed hot over the question of their adequacy. Trooping downstairs to a map room in order to study the so-called language boundary within which Hitler demanded immediate military occupation, the two men closed their encounter in acrimonious and desultory dialogue, the divergence of their views absolute and fundamental.

Dinner, consultation with advisers, and sleep brought no apparent change in Chamberlain's outlook. Next morning he drafted a letter to Hitler emphasizing the impossibility of his agreeing to any plan unless he had reason "to suppose that it will be considered in my country, in France, and indeed in the world generally, as carrying out the principle already agreed upon in an orderly fashion, and free from threat of force." [7] Hitler's reply, delayed for hours while Chamberlain anxiously paced the balcony at the Petersberg, maintained his earlier demand for the immediate military occupation of the Sudetenland. In the British delegation a rupture was considered, but Chamberlain eventually decided to request (from Ribbentrop, through Wilson and Henderson) a written version of the German demands. This would provide an official statement in the event of a breakdown, and equally important, might keep the door of negotiation open. Prepared for the possibility of a negative reply, the British were informed that a memorandum would be prepared, and were at length invited to discuss it at 10:30 that night.

Hitler's manner was by that time improved, but his demands were not. His memorandum called for a Czech evacuation and a German military occupation of the Sudetenland, up to a line determined by the German staff, to begin in two days' time—and without the removal of so much as a pig or cow. Chamberlain threw his copy on the table in disgust. The proposals were nothing less than an ultimatum, he protested, prepared by one who had for years inveighed against the so-called "diktat" of Versailles. Hitler's explanation that the document was clearly headed "Memorandum" drew from Chamberlain an acid retort that he was more impressed by its contents than its title. Bitterly reproaching Hitler for his failure to respond in any way to the efforts which he had made, Chamberlain noted that, apart from their substance, the form of the German proposals was wholly unacceptable. At that Hitler grabbed a pencil, toned down the asperity of the document by a few minor alterations in wording, modified his timetable by a few days, and grumbled to Chamberlain about his being the first man to whom he had ever made a concession. Hardly overcome by such generosity, Chamberlain stated clearly that he could neither accept nor recommend these proposals—but he would, as an intermediary, submit them to the Czechoslovak Government. There the matter rested when they parted at 2 A.M.

Chamberlain's attitude upon his return to London, September 24, is still somewhat uncertain in the light of conflicting evidence, but there is much to suggest that he favored acceding to Hitler's demands. Hoare maintains that the Inner Cabinet "at once decided that Hitler's new demands were unacceptable," a view strongly confirmed by the full Cabinet that evening.[8] But Duff Cooper, the soon-to-resign First Lord of the Admiralty, records his astonishment at Chamberlain's recommendation of acceptance,[9] and Under-Secretary Sir Alexander Cadogan describes himself as "horrified" to find the Prime Minister standing "quite calmly for total surrender." [10] The fact that Halifax's dramatic change of heart (from acceptance to rejection) on the night of September 24 came as a "horrible blow" to Chamberlain strengthens the view that the Prime Minister favored acceptance.[11] On balance, it seems most likely that Chamberlain along with Hoare and Simon) was prepared to accept the Godesberg terms. But some other members of the Cabinet (Duff Cooper, Halifax, Oliver Stanley, and Walter Elliot among them) could not stomach the crudity of the surrender and said so plainly. Consequently, Chamberlain wavered, hoping for the discovery of some intermediate ground. The relentless consistency which had earlier characterized his views on the Czech situation evaporated momentarily. Exasperated with Hitler, stung by the personal affront at Godesberg, and now vaguely aware of a German threat to Europe, he was also ready to believe, as later evidence suggests, that the issue was still insufficient to warrant war. Which way the pendulum would ultimately swing yet remained to be seen.

Whatever Chamberlain's personal views, there was much support for firmness. It appeared in the Cabinet, where Duff Cooper and Hore-Belisha advised immediate mobilization; in the British press, which came out strongly against the Godesberg memorandum; among the British people, where mass-observation surveys revealed a distinct hardening against appeasement; and not least of all in Prague, where the Czechs rejected the Godesberg provisions absolutely and unconditionally. Even Daladier and Bonnet, when they went to London on the evening of September 25, found Hitler's memorandum unacceptable and proposed a return to the Anglo-French Plan.

The apparent French commitment to resistance was not easily accepted by Chamberlain, however. Asking what France would do if Hitler refused to return to the Anglo-French Plan (a refusal he judged most likely), he was little consoled by Daladier's reply that France would do her duty. There followed an exasperated exchange of views in which Chamberlain tried to elicit what France would do militarily, and Daladier, irritated by open British doubts about French military power, asked sharply whether Chamberlain was ready to accept Hitler's demands passively. Through this grim bout of fencing Chamberlain and Simon couched their inquiries largely in terms of learning as much as possible about the military potential of France. But the tone and manner of their comments—bluntly, the way in which they tried to pin Daladier to the wall and get him to confess French military weakness—clearly suggests that in their minds there was no alternative to accepting Hitler's demands.[12]

Yet at the Cabinet meeting which followed (the third in twenty-four hours), Chamberlain seemed to be of another mind. He proposed, as Halifax had urged him to do, one final effort to reach agreement with Hitler. Next day he would send Wilson with a letter appealing to him to allow the details of the transfer of territory to be settled by an international body of Germans, Czechs, and British. If Hitler refused, Wilson would tell him that France would fight for Czechoslovakia and Britain would stand by France. This seemed to constitute a startling reversal of position, but its meaning was clear and unequivocal. And a Foreign Office statement of the following day, issued after a special session with General Gamelin, the French Chief of Staff, had bolstered Chamberlain's estimate of French military potential, was equally plain and positive.

The explanation for the reversal lies, perhaps, with the uncertainty and vacillation in Chamberlain's mind as he waded through this drawn-out crisis. But it is also possible that it was a diplomatic bluff—part of a last desperate effort to dissuade Hitler from war.[13] Strange it was that, when he announced his reversed position to the Cabinet on the night of September 25, not a single minister who had given him total support in his earlier position raised so much as the slightest objection. And none of the practical arguments for avoiding war, which had previously played so large a role in his thinking, had been substantially changed. By the night of September 27, when he broadcast to the nation, Chamberlain was back to the view that the quarrel was already settled in principle, and while he understood the Czech rejection of the Godesberg terms, he still thought it possible to arrange the transfer of territory in a way that would be fair to all. To accomplish this, he "would not hesitate to pay even a third visit to Germany" if he thought it would do any good.[14] To be sure, he explained in the same address that if he were convinced that any nation had made up its mind to dominate the world by force, he would feel that it must be resisted. But there is little evidence that he had yet reached that conclusion about Germany. War is a fearful thing, he added, and "we must be very clear before we embark on it, that it is really the great issues that are at stake." The way he said it revealed his own real doubt about the greatness of the cause. Long before, he had rejected Czechoslovakia as unworthy of a European conflict. He still thought it "horrible, fantastic, incredible" that Britain should be preparing for war "because of a quarrel in a far-away country between people of whom we know nothing." Whether he actually revised his view—even for a very short time—on September 25–26 may forever remain in doubt. But if he did, he soon returned to his earlier position and continued the diligent search for a way out.

Meanwhile, Wilson was having a terrible time with Hitler. Carrying a letter from Chamberlain which pronounced the difference between them one of form, not of principle, and urging a German-Czech conference which the British would attend if Hitler desired it, he found Hitler (5 P.M., September 26) in so vile a mood as to make conversation almost impossible. Yet the Führer grudgingly accepted the idea of a meeting if it was understood, in effect, that the Czechs would give way at every point. When informed of this, Chamberlain offered (through Wilson, at noon, September 27) to see that the Czech promises were carried out with reasonable dispatch, provided Germany agreed to a peaceful transfer of territory. Again in a lather of rage, Hitler posed two clear alternatives: total Czech acceptance or rejection of the German terms. It was only then, having delayed on his own initiative, that Wilson conveyed Chamberlain's warning about Britain standing firmly behind France.[15]

All hope seemed gone, a fact attested by Chamberlain's most reluctant agreement to the mobilization of the British fleet. But Chamberlain was not yet finished. Nor was Hitler. Instructing Halifax to alert the Czechs to a possible invasion the next day unless the German demands were accepted, then advising them to accept the Godesberg memorandum under a modified timetable, which he simultaneously sent to Henderson for submission to Hitler, the Prime Minister was awaiting a reaction to that initiative when a message arrived from Hitler. More conciliatory than before, the Führer gave assurances about the German occupation of the Sudetenland, offered to guarantee the new Czech frontiers, and left it to Chamberlain's judgment whether he should continue efforts to bring the Czechs to reason at the very last hour.[16] Chamberlain replied next morning: "After reading your letter I feel certain that you can get all essentials without war and without delay." Putting into operation the idea of a four-power conference which had occurred to him several days before, he offered to go to Germany at once to discuss arrangements with representatives of the Czech Government, as well as France and Italy if Hitler so desired.[17] A message to Rome besought, and soon received, the Duce's support for this proposal.[18]

Next afternoon, September 28, Parliament assembled to hear the Prime Minister's version of recent events. Appearing worn and haggard, he was well into his disheartening account when word arrived (a note was passed along the Treasury Bench until it reached him) that Hitler had accepted his proposal for another conference—to be held at Munich the following day. This touched off a spectacle of emotional relief perhaps unparalleled in Parliamentary history. Chamberlain himself acknowledged several days later "that the news of deliverance should come to me in the very act of closing my speech in the House, was a piece of drama that no work of fiction ever surpassed." [19]

The Prime Minister certainly shared in the overwhelming sense of relief. His air of confidence suddenly returned and even he— the staid old businessman from Birmingham—could not help but react emotionally to the spontaneous outburst of rejoicing which swirled around him. To crowds surging through Downing Street that night he tendered fatherly advice: go home and sleep quietly; things would be all right now. At the airport next morning he recalled his childhood and quoted nursery rhymes: "If you don't at first succeed, try, try, try again." And in this moment of triumph, lines from Shakespeare also seemed appropriate: "Out of this nettle, danger, we pluck this flower, safety." Riding on air in every sense of the word, Chamberlain then set out for Munich.

The four heads of government (Chamberlain, Hitler, Daladier, Mussolini) assembled at the Führerbau shortly after lunch, September 29. In discussion prolonged in part by the faulty organization of so hastily-called a conference, Chamberlain negotiated with some obstinacy on several points. These included the question of seating a Czech representative in the discussions (which was his original intention), the problem of guaranteeing Czech acceptance of the Munich provisions without knowing their official attitude, and the matter of providing compensation to Czechoslovakia for property and investments lost in the transfer of the Sudetenland. But his efforts were all in vain; his points were either openly discarded or sloughed over in semantical gymnastics. The mere fact of Munich meant that in all essentials Hitler had won his demands, and there was never a question of rejecting the basic proposals for an orderly transfer submitted by Mussolini but prepared in advance by German officials. The Prime Minister was only trying to salvage, in the midst of much confusion and without a single diplomatic lever to wield, what little he might from the final German triumph embodied in the document eventually signed about 2 A.M.[20]

What Munich did was to extort from Hitler a modification of the most offensive and provocative of the new conditions which he had insisted upon at Godesberg. The Sudeten territory was divided into four zones to be occupied progressively between October 1 and 7. Conditions of evacuation would be laid down by an International Commission in Berlin (composed of German, British, French, Italian, and Czech representatives), which would also determine the remaining territory of predominantly German character to be occupied by October 10, ascertain the territories in which plebiscites would be held, fix the conditions of the plebiscites, and finally delimit the frontier. A joint German-Czech Commission would handle the right of option into and out of the transferred territories. The four major powers would guarantee the new frontiers of Czechoslovakia, German and Italian participation hinging upon a settlement of the Polish and Hungarian minority questions in Czechoslovakia.

The extent to which the terms of the Munich Agreement constituted an amelioration of the Godesberg demands would soon become, and long remain, a matter of lively controversy.[21] Chamberlain considered the differences real. Having earlier accepted the principle of secession, what he sought in those last frantic days of September was an orderly, non-violent way for carrying it out. Munich provided that—at least when its terms were taken at face value—and he was satisfied that he had obtained his earlier objective.

But Chamberlain was ever mindful of the larger issue of Anglo-German relations and still apparently convinced that he could do business with Hitler on a personal basis. These preoccupations surely help to explain his separate approach to Hitler on the morning of September 30. Acting entirely alone, he sought the Führer out at his Munich apartment and engaged him in extended conversation over a wide range of international issues. According to the record of Hitler's interpreter, the only one which exists,[22] Chamberlain at length observed that it would be a pity if the Munich meeting should pass off with nothing more than a settlement of the Czech question. Hoping for some statement showing agreement between them on the desirability of better Anglo-German relations, he offered a declaration, which he had drafted himself, in which the two statesmen would resolve that consultation would be utilized in dealing with any future questions which might concern the two countries, and would declare their determination to continue efforts to remove sources of difference, thus contributing to the peace of Europe. Hitler agreed to sign at once, and the tête-à-tête was then concluded.

Precisely what passed through the Prime Minister's mind in this fleeting episode, and what he hoped to accomplish by the declaration, is quite uncertain. Ivone Kirkpatrick, who assisted Chamberlain at Munich, acknowledges his own incertitude, then offers the following as the most likely hypothesis: Chamberlain believed that the best chance with Hitler was to try to bind him to a public declaration and then to proclaim the belief that Hitler would keep his word. Iain McLeod cites evidence that it was done for American consumption, quoting Chamberlain: "If he [Hitler] . . . sticks to it that will be fine, but if he breaks it that will convince the Americans of the kind of man he is." [23] According to Ciano, Hitler reported Chamberlain's saying that the declaration was essential for the maintenance of his Parliamentary position, the implication being that some apparent progress toward a larger Anglo-German understanding was essential for making the sacrifice demanded of Czechoslovakia acceptable in Britain. It is possible that Chamberlain still believed in Hitler's sincerity; he later reported that it was in the Führer's apartment that he first discovered in Hitler a human being, and his reaction to the German duplicity of March, 1939, was certainly that of a man whose trust had been betrayed. It is possible, too, that he was carried away by the emotion of relief that war had been averted. But whatever the explanation, the action was characteristic of the man and provides considerable insight into his concept of international diplomacy.

The send-off accorded Chamberlain by the German people as he departed Munich was enough to stir the emotions of any man. Despite intermittent rain, a great throng gathered outside his hotel. Women wept, children threw flowers, men cheered themselves hoarse. His reception in Britain was still greater. To cheering crowds at Heston he read the text of his agreement with Hitler and described the Czech solution as the prelude to a larger settlement that would bring peace to all of Europe. Amid delirious uproar in London, he accompanied the King and Queen to the balcony of Buckingham Palace to wave to the multitudes below (who burst forth with rousing round after round of "For he's a jolly good fellow"). In Downing Street the surging mob clamored to see him. Chamberlain fully realized, Halifax testifies in his memoirs, that this popular enthusiasm was only momentary; yet he needed to acknowledge the greeting accorded him. "What can I say?" Chamberlain asked. "Say that you have come back with peace with honor, and go on to the balcony where Dizzy said it before," replied one of his staff.[24] So with this expression running through his tired, emotion-charged mind, Chamberlain stepped to the balcony and spoke those ill-fated words: "This is the second time in our history that there has come back from Germany to Downing Street peace with honor. I believe it is peace in our time." Two days before, upon setting out, he had rejected the phrase with impatience; one week later, he appealed to the House of Commons not to read too much into words used in a moment of emotional stress at the close of a long and exhausting day, during which he had driven through miles of excited, enthusiastic people. But the phrase stuck with him and soon became, in the popular mind, synonymous with Chamberlain and Munich. Such are the quirks of history.

The expressions of gratitude which then poured in to Chamberlain from all over the world (40,000 messages in all), to the accompaniment of thankful adulation in the press, further enhanced his conviction—from which he never wavered—that he had done the only right thing. Testimony to the general repugnance to war, not only in Britain and France but Germany as well, especially impressed him, and it is not surprising, given his own longstanding state of mind, that whatever other considerations there must be, the preservation of peace outweighed them all.

But other considerations there were, and they came quickly to the fore. They appeared in the press, where many journals combined their praise for Chamberlain's work in preserving peace with stark acknowledgment that Munich was a "diktat" arousing grave concern for the future—the future of Czechoslovakia, of peace, and of European democracy.[25] They appeared in the House of Commons, where an intense and dramatic four-day debate (October 3–6) found a number of speakers, from all parties, rising to pronounce Munich abject surrender to naked force, to blame the Government for betraying the Czechs, to charge it with allowing the League to die, and to chastise it for cold-shouldering Russia. Labor and Liberal members pushed the attack, sometimes in emotion-charged terms, such as Colonel Wedgwood's quoting of Patrick Henry: "Is life so sweet and peace so dear as to be purchased at the price of chains and slavery?"; Robert Gibson's characterizing Chamberlain as the Samaritan who took the clothes from the wayfarer and gave them to the robbers; and Geoffrey Mander's flat predicting that Chamberlain's policy would inevitably lead to war. Conservative criticism was also conspicuous. While Eden, Richard Law, and L. S. Amery expounded the bankruptcy of "stand and deliver" diplomacy, Churchill solemnly warned that Munich was not the end but only the beginning—"the first sip, the first foretaste of a bitter cup which will be proffered to us year by year unless by a supreme recovery of moral health and martial vigor, we arise again and take our stand for freedom as in the olden time." Through all of this ran the basic point that appeasement had dismally failed and that it must now be replaced by a new and different approach to foreign affairs.

On this general issue the resigning Duff Cooper had begun the debate, and his denial that it was possible to come to a reasonable settlement of outstanding questions with Germany set the tone for all that followed.

Chamberlain, of course, did not accept this view. Admitting that the path to appeasement was long and bristled with obstacles, still he thought it possible to make further progress "along the road to sanity" now that a settlement had been reached in Czechoslovakia. He saw "sincerity and good will" on both sides of the Anglo-German declaration, although he acknowledged that Britain could not afford to relax her rearmament program. In closing debate, October 6, he argued (in indirect reply to comments Churchill had made) that if British policy were based on the view that friendly relations with totalitarian states were impossible, that assurances given him personally were worthless, and that those states were bent on the domination of Europe, then war was inevitable. But that hypothesis he refused to embrace. The catchword "collective security," so popular with the Opposition, was to him only a return to entangling alliances and power politics—"a policy of utter despair." [26] In short, the experiences of September had in no way shaken his faith in the validity of appeasement.

It is on this count that Chamberlain is most difficult to fathom —and indeed most open to criticism. The much-debated question of whether he had any real alternative, given the circumstances of September, but to accept the terms of the Munich Agreement is one on which it is altogether possible to offer alternative answers and to build up convincing cases for each—all in a hypothetical vein, of course. Whether Hitler would have backed down if confronted with British intransigence; whether France would have followed Britain in a policy of firmness; whether the German opposition to Hitler could have taken effective action against him; and a host of related questions will always remain unanswered. The best that can be said here is that Chamberlain, in reviewing the situation in September, had little substantial ground on which to take a different line. Similarly, the question of whether it would have been better had Britain fought in 1938—a controversial issue so much-discussed and commonly-known as to warrant no more than passing mention here[27]—is subject to alternative responses, each of which can be made convincing depending upon which segment of the evidence is emphasized. Whether the Czechs could have repelled a German attack; whether British armaments were, in comparison with German armaments, relatively weaker or stronger in 1938 than in 1939; whether the British people (and the Dominions) would have rallied behind a war for the Sudetenland; indeed, whether the war which broke in 1939 was a certainty in 1938; and similar questions likewise remain unanswered. Again, however, Chamberlain had greater grounds for doubt than confidence. Whether greater efforts on Chamberlain's part to revitalize and utilize the League of Nations would have improved Britain's position materially is entirely open to debate. So is the question as to whether closer contacts with Russia, which Chamberlain never seriously considered because of a combination of prejudice, distrust, and ignorance (see pp. 181–83), would have strengthened Britain's hand in any practical way. Certainly both were deserving of effort—much more than Chamberlain believed. But in the midst of uncertainty, one thing at least is clear: after all the vicious treatment (both personal and policywise) which he received at Hitler's hands during September, Chamberlain had a reasonable, indeed a compelling alternative to continuing to believe in the decency and trustworthiness of the Führer, and thus the efficacy of appeasement.

Feiling puts it well: "Simple he was . . . and obstinately sanguine in that he was bent on finding decency even in dictators." [28] Despite Hitler's behavior and the warning voices of his critics, Chamberlain was simply not prone to suspect really evil intentions. Willing to allow that German leaders often alienated sympathy by the way in which they treated even good causes, he thought their behavior partly due to the conviction that "nobody loves them." So Munich was barely past when the Prime Minister (and Simon and Hoare as well) began suggesting in public speeches that Germany should make her demands known in order that negotiations might be pursued. He was now prepared to consider the return of German colonies—although the basis on which it could be done was rather sticky. For Chamberlain, appeasement still soared in the heights it had reached at Munich.

CHAPTER XV

Munich Winter

IN THE PERIOD AFTER MUNICH, CHAMBERLAIN'S OUTLOOK AND policy seemed to become, in one sense, increasingly ambivalent. This derived in part from his studied effort at a dual approach, defense and appeasement. It stemmed from an apparent divergence between what he sometimes felt as a person—a sensitive one at that—and what he thought it essential to feel as a statesman. Most significantly, perhaps, it sprang from the ever-increasing problem of reconciling belief (based on tangible evidence) and hope. In another sense, however, Chamberlain's perspective and direction were simple and consistent. Whatever he believed at particular moments, whatever his feelings and reactions to specific situations, his hope of securing peace and stability remained dominant. The steady pursuit of that hope accounts for much of his activity during the winter of 1938–1939.

Vacationing on the Tweed and "trying to forget Europe," he was not, in mid-October, a relaxed and satisfied man. As the excitement and hysteria of Munich subsided and many more Englishmen than before began thinking and talking hard common sense—which was perhaps the most important effect of the debate in the Commons, October 3–7—Chamberlain was troubled about a number of things. The division which appeared in his party was especially disconcerting. Though still small in number and in no way dangerous to his Parliamentary majority, the potent minority which could no longer accept the Prime Minister's view of things included powerful names (Churchill, Eden, Duff Cooper, and Amery, for example) and some men who in the past had stood very close to Chamberlain.[1] The talk about "betrayal," however inaccurate he deemed it, bothered him intensely—a fact which prompts recollection of Professor Namier's later sagacious observation about Munich: "The more there was of doubt lurking deeper down, the greater was at first the annoyance and irritation with anyone who dared to give expression to it."[2] The suggestion that he ought now to reconstruct his Cabinet so as to attain a greater unity in foreign policy, advice which came from one as close to him as Halifax and which he steadfastly refused to heed, cast a certain kind of doubt upon his personal judgment and the course he chose to follow. Uncomplimentary references generously offered in public speeches by Hitler and Mussolini were hardly reassuring. Nor was there any comfort in the fact that the International Commission established in Berlin to settle all questions arising out of the transfer of the Sudetenland accepted with monotonous regularity the harsh terms dictated by Germany.

The effect of all these things was to force from Chamberlain an admission that ". . . we are very little nearer to the time when we can put all thoughts of war out of our minds, and settle down to make the world a better place." [3] But he did not conclude from this that his policy stood in need of change; rather, it must be pursued more diligently. It was not that his prescription for European ills had proved ineffective; it must simply be administered over a longer span of time and given more opportunity to do its work. Never doubting that time and effort would at length achieve the end he had in view—and in the process, of course, vindicate his judgment—he wrote his sister of his intentions: "In the past, I have often felt a sense of helpless exasperation at the way things have been allowed to drift in foreign affairs, but I am now in a position to keep them on the move, and while I am P.M. I don't mean to go to sleep." [4]

His determination to "keep things on the move" conditioned Chamberlain's attitude toward Cabinet composition. None of his appointments (Stanhope at the Admiralty, Runciman as Lord President, John Anderson as Privy Seal, and several months later, Chatfield in Co-ordination of Defense and Dorman Smith in Agriculture) reflected the wishes of party or youth. The possibility of Eden's return he quickly dismissed, and other dissident Conservatives were not considered. Chamberlain sought more support and power for his policy; running battles in the Cabinet would only slow his pace. As for youth, he found the men on the back benches "meagre in the extreme." If talent were there, he did not see it for it did not fit into his scheme. Chamberlain was also loath to consider the creation of new posts, such as a Ministry of Supply which was being pressed on him from various quarters; organizational rearrangements must be avoided at a time when he wished to press on with other things. The result of his attitude was considerable discontent among some junior ministers and a good deal of grumbling in the House of Commons—indeed to the extent that, by December, he was wondering whether he could get on with this "uneasy and disgruntled House" without an election. But the back-benchers were pacified by domestic moves (such as the ditching of the Milk Bill and the doubling of the barley subsidy) and mollified by the increased pace of rearmament, which had a favorable effect on unemployment figures. And the Prime Minister himself was soon preoccupied with other things.

Shortly after Munich, where Chamberlain and Mussolini had managed a bit of conversation about Spain, the British received from Italy a request that the Anglo-Italian Agreement of April be implemented, on the grounds that Italian infantrymen were being withdrawn from Spain. Chamberlain was agreeable, so when the Commons reassembled in early November, he announced that the time was ripe "to take a further step forward in the policy of appeasement" (to promote peace in the Mediterranean as a "long step" toward peace in general) by bringing the pact with Italy into force. Ten thousand infantrymen had been removed from Spain, he explained, and he had "definite assurances" from the Duce that the remaining Italian forces would be withdrawn when the non-intervention plan became operative. In his view the Spanish question was no longer a menace to the peace of Europe—the criterion he now adopted for a "settlement" of the Spanish problem—so there was no valid reason for delaying longer enforcement of the pact.

The Prime Minister's motion that the House "welcome the intention" of the Government to bring the agreement into operation reopened the whole question of Anglo-Italian relations which had been so bitterly debated during the spring and summer of 1938. It was soon apparent that the opponents of the Italian pact (the Laborites, Liberals, and some dissident Conservatives) had lost none of their fervor, and the criticism to which Chamberlain was subjected was acid in the extreme. In addition to Labor charges of spineless surrender, continued betrayal, and naive credulity, Eden forcefully denied that the essential condition which Britain had laid down as a prerequisite to enforcement had been satisfied. But when the critics had had their say, Chamberlain's motion prevailed by a substantial majority (207 votes), and the Prime Minister was free to implement this "further step" toward appeasement.

It is a striking fact that, although Chamberlain's description of what constituted a settlement in Spain—a definition which he had carefully avoided earlier—left much to be desired in the way of precision, no apparent concern about this was to be found among his supporters. At least it did not reflect in the debate or the vote. It is this sort of thing which raises a real question concerning the extent to which Chamberlain had a *carte blanche* to do essentially anything he liked, and opens the way for the view that there existed in the Commons an effective body of Conservative "yes-men," a "mass" of Conservative members devoted to blind followership, wherever that might lead. To the degree that this was true, there were surely a number of reasons for it—ranging all the way from rigid party discipline to honest faith in Chamberlain and deep distrust of the Opposition. Few of these reasons need relate directly (in a personal sense) to Chamberlain. But recognition of the situation is essential to understanding Chamberlain's ability to push on with his program without serious internal interruption.

One aspect of Chamberlain's effort to improve Britain's relations with Italy was the need to soothe the various irritations in Franco-Italian affairs. This was one of the reasons, among others, which prompted him to visit Paris—having obtained an invitation on his own initiative—in late November. He summarized his motives in a letter to his sister shortly after the arrangements had been made:

> I felt it to be the right thing for many reasons—to give French people an opportunity of pouring out their pent-up feelings of gratitude and affection, to strengthen Daladier and encourage him to *do* something at last to put his country's defenses in order, and to pull his people into greater unity, to show France, and Europe too, that if we were anxious to make friends with Germany and Italy, we were not on that account going to forget our old Allies, and finally to make it possible for me to go to Rome in January, which is what I am trying to arrange.[5]

Accompanied by Halifax—a new departure in his diplomatic travels[6]—Chamberlain exchanged views with Daladier and Bonnet at the Quai d'Orsay on November 24. Their discussion of defense measures, Franco-Italian relations, the guarantee to Czechoslovakia, and other less pressing issues resulted in a "complete identity of ideas" on the general orientation of policy. Agreement had not in fact been easy, for a basic difference had arisen over the guarantee to Czechoslovakia. While the French envisaged a joint and several guarantee, in which Anglo-French responsibility would not depend on Italian or German cooperation, the British insisted upon a general guarantee that would operate only if three of the four guarantors were prepared to act. (Russian participation was discussed obliquely but not anticipated.) Daladier pled the case of a moral obligation to Czechoslovakia and the spirit of the Anglo-French Plan of September. But Chamberlain would acknowledge only the practical side of the question and the letter of the Anglo-French declaration. It was never intended that the guarantee should be unconditional, he argued; further, its manner of operation had not been previously specified. Though less than satisfied, Daladier had given way.[7]

So the outcome of the conversations was gratifying to Chamberlain—as was the enthusiastic welcome accorded him by the people of Paris. He was also pleased to learn that Ribbentrop was about to visit France to sign a declaration along the lines of the Chamberlain-Hitler agreement of September 30, but the official record makes no mention that he revealed his own intention to visit Rome. That was very much in his mind, however, and the announcement was made only a few days after his return from Paris.

That Chamberlain should go to Rome to see the Duce was, for a good many Englishmen, uncomfortably reminiscent of Munich. It provoked in sections of the British press a protest which did not at once subside and which indeed became more intense and vitriolic as the time for the visit drew near.[8] Exemplifying this feeling, the Liberal *News Chronicle* (January 3) sarcastically admonished the Prime Minister, who seemed so fond of nursery rhymes, to read the one beginning "Will you walk into my parlor? said the spider to the fly." Nor was the idea quietly accepted in the House of Commons, where the view that Chamberlain seemed bent on proving himself more an acrobat than a diplomat was expressed in a dozen caustic ways. Vernon Bartlett (independent) put it well: since it was Italy which had demands to make, not Britain, it was very doubtful whether the best way of keeping those demands within the bounds of moderation was for Chamberlain to go to Mussolini instead of Mussolini coming to Chamberlain. But Italy was, in Chamberlain's view, the end of the Axis on which it was easiest at that moment to make an impression. A tête-à-tête with Mussolini might not only be worthwhile in itself, in terms of pushing for an armistice in Spain and assuring peace in the Mediterranean; it might be "extraordinarily valuable in making plans for talks with Germany." And in order to achieve the ultimate end he had in view, he ardently hoped for "some way of getting a move on." [9]

Despite his hopes and desires, Chamberlain was not without his moments of depression during these months. The demise of Czechoslovakia continued with the Vienna Award (an arbitral award, supposedly, handed to Hungary by Germany and Italy) and the steady slide of the rump Czech state under German domination. A guarantee of what remained, about which Chamberlain had been lukewarm in the first place, had thus become increasingly difficult. The savage anti-Semitic pogrom carried out by the Nazis in mid-November profoundly shocked British opinion and left the Prime Minister aghast at such "barbarities." Hitler's sarcastic references to British "governesses" and "umbrella-carrying types" were hardly designed to curry English favor, and Chamberlain admitted (to the Foreign Press Association, December 13) his grave disappointment with the venomous attacks in the German press and the failure of the Führer to make the slightest gesture of friendliness. To make matters worse, Mussolini was emulating Hitler, writing offensive articles about "Dialogues on the Thames" which held the democracies up to ridicule. And the rigged outcry for "Nice, Tunis, Corsica" which began to emerge from the Italian Chamber of Deputies did not bode well for any improvement in Franco-Italian relations.

Nor was Chamberlain free from worries at home. Agriculture was grumbling about milk and grain supports, and party discontent with the Cabinet's composition persisted. A mid-November by-election in the Bridgwater Division of Somerset resulted in a serious blow to the Government's electoral prestige when the well-known journalist Vernon Bartlett, standing as an anti-Munich independent in a straight fight with a Chamberlain supporter—in a constituency where the Conservatives had held a 10,000-vote majority and in a campaign in which foreign policy played a major role—won a 2000-vote victory.[10] Anxiety about the international situation in general and Chamberlain's policy in particular continued undiminished in important sections of the press (especially in signed articles by respected figures in the periodical press). And the Opposition in Parliament tenaciously and consistently challenged the validity of appeasement, a Labor motion of no-confidence on December 19 concentrating its attack upon the Prime Minister personally. Stung by charges of "grave misjudgments" which had brought the nation into dire peril, Chamberlain said of appeasement:

If that policy, having had a full chance of success, were nevertheless to fail, I myself would be the first to agree that something else must be put in its place. But I have been getting a great number of letters which convince me that the country does not want the policy to fail, and whatever views may be expressed in this House, I am satisfied that the general public desire is to continue the efforts we have made.[11]

This statement reveals three significant elements of Chamberlain's thinking, all of which are clearly questionable: appeasement had not yet had a sufficient trial to warrant judgment; appeasement must be pursued because the British people did not want it to fail; his own estimate of British opinion would take precedence over anything said in the Commons. There were many who felt that appeasement had already been tried and had obviously fallen short, inasmuch as the dictators were not responding to it in the way that had been hoped. The matter of whether the British people wanted appeasement to succeed (which of course they did) had no relationship whatever to the question of whether it could succeed. And a democratic leader's assumption of full responsibility for interpreting the wishes of his people without reference to his parliament is always fraught with dangers. But Chamberlain apparently did not—or would not—see beyond the general hope for success, and it was this sort of outlook which points at length to the conclusion that he did not really comprehend the danger of the German menace to Britain and to Europe. Hope was now the dominant component of his mind, and it helped to blind him to considerations of another sort. This is further demonstrated by his flat insistence in the same address that his policy "has been right all along"—and this despite the fact that just three days before, the Cabinet had received, and took very seriously,[12] a report of extensive plans which the Germans were developing for a surprise air attack on London.

Privately wearying of his one-sided efforts, and occasionally revealing his weariness in public, Chamberlain always returned to the opposite view. A flash of doubt across his mind always seemed to rekindle a determination that doubt there must not be, and the more that doubt arose, the greater became his efforts to resist it; so that at length his hopes appeared to spring not so much from positive bases as from an intense personal determination, almost psychopathic in nature, to resist the encroachments of any kind of negative or pessimistic feeling. Thus for example, while he appears on occasion to have had certain private doubts about Mussolini, he would not permit that doubt to condition his thinking, and felt it necessary to berate his opponents in Parliament for their discourteous behavior in even suggesting that the Duce might invite him to betray vital British interests.

Chamberlain's Christmas card for 1938 pictured his airplane gliding over a cloud bank on the way to Germany. A short time later he was back on the plane, again accompanied by Halifax, headed for Italy and a visit with Mussolini. The conversations in

Rome, January 11–13, wandered (there was no agenda) over the entire range of Anglo-Italian relations, with Chamberlain making a special effort to elicit from the Duce any information or opinions he might have about Hitler's future intentions.[13] If hopeful of weaning Italy away from her Axis connection, which seems to have been clearly in his mind, or even obtaining Italian support for the guarantee to Czechoslovakia, Chamberlain made no progress whatever. The conversations were drab and in no way decisive. According to Ciano—and the official British record does little to contradict this view—"the visit was kept on a minor tone, since both the Duce and myself are scarcely convinced of its utility." [14] Later he described the talks to Ribbentrop as a "big lemonade" and an "innocuous farce." Though such a description may appear contrived for political effect, especially since the German ambassador in Rome took a more serious view, it seems significant that Mussolini was so uninterested in what was going on that on the final day of Chamberlain's stay he chose to go skiing instead of attending the farewell banquet.

Chamberlain, however, pronounced himself fully satisfied. He achieved all that he expected, and more, he wrote his sister upon his return, and believed his journey had definitely strengthened the chances of peace. He found Mussolini straightforward and considerate—despite the fact that others with him thought the Duce occasionally curt and discourteous—and emphatic in his assurances that he wanted peace. Coincidental with Chamberlain's visit, some prominent Italian newspapers were blatantly boasting that four Italian divisions (including the Littorio Division, composed of the very veterans whose alleged withdrawal had been considered by the British Government as sufficient ground for bringing the Anglo-Italian Agreement into force) were leading a new Franco offensive in Spain. But suspicion of Mussolini's professed good will was apparently still quite distant from Chamberlain's mind.

One success he did achieve, the political effect of which was hard to assess, but in which Chamberlain was inclined to put much stock: he appeared to reach the Italian people. (In this, both in his own calculation and the response of the Italian populace, he was interestingly reminiscent of President Woodrow Wilson and his notable journey to Italy some years before.) Crowds thronged the streets to see him, and even Ciano recorded: "The welcome of the crowd was good, particularly in the middle-class section of the city, where the old man with umbrella is quite popular." [15] An end which he seems to have felt significant was served when he tried to warn Hitler, through Mussolini, that "it would be a terrible tragedy if aggressive action were taken under a misapprehension as to what lengths the democracies might be prepared to go." The Duce, however, was already entertaining his own aggressive intentions, and it is doubtful that the warning made much of an impression upon him.

Reporting on Rome to the House of Commons, January 31—in a message which, according to Ciano, had earlier been submitted to Mussolini for his approval [16]—Chamberlain made his satisfaction obvious. He saw appeasement "steadily succeeding," and cited as evidence both his meeting with Mussolini and Hitler's speech to the Reichstag on January 30, from which he "very definitely got the impression that it was not the speech of a man preparing to throw Europe into another crisis." [17] Remarks of this tenor did not, of course, go long unchallenged, but the protests of his critics only seemed to stir in him a greater sense of confidence.

This set the tone for a number of speeches delivered elsewhere by Chamberlain and other ministers during February and early March. Over the protests of Halifax and without participation by the Foreign Office, they sought to create in Britain a wave of confidence, Chamberlain, Simon, and Hoare consciously competing (or so it seemed) in issuing optimistic statements to the country. Most exemplary perhaps was Hoare's address to his constituents at Chelsea, March 10, in which he translated Chamberlain's wish that he emphasize the great possibilities of peace into talk about a possible "golden age." That same day Chamberlain told a group of press correspondents that Europe was settling down to a period of tranquility. They either had little comprehension of the totalitarian threat, or feverishly sought to subdue whatever grasp they had—in either case an alarming situation. This is all the more difficult to understand since there were times when Chamberlain appeared to be much less credulous than his public utterances suggest—like the conversations in Rome, when he was acutely anxious to learn what Germany's next aggressive step might be. But so far from finding it possible to admit that his policy was based on misconception and must soon be radically refashioned, there is little to suggest that he even questioned its validity in his own mind.

It is possible, of course, that Chamberlain hoped to create confidence, both at home and abroad, by talking it into being. It is more likely that, following his depression of December, he revived in spirit and determination and saw again what were to him sufficient bases on which to build a hopeful outlook. (One seeking vainly for oases in the desert sometimes observes them when they do not in fact exist.) The extent to which he actually trusted the dictators still remains in doubt, partly because he was not entirely sure himself. But there is no question that he put considerable reliance in the deterrent forces which might have been expected to exercise a restraining influence upon them.[18] Important among these were the peaceful sentiments of the German and Italian people; and Chamberlain's hope to exploit this force—in the belief that it was indeed a potent force, even in a totalitarian country—helps to explain both his interest in and satisfaction with his traveling diplomacy. Surely these people who had come so close to war in September would henceforth resent and resist it.

His estimate of Germany's economic situation contributed to his rising confidence. Experienced travelers, indeed Nazi leaders themselves, spoke of economic crisis, hardly a time in which to make trouble and risk war. Besides, efforts to improve Britain's economic relations with Germany, undertaken with Chamberlain's blessing shortly after Munich, had begun to make headway. Negotiations between the British and German coal industries had recently (late January, 1939) resulted in an agreement in effect dividing coal export markets. After numerous proposal exchanges, the Federation of British Industries and the Reich Federation of Industry were scheduled to meet in Düsseldorf in mid-March, and Oliver Stanley, President of the Board of Trade, was set to visit Berlin about the same time. Surely improved economic relations would have a favorable effect on political relations.[19]

Most important, perhaps, in Chamberlain's return to confidence was his growing trust in the gathering strength of British rearmament. A most disturbing aspect of the Munich crisis had been the revelation of deficiencies in Britain's defenses, and the Munich debate disclosed a nearly unanimous demand that rearmament be pushed forward with all celerity and force. The months which followed witnessed not only an extension of British plans but some real progress in the filling in of those plans, particularly in the area of aircraft production. The seed which Chamberlain had planted in his defense efforts of 1936 finally began to bear fruit; rearmament was gradually geared to eventual military action.[20] By February, 1939, Chamberlain was writing that Hitler had "missed the bus" at Munich; "they could not make nearly such a mess of us now as they could have done then, while we could make much more of a mess of them." [21] And in a speech at Blackburn, February 22, he quoted Shakespeare again: "Come the three corners of the world in arms, and we shall shock them." [22]

Other factors may have played a role in Chamberlain's thinking: Roosevelt's slowly growing momentum in shaping American opinion, his belief in Mussolini's persuasive influence with Hitler, even Poland's second thoughts about her earlier bargain with Germany. But whatever the explanation, his confidence appears to have been genuine, his hope entirely real. As he wrote his sister, February 19, in words so characteristic of him: "With the thrush singing in the garden, the sun shining, and the rooks beginning to discuss among themselves the prospects of the coming mating season, I feel as though Spring were getting near. . . . All the information I get seems to point in the direction of peace." [23] And there is much to suggest that he had come to believe that he alone could save that peace. Anticipating his seventieth birthday (March 18) and recalling his father's collapse at that age, he hoped for "a few more years" in which to save his country. Small wonder that the events of March and April came as such a blow to him.

CHAPTER XVI

The Descent to War

THOUGH TROUBLE HAD BEEN BREWING FOR WEEKS AND HAD REACHED crisis proportions five days before, the sudden German invasion of Czechoslovakia on March 15, 1939, stunned all of Europe.[1] To many Englishmen who had not believed the warning signs, it came as a rude awakening to the menace of Nazi methods to European freedom and security. To those who expected peace on the basis of Munich it came as hideous disillusionment.

In his address to the Commons that same afternoon, however, Chamberlain succumbed to the weight of ignorance and hope. Knowing little about what had actually happened, and wishing in any case to put the best construction on it, he quickly dismissed the idea of a "moral guarantee" to Czechoslovakia and explained that the Czech state had come to an end as a result of "internal disruption"; that freed the British Government from any obligation. Though conceding that the changes wrought in Czechoslovakia were not in accord with the spirit of Munich, he hastened on to say:

> Do not let us on that account be deflected from our course. Let us remember that the desire of all peoples of the world still remains concentrated on the hopes of peace. . . . Though we may have to suffer checks and disappointments from time to time, the object that we have in mind is of too great significance to the happiness of mankind for us lightly to give it up or set it on one side.[2]

This was the dialect of appeasement. It was that day an alien tongue in the House of Commons, and member after member rose to castigate the Prime Minister for his remarkable state of detachment and to challenge him to acknowledge the demise of appeasement and seek through common action with other nations to arrest the black death of totalitarian aggression. Labor and Liberal members found Chamberlain's attitude "incredible." As Sydney Silverman put it: any man who, seeing what had happened since Munich, could still say that appeasement was right either deliberately meant to mislead the House and country or was intellectually incapable of understanding what was going on in the world around him. Violent attacks came from those who had earlier criticized Munich, but a number of Conservatives, not all of them dissidents heretofore, also joined in the condemnation of appeasement. Eden was convinced that only a drastic reversal of policy could head off European anarchy and universal tragedy. Commander R. T. Bower flatly declared: "This plan of appeasement has failed," while Richard Law and Duncan Sandys made identical points just as abruptly. There was a perceptible change of temper in the House at large, a clear indication that many Government supporters were deeply disturbed and genuinely unhappy about the views and tactics of their leaders. Sir John Simon tried to defend the Government by arguing that there was still no alternative to the policy pursued at Munich and admonishing the members about the necessity of avoiding extensive and undefined commitments. This provoked savage criticism and aroused the House to a pitch of anger rarely seen. "Never has a Minister . . . given such an exhibition of complete and hopeless political bankruptcy," stormed William Gallacher (Communist) in expressing a sentiment widely shared by many who normally did not agree with Gallacher's political views. Vyvyan Adams (Conservative), fearing that Hitler might next threaten to bomb London or Leeds or Liverpool if Britain did not give Germany a colony, proclaimed: "In God's name . . . let us not give way to that kind of threat." J. J. Davidson (Labor) raged: "I want to say plainly to the Government that when the time does come to make some defense of their own interests, I will advise the workers to see the Government in hell before they undertake the job which should have been dealt with long ago." [3]

Equally important, there followed throughout the country an explosion of public opinion, impossible to trace with precision, but forcefully reflected in the volume of acute criticism which spurted from the British press. The overwhelming sentiment was that Munich had been reduced to utter mockery; appeasement was totally discredited and must be abandoned at once. The Conservative *Daily Telegraph* (March 16) and the Unionist Cardiff *Western Mail* (March 16) exemplified the sentiment of most journals when, in demanding a change in British policy, the former asked: "Who can appease a boa-constrictor?" while the latter proclaimed further talk of appeasement "greater folly than reading a tract to a Bengal tiger." Those journals which, at the time of Munich, were prepared to give the policy a "fair trial," now recognized its futility. Even the pro-Government *Times* (March 17), long in the vanguard of appeasement, at last saw Nazism revealed in all its cunning and ruthlessness, and found it a "wholly natural impulse" that would urge the other nations of Europe "to confer forthwith on the best means of defending together all that they are agreed on holding sacred." Those newspapers which had earlier warned of this unfortunate outcome were in a stronger position for telling criticism than ever before. The Liberal *Manchester Guardian* (March 16) expounded on the final shattering of Chamberlain's "dream fantasy"; the Liberal *News Chronicle* (March 16) reiterated the "utter futility" of appeasement; the Labor *Daily Herald* (March 16) saw Prague as merely "the postscript to Munich." Dozens of other journals around the country—like the *Liverpool Daily Post,* the Bradford *Yorkshire Observer,* the *Glasgow Herald* and the *Leeds Weekly Citizen*—read the evidence exactly the same way. Everywhere it was agreed that appeasement must be replaced by some sort of vigorous, and quite probably collective, action. Here and there, especially in Opposition journals of course, it was noted that the alternative to an abrupt change in policy was a change in prime minister. The forcefulness and virtual unanimity of this judgment could not help but weigh heavily on Chamberlain, who long had prided himself as a keen interpreter of the country's mind.

March 16 brought no apparent change in Chamberlain's outlook (at least his replies in the Commons to questions about the Czechoslovak situation were distressingly non-committal), and his failure to gauge the changed temper of the nation precipitated a crisis within the Conservative Party. Throughout the day criticism of his apparently stubborn refusal to be deflected from appeasement continued to grow until his position as Prime Minister and leader of the party was clearly in jeopardy. Besides their own sudden disenchantment with appeasement, most Conservatives undoubtedly realized the political implications of holding to a policy which had been sorely discredited in the eyes of the electorate. Halifax for one recognized the signs of party disobedience, and in the moment of crisis put the issue squarely to Chamberlain: unless a clear and unequivocal statement of Britain's attitude toward German aggression were forthcoming, he must expect insurrection in the party and the House.

Still other forces played upon Chamberlain. Representations came in from the Dominions, which hitherto had counseled against Continental involvement. The Foreign Office passed the limit of restraint and sternly urged, indeed demanded, a stronger posture. Even Nevile Henderson, the British ambassador on whose optimistic diagnosis of the German situation Chamberlain had so long relied, saw that a new attitude toward Germany would be necessary. Gradually it dawned upon Chamberlain that he had been cheated; surely he was entitled to consultation if Hitler thought Munich should be undone. And no manner of mental gymnastics could reconcile the incorporation into the Reich of seven million Czechs with Hitler's oft-professed aim of including only Germans. Chamberlain had no choice but to change his view.

The change was announced in his Birmingham address of March 17. Casting aside a long-prepared speech on domestic questions, he set out to correct the error of his judgment in the House of Commons two days before. He would not recant on Munich, but now the case was different. It caused Britain to ask: "Is this the last attack upon a small state, or is it to be followed by others? Is this, in fact, a step in the direction of an attempt to dominate the world by force?" While there was hardly anything he would not sacrifice for peace, he must except "the liberty that we have enjoyed for hundreds of years." And while he was not prepared to enter into "unspecified commitments operating under conditions which cannot be foreseen," there could be "no greater mistake" than to suppose that Britain had so lost its fiber that it would not do its utmost to resist domination of the world by force.

A definite contradiction to the mood and policy of his earlier statements, Chamberlain's Birmingham remarks still did not launch a new crusade. They pointed in a new direction but that was all. There was no decision on support to be offered other potential victims of aggression, cooperation to be sought with other powers, or sacrifice to be demanded from the British people. While Chamberlain reluctantly pondered these matters, the pace was forced by Romania's report of an economic ultimatum from Berlin. Halifax sought at once an "expression of opinion" from the Foreign Ministers in Paris, Moscow, Warsaw, Ankara, Athens, and Belgrade. The replies received covered the whole gamut of evasion, save for the Soviet proposal that delegates from Britain, France, Russia, Poland, Romania, and Turkey meet at once, possibly in Bucharest, to discuss the possibilities of common action. But the British dismissed this idea, with some very unconvincing arguments,[4] in favor of a proposal of their own. That proposal was drafted by Chamberlain himself, who wrote about it to his sister on March 19:

As soon as I had time to think, I saw that it was impossible to deal with Hitler after he had thrown all his assurances to the winds. . . . I have worked out a plan which . . . is pretty bold and startling, but I feel that something of the kind is needed. . . . As always, I want to gain time, for I never accept the view that war is inevitable.[5]

This "bold and startling" plan called for France, Russia, and Poland to join with Britain in signing and publishing a formal declaration that, in the event of a threat to the independence of any European state, the four powers would consult at once on measures to be taken to organize common resistance. Poland torpedoed it, refusing to associate with Russia in any way which might provoke Hitler. So Chamberlain's first idea died quickly.

Anticipating possible failure, Chamberlain and Halifax agreed with Bonnet in London, March 22, on a line to be followed thereafter. Romania must resist German aggression, and Poland must support her. In order to encourage a Polish commitment to Romania, Britain and France would give a private undertaking to Poland, after which the Poles should raise no objection to Anglo-French efforts to secure Soviet aid. The implication was clear. It was best to make sure of Poland, regarded in the Cabinet as a more formidable military power than Russia.[6] An attempt to secure Russian aid could be made later.

As days passed, the pressure on Chamberlain for positive action grew to very great proportions. March 22 saw Hitler wrest Memel from Lithuania and assume responsibility for the "protection" of Slovakia. This stirred the Poles to push in London for a bilateral agreement along the lines of Chamberlain's intended four-power declaration. Other small powers awaited a lead from Britain. A flood of rumors concerning German demands on Warsaw, Polish mobilization, and German troop concentrations on the Pomeranian frontier began to pour into London. Halifax, with unaccustomed doughtiness and modest support from Hoare, pressed for an entirely new National Government, to include Churchill, Eden, and the leaders of all parties. Question periods in the House of Commons were characterized by widespread and unrestrained impatience to hear what course of action the Government proposed to take. Public speakers of all political hues demanded immediate and vigorous action. Deputations visited Chamberlain to urge boldness and resolution. And the outcry in the press for positive achievement persisted in direct proportion to Chamberlain's failure to come up with anything definite. Indeed, a veritable revolution in feeling and opinion had occurred in Britain within the course of a few days,[7] and the psychological impact upon ministers who themselves were badly shaken and converted to the view that "something" must be done was exceedingly strong.

In daily meetings of the Cabinet, the need for definite action was painfully apparent to all. There was general agreement that a line should be laid down and Berlin told that to cross it would mean war. But the location of the line was still the object of extensive controversy. March 27 brought a decision to proceed along the path envisaged by Chamberlain, Halifax, and Bonnet five days before, with Poland now considered as the primary object of German aggression. After two days of waiting for French concurrence, the British proposed to Poland and Romania (late evening, March 29) that if they were to fight to defend their independence, Britain and France would aid them, provided that Poland helped Romania, if necessary, and that Poland would promise reciprocal support to Britain and France in case of attack by Germany or in case they went to war to resist German aggression anywhere in western Europe or Yugoslavia. Britain and France, it was added, would maintain friendly contact with Russia to prevent her from lapsing into isolation and to assure her benevolent neutrality and possible support.[8]

Next day, however, a German attack on Poland appeared so imminent that this proposal was superseded by a telegram seeking Poland's approval of a unilateral British guarantee. It was this guarantee which Chamberlain announced in the Commons, March 31, in what was surely one of the most remarkable declarations in the history of British foreign policy:

> . . . In the event of any action which clearly threatened Polish independence, and which the Polish Government accordingly considered it vital to resist with their national forces, His Majesty's Government would feel themselves bound at once to lend the Polish Government all support in their power. They have given the Polish Government an assurance to this effect.[9]

While some questions concerning the drafting of the guarantee remain uncertain (including those with regard to the origin of the idea and what precisely it was meant to accomplish),[10] Chamberlain's involvement was undoubtedly great. The evidence available suggests that it was an improvisation drafted on the afternoon of March 30 by the Prime Minister himself, with assistance from Halifax and Cadogan,[11] in reply to a Parliamentary question, due to be answered the following day, asking what action the British Government would take in the event of a sudden (and expected) German attack on Poland. According to William Strang, it seems to have "sprung fully grown from the Ministerial mind," without any canvassing of military or political advisers, and "was designed, no doubt, among other things, to meet what was recognized to be an imperative demand by public opinion that Poland should not be allowed to go the same way as Czechoslovakia." [12] Halifax later explained it simply as an attempt to make it "unmistakably clear" to Hitler "that the particular acts of aggression which he was believed to have in mind would result in general war." [13]

The guarantee to Poland completely reversed Chamberlain's Birmingham stand against "new unspecified commitments operating under conditions which cannot be foreseen" and moved very close to placing the ultimate decision on Britain's involvement in war into Polish hands. Chamberlain himself acknowledged in the Commons, April 3, that this was a landmark reversal of British policy, so important that it would "have a chapter to itself when the history books come to be written." [14] He seemed to sense the full implications of the pledge and was somewhat reluctant to give it. But he felt compelled to act in response to public demand, the pressure in Parliament and party, the conversion of a Cabinet majority to deterrent action, personal indignation at having been double-crossed by Hitler, and increasing appreciation of the real menace posed by Nazi brutality. These factors could hardly fail to move any prime minister, especially one of whom it had been widely and bluntly said that if his policy did not change, he himself must be changed.

The guarantee to Poland won hearty approval in the British press and the House of Commons. But there was also widespread insistence that it must be understood as only a first step in organizing the forces of Europe against aggression. The *Manchester Guardian's* (April 1) view that the Government must lose no time in passing from its "interim policy" to the "final scheme" was expressed with equal effect in a wide variety of journals, while in the Commons Arthur Greenwood (deputy Labor leader), Sinclair, Churchill, Lloyd George, Hugh Dalton and others spoke forcefully to the same point. Chamberlain acknowledged this on April 3; "the matter could not end where it stands today" for if domination of the world by force were indeed the intention of the German Government, it is quite clear that Poland would not be the only country which would be endangered, and the policy which has led us to give this assurance to Poland, of course, could not be satisfied or carried out if we were to confine ourselves to a single case which after all, might not be the case in point.[15]

He was prepared to welcome the cooperation of any country, whatever its internal system of government (an obvious reference to Russia) in resistance to aggression. This did not mean, he carefully explained, that he was now any more a man of war than he had been in September. Indeed, it was his ardent hope that "our actions, begun but not concluded, will prove to be the turning point not towards war, which wins nothing, cures nothing, ends nothing, but towards a more wholesome era, when reason will take the place of force." [16] But he felt it imperative now for Britain to make her position clear and unmistakable, whatever the result might be.

An opportunity to extend the guarantee policy arose much sooner than Chamberlain expected. Without a word of warning, Italy invaded Albania on April 7 (Good Friday). The British demanded the "frankest and fullest" explanation, and Chamberlain, gravely disillusioned, wrote his sister with his freezing gift of understatement: "I am afraid that such faith as I ever had in the assurances of dictators is rapidly being whittled away." [17] Two weeks before, he had written to Mussolini asking his aid in reestablishing trust and assuring peace. This was the Duce's reply. Yet, in the face of the German danger, or in relation to the role he had cast for Italy, Chamberlain decided to minimize the Italian threat. He refused to denounce the Italian agreement and assumed an attitude which not only raised a question as to whether this was his "soft" reaction of March 15 all over again, but whether he had been genuinely converted to the stronger position which his words and actions of March 17–31 had seemed to indicate.

This did not last long, however. A storm of protest similar to that which followed the crushing of Czechoslovakia arose from the British press. Reports from British envoys in the Balkans registered Greek fear of an Italian attack on Corfu and Turkish disappointment that Britain had not given a definite lead. Churchill, who according to his own testimony became much closer to Chamberlain after the Birmingham address, undertook to impress upon the Prime Minister personally the need for some statement which would produce the same united front which had emerged in the case of the Polish agreement; and Halifax plugged for a tightening of mutual obligations of support between Britain and France on one hand, Greece and Turkey on the other. An alarmed Daladier saw good reason to expect an Italo-German offensive from the North Sea to Egypt. The upshot of all this was that Chamberlain and the Cabinet eventually decided to extend to Greece a guarantee similar to that given Poland. That Romania was also included in the pledges announced by Chamberlain in the Commons, April 13, was largely the result of French insistence, Daladier standing unusually firm in the diplomatic pork-barrelling which preceded agreement that both Britain and France should guarantee both Greece and Romania.

In announcing the guarantees in the Commons—in language identical to that of the Polish pledge—Chamberlain was considerably less than reassuring to many members of the House. He was still "unwilling to believe" that his efforts to remove suspicions, promote good will, and keep the peace "will not even yet bear fruit," however discouraging the outlook might seem at the moment.[18] His determination to avoid a division of Europe on ideological grounds, one thing which had been constant with him, still weighed heavily in his mind. He was able to see hope— with Chamberlain hope was indeed eternal—where few others could find it. In one sense, the very acts of guaranteeing Poland, Greece, and Romania can be viewed as placing significant barriers in the way of Hitler and Mussolini so as to incline them more readily toward hoped-for agreement. But the seizure of Czechoslovakia and Albania moved the British Parliament and public to a point where they would no longer tolerate the policy of paying compliments to the dictators, assuring them of British good will, and ignoring steps to protect their neighbors. Under the impact of events, and the pressure which generated from Parliament and public because of them, Chamberlain was forced, however reluctantly, to move along a different course.

Spurred in part by his own appreciation of the need to improve the nation's military posture and borne along on the tide of resistance which events had created, Chamberlain accepted, during the month of April, significant military measures, two of which had long been in the wind. Important policy decisions involved a definite program for an expeditionary force to the Continent, doubling the Territorial Army, shifting priority in the air program from bombers to fighters, plans for naval operations in both the Mediterranean and Atlantic, and methodical staff talks with the French. April 20 brought an announcement of the establishment of a Ministry of Supply, long sought by the Liberal Party, with some support from Labor and the dissident Conservatives, as well as the Secretary of State for War, Hore-Belisha. (Disappointment and dismay sprang, however, from Chamberlain's nomination of Leslie Burgin, Minister of Transport, to fill the post. Churchill had been widely-regarded as the obvious man for the job, but Chamberlain did not want to risk "any possibility of easing the tension and getting back to normal relations with the dictators" by making an appointment that "would certainly be regarded by them as a challenge." [19]) Finally, there followed one week later the introduction of conscription, a measure long and earnestly resisted by the Prime Minister. But the strength of Parliamentary feeling (Labor excluded), the insistence of Hore-Belisha, and perhaps most important, the frank admission of the French that this alone would convince them of Britain's resolution, brought Chamberlain to see that he must take the step.

Measures of military preparedness aside, the central question asked in Parliament and the press after the guarantee to Poland was "What about Russia?" It was widely acknowledged, even by Chamberlain—in word if not by deed—that the peace front now begun must be developed with utmost speed and vigor. Likewise, it was obvious that effective aid for Poland and Romania, in the event that Britain's guarantees should be called into operation, could only come from the east, from the association of Soviet Russia with the peace bloc. This was a most difficult fact for Chamberlain to accept, for his attitude toward Russia, whenever he could bring himself to think of her at all, had long been negative in the extreme. But Chamberlain was a statesman cornered by reality, and the pressures upon him offered no alternative but to approach the Soviet Union. The British negotiations with Russia during the summer of 1939 have been fully described in a number of works;[20] the central purpose here will be to indicate Chamberlain's attitude toward them.

From the moment he became Prime Minister, Chamberlain believed that the peace of Europe depended upon friendly discussion among the four great powers: Britain, France, Germany, and Italy. Russia was excluded from his thinking. Her participation would make 1914 all over again, effecting the encirclement which might be Hitler's pretext for an early war. Moreover, he believed Russia to be weak, both actually (the effect of the military purges) and potentially (the weight of tremendous domestic problems). Further, he distrusted her motives, suspecting that she would be very happy to see the Western democracies and Germany locked in a deadly bourgeois war, and was, at the very least, content merely to fish in troubled waters for the sake of promoting her own selfish ends. The extent to which his view of Russia sprang from ideological prejudice as opposed to political suspicion (an honest, realistic—as he saw it—interpretation of military and intelligence reports) has long been the object of controversy. Surely both were involved, the latter perhaps more so than the former, but the line between the two defying demarcation and the scope of his prejudice especially difficult to assess since it appears to have been more subconscious than conscious in nature. But in any case, his resulting attitude was clear. Thus in the circumstances of the *Anschluss*, Russia's guarded initiative was taken very lightly. So were reports of her willingness to stand by Czechoslovakia during the September crisis. There was never a question of inviting Russia to Munich, especially since Hitler was no more interested in her presence than Chamberlain. The German occupation of Prague would seem to have changed things somewhat, but when Polish intransigence precluded quick collaboration with Russia, Chamberlain and his colleagues deemed it best to make certain of Poland and leave cooperation with the Soviet Union to be contemplated later.

His unchanging attitude was revealed in a letter Chamberlain wrote his sister, March 26:

I must confess to the most profound distrust of Russia. I have no belief whatever in her ability to maintain an effective offensive, even if she wanted to. And I distrust her motives, which seem to me to have little connection with our ideas of liberty, and to be concerned only with getting every one else by the ears. Moreover, she is both hated and suspected by many of the smaller States, notably by Poland, Roumania, and Finland.[21]

Of Poland's anxiety to avoid entanglement with Russia, he wrote a few days later: "I very much agree . . . for I regard Russia as a very unreliable friend . . . with an enormous irritative power on others." [22] But there were potent factors working in the direction of negotiating with Russia. The demand for Russia's inclusion in the peace bloc was a cardinal feature of the Commons debate on April 3, Churchill and Lloyd George impressively sustaining Labor-Liberal appeals by pointing out both the political and military value of Russia's participation. It was much intensified on

April 13 when Chamberlain, speaking with great forbearance toward Italy despite her Albanian action, was so vigorously interrupted by cries of "What about Russia?" that he momentarily deserted his prepared typescript to "ask the House to believe that without any prejudice, without any preconceived ideological notions," he was working to the utmost of his ability to marshal the forces of peace against aggression.[23] Subsequently, fifteen speakers of diverse political loyalties (including Attlee, Sinclair, Churchill, Eden, Hugh Dalton, Haden Guest, Vernon Bartlett, and Ben Riley) pushed in different ways toward a single conclusion: specific arrangements for cooperation and combined action among both larger and smaller nations must be made at once, and Russia's inclusion was vital. The same intense concern for Russia's cooperation had pervaded the British press since the guarantee to Poland,[24] and a Gallup Poll showed 92 percent of the Englishmen canvassed to be in favor of a British alliance with Russia. Closer still to Chamberlain, anxious Cabinet colleagues (Halifax and Chatfield in particular) pressed the matter upon him. And from Paris came steady French encouragement for the opening of talks with Russia. All these factors, combined with the common-sense logic of the situation, finally persuaded Chamberlain that an approach to Russia, however distasteful, simply must be made.

The first British proposal, April 15, was guarded and vague. It provided that if any neighbor of Russia should be attacked, "the assistance of the Soviet Government would be available, if desired, and would be afforded in such a manner as would be found most convenient." [25] Russia's reply of April 17 demanded a full-scale alliance for mutual defense with Britain and France, coverage for all the border states between the Baltic and Black Seas, and immediate military conversations. The startled British thereupon consumed three weeks trying to reconcile the following objectives (as summarized by Halifax): not to forego the chance of receiving help from Russia in case of war; not to jeopardize the common front by disregarding the susceptibilities of Poland and Romania; not to forfeit world sympathy by giving a handle to Germany's anti-Comintern propaganda; not to endanger the cause of peace by provoking Germany. They experienced no success, and the British response to Russia, May 8—which called the Russian proposal "logically complete" but too little cognizant of "practical difficulties"—was merely a re-cast formula of their original proposition.

Meanwhile, Chamberlain was under intensifying pressure from Parliament and the press to get the negotiations moving. Questioned repeatedly in the House of Commons, he sometimes offered placid replies, as on May 2: "We are carrying on discussions of a perfectly friendly character. There must necessarily be a great many details which have to be considered, and there are other Governments to be considered. . . . There is no want of good will on the part of His Majesty's Government." [26] At other times he vented a peevish displeasure on his questioners—as on May 5, when the replacement of Litvinov by Molotov in the Soviet Foreign Ministry prompted Attlee to charge that delays were causing uncertainty: "I do realize that uncertainty is being created by a number of people who are all the time suggesting that if there is any fault it must be the fault of the British Government." This "purely partisan attitude" was not "conducive to the interests of this country, but I cannot be held responsible for that." And when another member suggested that Chamberlain make personal contact in order to get Stalin's own view, the Prime Minister snapped back: "Perhaps the hon. Member would suggest with whom I make personal contact, because personalities change rather rapidly." [27] At best lukewarm about the conversations with Russia, Chamberlain resented attempts to push him faster than his own reluctant judgment would permit him to go.

Indeed, with one eye on Germany, Chamberlain ordered Nevile Henderson back to his post in Berlin (from which he had been withdrawn in mid-March) with the express purpose of explaining British conscription before it was announced in the House of Commons. Hitler's response was a venomous speech in the Reichstag (April 28) denouncing both the Anglo-German Naval Agreement of 1935 and the German-Polish Non-Aggression Pact. Chamberlain's hopes were shaken anew: "He finds it so easy to tear up treaties and throw overboard assurances, that no one can feel any confidence in new ones." [28] Hardly a novel deduction by this time, his moderate tone suggests that Chamberlain was still having some difficulty bringing himself to accept what was so obviously true.

The successful conclusion of a British mutual assistance pact with Turkey in mid-May (exchanges had begun shortly after Prague and proceeded without serious difficulty) turned attention once more to the Russian talks. An impasse had been reached, the Russian reply of May 15 offering no compromise in the original Soviet position. The effect of this was great temptation for Chamberlain and some of his Cabinet colleagues to abandon the talks entirely. But after "many meetings and searchings of heart" (Hoare's words), it was decided to continue on the Soviet basis.

Undoubtedly instrumental in forcing this decision was the May 22 signing of the Italo-German "Pact of Steel," signs of a developing crisis over Danzig, and intense agitation in Parliament and press.

The May 19 debate in the Commons found Chamberlain under heavy attack from Lloyd George, Attlee, and Sinclair for (in the former's words) "political snobbery" and "staring this gift horse [Russia] in the mouth." Stung by their thrusts, Chamberlain reacted obstinately and refused to explain with any precision the status of Anglo-Russian contacts. This only whetted the critics. Churchill could not understand why, if Britain was prepared to ally with Russia in time of war, she would shrink from allying with her in time of peace, especially since by that very act she might prevent the outbreak of war. Eden was equally perplexed, and Sinclair rose to convey "the impression of blank astonishment and deep disappointment . . . felt abroad by men of all parties, by all friends of peace and justice," at the Government's attitude toward Russia.[29]

The tone of the press was no less anxious. The Labor *Daily Herald* (May 8) was most emphatic: "The country is determined to have a Russian alliance. The country must have its Russian alliance!" The Government could continue to "refine formulas or elaborate compromises" only at the cost of betraying national interests, it stormed (May 24). This was more than partisan diatribe. The Conservative *Daily Telegraph* (May 20, 22) took essentially the same position, and the Conservative-leaning *Observer* (May 21), long a mouthpiece of appeasement, saw the argument for a Russian alliance leading "irresistibly to a consummation which shall put the final seal on a convincing, businesslike, decisive 'encirclement for defence' against Germany." Britain could not feel secure without Russia, the Liberal Bradford *Yorkshire Observer* (May 20) and the Liberal *Liverpool Daily Post* (May 25) declared. And Conservative opinion had begun to accept that fact despite Chamberlain's refusal to recognize national opinion on the point, the *Yorkshire Observer* added. An alliance with Russia was "the most obvious means of checkmating aggression," the independent *Glasgow Herald* (May 11) exhorted, while the Unionist Cardiff *Western Mail* (May 24) expressed keen disappointment that no agreement had yet been reached. "What is Chamberlain up to now?" the *Sunday Pictorial* (May 14) asked. "Is he dreaming of turning our friends into enemies and our enemies into friends?" And so it went in a wide range of dailies and periodicals alike.

Now cloaking the whole project under the Covenant of the League of Nations—a curious maneuver in view of Chamberlain's earlier estimate of the League, undertaken apparently for the purpose of face-saving—the British accepted (May 25) the principle of mutual assistance and offered to "concert together as to the methods by which such mutual support and assistance could, in the case of need, be made most effective." [30] Russia rejected this as cumbrous and vague, re-emphasized her original position, and added that a political pact must be preceded by a military convention. Again Chamberlain was disheartened and "not at all sure he would not call the whole thing off." [31] Finding the recall (for consultation) of Ambassador William Seeds impossible because he was not well, Chamberlain decided to send a Foreign Office official, William Strang, to Moscow with full information about the British attitude on all outstanding points. Eden had offered to go, and it was widely suggested that a major minister should be sent. But Chamberlain's distrust of Russia's hard bargaining made him unwilling to consider such an "upscaling" of the conversations.

A June 15 British compromise called for immediate action by the three contracting parties if one of them went to the assistance of another state which had consented to receive aid. Arguing that a British refusal to guarantee the Baltic states would put Russia in a "position of inequality," the Russians rejected this in favor of a simple defensive pact covering only direct attack on one of the signatories. That was of no use to the British in protecting the states already guaranteed, so they countered (June 22) that the alliance should operate in any case of aggression which menaced the security of one of the contracting parties. But this proposal faltered for lack of agreement on who should decide the moment to act had come.

The first three weeks of July, though filled with continued wrangling over the form and content of what was nearly agreed in principle, brought no appreciable advance. The British slowly conceded one point after another, but without any corresponding concession from Russia. Again Chamberlain questioned the wisdom of continuing the negotiations, and was nearly prepared to tell Russia (as Halifax put it) "to go jump into the Baltic Sea or any other sea they can find. . . ." [32] But the enormous interest of the British public and (again in Halifax's words) the "constant pressure from all their [the Government's] friends" [33] kept him going until July 23 brought a startling reversal in Russia's position. Suddenly seeing no "insuperable difficulties" in the political discussions, Russia requested immediate military conversations. Since the British had already decided upon this tactic themselves, should the political conversations break down, their assent was quickly given.

While the Anglo-Russian negotiations teetered on the brink of collapse, Chamberlain was engaged with a limited German contact—knowledge of which probably helps to explain the sudden change in Russia's attitude. During the third week of July, Helmut Wohltat, a leading official of Göring's economic staff, visited London and listened to Horace Wilson expound a comprehensive program for Anglo-German cooperation which touched upon a non-aggression pact, a limitation of armaments, economic arrangements, and colonial questions. Wohltat also met with R. S. Hudson, the Minister of Overseas Trade, who spoke of Anglo-German cooperation in world markets, a delimitation of spheres of interest (to avoid deadly competition), and a possible British loan to Germany. The general British objective was a broad Anglo-German agreement on questions of such importance that issues like Danzig and Poland, being relegated to the background, would lose much of their acuteness. That Chamberlain approved all of this, and perhaps himself had drafted the plans which Wilson presented, is all but verified by Wilson's offer to Wohltat to meet the Prime Minister "then and there" for an endorsement of the program.[34] (Wohltat declined.)

Nothing came of the Wohltat visit; German officials showed no interest in what the British had to say. But the incident provides significant evidence that the new policy which Chamberlain adopted after Prague had by no means obliterated his hope for reconciliation with Germany. Previously he had pursued appeasement publicly while occasionally warning Hitler in private; after March, 1939, he warned him publicly and clung to a hope for appeasement in private. He worked to make it clear to Germany that his whole course of action was defensive, and still believed that, while he must convince Germany that her chances of winning a war were too remote to make it worthwhile, "the corollary to that must be that she has a chance of getting fair and reasonable . . . treatment from us and others, if she will give up the idea she can force it from us, and convince us that she has given it up." [35]

An important point to note, however, is that the concessions to Germany envisaged in the Wohltat talks were to be offered primarily at the expense of Britain, not some other nation. The Danzig situation had grown increasingly tense during the month of July, as the Germans remilitarized the city and the Poles fought back through restrictive economic measures. But there was no hint of British retreat from the position taken up on Poland. Chamberlain assured the Commons, July 10, that Britain was "firmly resolved" to carry out her guarantee, and several times in the days which followed, Germany was officially warned that Britain would support Poland should she feel compelled to resist unilateral German action in Danzig. A solution to the Danzig question along the lines of Munich was "not good enough," Chamberlain wrote his sister in mid-July. Indeed, he doubted "if any solution short of war, is practicable at present." To be sure, he quickly added that "if the dictators would have a modicum of patience, I can imagine that a way could be found of meeting German claims while safeguarding Poland's independence and economic security." [36] But this referred to the future—a future which never came. And even if Chamberlain himself had wavered, the state of public feeling in Britain would not have permitted him to repeat what he had done the previous September. His recognition of this, along with a general understanding in the Cabinet that to retreat from the Polish guarantee would merely land Britain back in the difficulties from which she had, by the guarantee, sought to extricate herself, ruled out any possibility of a "Polish Munich." Anyway, Chamberlain was not inclined to think the danger near. Though predicting a war of nerves, he doubted that Hitler would face the real thing—thus his self-assurance in forcing the debate on the rising of Parliament, August 4, into an issue of confidence, and his optimistic departing, twelve days later, for a holiday in the Highlands.

Back on the Russian scene, things were about to happen. After a slow sea journey to Leningrad, the British (and French) military mission arrived in Moscow on August 11. The talks began auspiciously, despite the British mission's instructions to "go very slowly" and "treat the Russians with reserve." But they came to a sudden halt on the third day, when Russia asked the crucial question: In the event of German aggression, would Russian troops be permitted to move across Poland and Romania?[37] The talks adjourned while the British reluctantly, and the French more eagerly, sought an answer from Poland. Six days in coming, it was flatly negative. And by then more shocking news was ready for the world to hear.

On August 23 the Russians announced their astounding non-aggression pact with Germany. A possible outcome of evolving Nazi-Soviet contacts (of which the British were at least vaguely

aware) which once or twice had crossed the minds of British officials, it had never been taken seriously. Occupying a favorable
bargaining position, the Soviets had decided at length that they
had more to gain, for a time at least, by an association of sorts
with Germany. Whether a more positive British approach to the
negotiations with Russia would have produced a different result
will long be debated but may never be known.[38]

Reflecting perhaps his steady skepticism of the value of Russian assistance, Chamberlain was less perturbed by this shocking
turn of events than many of his colleagues. Indeed, he seemed
somehow strengthened by it. Writing to Hitler in language which
epitomized firmness and clarity, he warned:

> Whatever may be the nature of the German-Soviet Agreement, it can-
> not alter Great Britain's obligation to Poland which His Majesty's Gov-
> ernment have stated in public repeatedly and plainly, and which they
> are determined to fulfill. . . .
> It has been alleged that if His Majesty's Government had made their
> position more clear in 1914, the great catastrophe would have been
> avoided. . . . On this occasion there shall be no such tragic misunder-
> standing. If the need should arise, they are resolved and prepared to em-
> ploy without delay all the forces at their command, and it is impossible
> to foresee the end of hostilities once engaged.[39]

Direct German-Polish negotiations, resulting in a settlement that
could be guaranteed by other powers, was the only way he now
saw to avoid plunging Europe into war.

In the House of Commons, August 24, Chamberlain reaffirmed
that Britain's obligations remained unaltered. If Britain was
forced, he carefully explained, despite all her efforts for peace, to
embark upon a struggle of untold misery, she would be fighting
not for the "political future of a far-away city in a foreign land,"
but for the preservation of those principles of justice and freedom
for which she had always stood. How different were these words
from his remarks of a year before about a quarrel in a far-away
country (Czechoslovakia) among people of whom Englishmen
knew nothing![40] The House was solidly behind him, irrespective
of party. So was the press, where determination to honor Britain's
pledge was everywhere—and firmly—expressed.

In the week of peace which remained, Chamberlain's efforts
were devoted to two ends: to persuade the Germans and Poles to
negotiate, and to make it clear that Britain would stand by her
pledge to Poland. He had not abandoned hope of somehow
reaching accommodation with Germany, but he knew well that

no policy other than the one pursued would have been tolerated by the British people, now exceedingly tired of being described as weak, unreliable, and degenerate and plainly determined to fight rather than to retreat again.

Britain signed a formal Agreement of Mutual Assistance with Poland on August 25. That same afternoon Hitler, in one of the striking changes which were so formidable a part of his temperament, sent the British a message about a "large comprehensive offer" once the urgent Polish situation was settled. The British reply (August 28), studied almost continuously in the Cabinet for two days, held that everything depended on the nature and method of the settlement with Poland. In response to Britain's urging of direct negotiations with Poland, Hitler demanded (August 29) the presence of a Polish representative, with full plenary powers, in Berlin the following day. This the British rejected as unreasonable, and recommended to Poland the use of normal diplomatic channels. Their request for a list of Germany's demands was grudgingly honored only on the evening of August 31, by which time the Germans regarded their proposals "neglected" and the whole negotiation off.

Meanwhile, Birger Dahlerus, a Swedish manufacturer, was shuttling back and forth between Berlin and London, carrying unofficial messages from Göring to Halifax and back. The sum total of his story[41] shows the British determined to stand by the guarantee to Poland, but willing to tolerate these somewhat unorthodox contacts lest there be in them a remote chance of preserving peace. Indeed, Chamberlain later (September 10) wrote that the communications with Hitler and Göring looked "rather promising" for a time. He did not think that Hitler was "merely talking through his hat" or "deliberately deceiving us while he matured his schemes," but believed that the Führer "did seriously contemplate an agreement with us, and . . . worked seriously at proposals . . . which to his one-track mind seemed almost fabulously generous." [42] This assessment apparently showed through Chamberlain's remarks to the Commons on August 29, for his account of contacts with Hitler stirred considerable uneasiness among the "anti-Munichers," who were alert for anything savoring of surrender or suggesting that Hitler was yet to be believed. While standing by his position on Poland, Chamberlain still held hope that the crisis could result in something besides war.

The German invasion of Poland at dawn, September 1, was followed that afternoon by a British warning that unless Germany suspended all aggressive action and withdrew her forces,

the British obligation to Poland would be honored "without hesitation." Chamberlain then told the House of Commons at 6 P.M.
—in a speech conveying a world of shattered illusions—that if the
reply to this "last warning" was unfavorable (and he doubted it
would be otherwise), the British ambassador in Berlin would ask
for his passports. This talk about a last warning and asking for
passports left the House puzzled. The plain fact was that by the
terms of the agreement with Poland, Britain should by now have
come to her aid.

Thus began a 36-hour period of acute suspense and tension,
during which the Government's delay produced a widespread
fear that it intended to scuttle—and an equal determination that
it must not. Chamberlain's statement to the anxious and restive
Commons on the evening of September 2 did nothing to relieve
the strain. Members listened with amazement, stupefaction, then
exasperation, as he spoke of Germany's failure to reply to the
British note, a belated Italian proposal for a conference, and his
Government's willingness to regard the situation as being the
same as two days before if Germany would agree to withdraw her
forces from Poland. A smell of betrayal was in the air, and as a
ripple of revolt spread across the jam-packed Commons, Arthur
Greenwood, deputy Labor leader, rose to demand that Chamberlain tell the House at noon "tomorrow" (September 3) whether
Britain's promises were in the process of fulfillment; delay was
imperiling her national honor—and human civilization as well.
Universal cheers went up, and Chamberlain felt it necessary to
speak again. His reassurance that the Government was not
weakening seemed to impress almost no one, and he sat down
again without applause. At length the House adjourned amid
mingled feelings of astonishment, hostility, and dismay.

Chamberlain's statement left even his Cabinet colleagues
"aghast" (Hore-Belisha's word). They had earlier agreed on an
ultimatum to expire at midnight, and were unaware of last-
minute appeals from Paris which had led Chamberlain to make
so halting and ambiguous a statement. Consequently, they
pressed for another meeting, duly held from 11:30 P.M. to 1:30
A.M. Warnings from Halifax and the Chief Whip made it clear
to Chamberlain that, unless he clarified his position, the Government could not maintain itself in the House next day. The result
was agreement on an ultimatum to Germany to expire at 11 A.M.
next morning.

Shortly after 11 o'clock, September 3, Chamberlain broadcast
to the nation. An hour later he addressed the House of Commons.

It was a sad day for all, especially for him, he remarked to the latter group. Everything he had worked for, everything he had hoped for, everything he had believed in during his public life had crashed into ruins. Britain was at war with Germany. His hopes for peace were dead.

Chamberlain's exact position during those last two days of peace defies precise description—possibly because his position was not exact. He fully realized the need to stand firm, and much can (and has) been said about the need to coordinate British action with that of an unsure and hesitating France as the basic explanation for the British delay in honoring the pledge to Poland. And it does appear that Chamberlain dismissed, on the night of September 2, a final clandestine "offer" from Hitler[43] when it became clear that France was prepared to move. On the other hand, by his own admission, "complications" causing delay included the secret communications with Hitler and Göring through a neutral intermediary, and the conference proposed by Mussolini.[44] This suggests that September 1 and 2 found him still on the verge of seduction, still prepared to consider and perhaps accept some last-minute offer advanced by one of the dictators. How long he might have waited is impossible to say, but implacable pressure from the Commons and Cabinet on September 2 left him with no alternative but to take the final step toward war.

CHAPTER XVII

The Final Year

THE OUTBREAK OF WAR CAME AS A TERRIBLE SHOCK TO CHAMBER-lain. It had, however (so he wrote his sister, September 10), one "comforting" effect. While peace endured he felt himself indispensable, for "no one else could carry out my policy." Now this had changed and "half a dozen" people could take his place.[1] But this did not mean that he intended to step down quickly. Despite his intense hatred of war, the torment it caused him to wage it, and his knowledge that he was not proper material for a war minister, he remained in office until forced aside in May, 1940, and occupied a Cabinet post until a few weeks before his death six months later.

A number of things kept Chamberlain going. One of them was his characteristic optimism, which now took the form of believing the war might end before a holocaust set in. The very nature of the "twilight war" (a phrase which he coined) encouraged him in this view. Setting Poland momentarily aside, his thinking ran like this: the longer the German attack was delayed, the better prepared the British and French would be to meet it. Realizing at length that they could not win, the German people might force an abandonment of aggression, conceivably destroying Hitler and Nazism in the process. The former view he often stated in public; the latter (far more unsound) proposition he reserved for private conversation, but he appeared to embrace it firmly. By the end of the year he was obliged to admit that German morale was stiffening—to the point where he came to wonder "whether we shall do any good with them unless they first get a real hard punch in the stomach." [2] But he still did not believe that Hitler would risk a frontal attack on the Maginot Line, or even a swing to the north of it. That would be a foolish gamble fraught with political as well as military dangers. Such reasoning (if that is what it was) on Chamberlain's part can only be characterized as vain hope or wishful thinking. But it demonstrates a temperament which, shrinking by nature from the carnage of all-out war, was able to find solace in an unsubstantial supposition that victory might be won without it.[3]

Though potentially contradictory to his avoidance-of-holocaust hope, Chamberlain did not waver in his view that no peace was possible while Hitler was spared and Nazism remained. "The only chance for peace is the disappearance of Hitler and that is what we are working for," he wrote on October 8.[4] This was reconfirmed a month later: "It is essential to get rid of Hitler. He must either die, or go to St. Helena, or become a real public works architect, preferably in a 'home.' His entourage must also go, with the possible exception of Göring, who might have some ornamental position in a transitional Government." Once the Nazis were gone, Chamberlain did not expect to find "any serious difficulty in Germany over Poland, Czechoslovakia, Jews, disarmament, etc." [5] In this he seemed to show, like so many others, real misunderstanding about the extent to which Nazism had become an expression of German national feeling rather than a momentary rash afflicting the German body politic. But he could not believe that Hitler's ruthless exploits would continue to receive support from the German people, nor did he think their morale could remain high in the absence of striking military success.

His attitude toward Nazism is one explanation for Chamberlain's unwillingness to respond to any of a number of peace overtures (so-called) which came forth during the early months of the war. Ironically perhaps—though certainly to his credit—the Prime Minister who had been so ready to make concessions to maintain the peace was not prepared to make similar concessions to end the war. So long in coming to the point of disbelieving Hitler, there was for him no turning back once that point was passed. That was the nature of Chamberlain's ways. It has often been said in his defense that the one great thing he did was to unite the people of Britain in the belief that there was no alternative to war. Surely he shared that view himself. Thus he resisted, sometimes quite bluntly, all suggestions for a negotiated peace which came from Germany,[6] from neutrals (including the Dutch and Belgian monarchs), and from a variety of Englishmen. Twice during October he made it clear in the House of Commons that Poland was only the occasion, not the fundamental cause, of British action. Experience had shown that no reliance could be placed on the promises of the existing German Government. Only deeds, not words, had meaning. Besides, the peace offensive was Hitler's most potent propaganda weapon. So war there must be—but hopefully of the character that Hitler would be made to lose it by being convinced that he could not win it, and this before he had led all of Europe to destruction.

Ironically again, the very existence of twilight war had the effect of increasing the pressure for surrender, and Chamberlain knew it. Its sheer tedium and apparent pointlessness sorely tried people's nerves; their resolve weakened, their frustration heightened, their unanimity (of September 3) diminished. Hardships and uncertainties were more resented than they would have been in the face of mortal danger. Hundreds of letters besought him to "stop the war"; Lloyd George pleaded in the Commons for consideration of peace proposals; and Labor appealed in November for negotiated peace. The Government was widely reproached for not defining clearly the terms it would accept. In these circumstances, Chamberlain came to fear German propaganda more than German arms, but there was never a hint of flinching. "To us in Europe life had become absolutely intolerable, and it is to restore the possibility of living any civilised life at all that we have got to put an end to Nazi policy," he wrote a friend in late September.[7] That remained his fixed position.

If Chamberlain needed support for his view, he got it from Winston Churchill, whom he had asked to join the Cabinet as First Lord of the Admiralty on September 1. Almost at once Churchill became a moving force, a tower of strength, and far from resenting it, Chamberlain proceeded to place a heavy load of responsibility upon him. There were still occasions when Churchill's restless mind and proclivity for argument tried Chamberlain's patience, but he was now prepared to dismiss this as the price to be paid for the asset of Churchill's ability, personality, and popularity. Their opinions on policy matters almost always agreed now—though they often arrived at them in very different ways. Equally important, they shared a mutual trust, so that their personal relations were relaxed, almost cordial. As the winter wore on and the strains of war expanded, Chamberlain looked increasingly to Churchill for aid and advice. He took him to the Supreme War Council in Paris (February) and two months later arranged for him to preside over the Military Co-ordination Committee, which supervised the general conduct of the war.[8] And while he continued privately to prefer Halifax as his eventual successor, Chamberlain did much to open the way for Churchill's emergence and duly offered support to him when his own collapse was finally at hand.

Churchill aside, Chamberlain's wartime Cabinet-making was hardly adequate. Eden also returned (as Dominions Secretary) with the outbreak of war; otherwise, with the exception of a few minor offices, the ministry remained at first unchanged. Overtures to Sinclair (Liberal head) and Labor leaders got nowhere. Long distrustful of Chamberlain, they gave him no reason to believe that national unity could be achieved under his leadership. Indeed, as the months passed by, their constant attacks on what he deemed to be necessary, if unpopular actions, caused the Prime Minister some of his greatest discomfiture and personal frustration. Within his own party, Chamberlain saw no new faces he wanted, and when in time new men were required, the ones he chose were usually qualified by age and experience, but seldom by vigorous temperament or acknowledged keenness of foresight. In fact, one who seemed to qualify on the latter grounds (Hore-Belisha, the Secretary for War) he was forced to remove in January, 1940, because his self-confidence and assertiveness made him unacceptable to commanders in the field.[9] The unpleasant episode did nothing to ease Chamberlain's conservative outlook on Cabinet personnel. This was one factor in his inability to win back many of the dissidents in his own party, a circumstance which later contributed to his downfall.

It was not that Chamberlain gave no thought to Cabinet reorganization. Indeed he had to do so, for considerable criticism arose from his failure to streamline the body along the lines of the Lloyd George model of 1917 (a small War Cabinet of ministers without departments).[10] But what he sought was a Cabinet that "would work," and considering the personalities he had at hand, and the organizational changes which had occurred since 1917 (notably the establishment of a joint planning system running up from the Service departments to the Cabinet), he saw no need for major overhaul. He would not force change solely for the sake of creating an impression. Occasional changes did occur, such as the creation of a Ministry of Food and the retiring from the War Cabinet of the Minister for Co-ordination of Defense. But these were piecemeal and routine, not indicative of any large and sweeping effort.

In military matters, Chamberlain's efforts were seemingly competent but likewise unspectacular. His work on behalf of rearmament, in which he had long stood in advance of many of his countrymen, went forward unabated—and it is a measure of his accomplishment that his program required little substantial change during the war years. He visited the troops in France (mid-December), inspecting barracks, pillboxes, and breastworks and listening to the needs of commanders. Through the Supreme

War Council in Paris he sought to coordinate Britain's military efforts with those of France. He responded to the plight of Finland (attacked by Russia in late November) by sending what arms and materials he found it possible to spare—and to get to their destination without violating Norwegian and Swedish neutrality—all the while believing that a Soviet conquest of Finland would be of no assistance to Germany.[11] In a different but related vein, he tried to impress on Roosevelt, through the President's emissary Sumner Welles, the British need for security and the danger posed by Nazism. The inadequacy of production and gaps in the blockade of Germany, two of the points on which much criticism was centered, were not entirely subject to the Prime Minister's direct control. The former was connected—nebulously perhaps, but in a very real sense—with the imperfections of a democratic nation ill-prepared for war; the latter with the great (though understandable) reluctance of neutrals to abandon their neutrality.

A combination of factors worked against Chamberlain, among them the very nature of the twilight war, which left so many uncertain about what would happen in the future and what should be done to meet it. Still more basic was the growing lack of confidence in his leadership, which sprang in part from his earlier record but more directly now from his constant cringing at the horrors of war, his unwillingness to wage it strenuously, and his apparent inability both to grasp the nature of, and gird the nation for, the peril now impending. The negative impact of his reluctance to sanction aggressive action (such as the bombing of German targets) was reinforced by the tardy and ineffective nature of many British defensive operations. Chamberlain's personal inadequacies—his personality traits which alienated so many, his limited knowledge of the organization necessary for war, his lack of massive intellectual power—took on a graver meaning than before, and the sentiment began to build that Chamberlain had neither the experience, the imagination, nor the will to lead the nation in arms. A colleague later put it well: having never heard the sound of trumpets, he could give no inspiring trumpet call to others. Slowly at first, but with a depth of feeling which at length burst forth with sudden and (to many) surprising fury, the Parliament, and at a somewhat slower pace the nation at large, became restless and critical.

The spring of 1940 brought a deepening demand for more effective planning and coordination in the nation's war effort and more vigorous prosecution of the war. It also brought increasing frustration when these were not forthcoming. Dissident groups (the anti-Munich Conservatives, the 1922 Conservative Committee, a Watching Committee of Conservative M. P.s, an All-Party Action Group) began to reappear, increasingly committed to the proposition that Chamberlain must, in the national interest, be forced from office.[12] Their convictions were solidified as Chamberlain, in public utterances, demonstrated all too clearly his inadequate grasp of things. Most infamous—and highly damaging—in this regard was his April 5 address to the Central Council of the National Union of Conservative and Unionist Associations, in which he spoke with intemperate optimism, showing no premonition that Europe was on the eve of disastrous events and assuring his hearers that the Anglo-French position had so improved that it could now be safely said that Hitler had "missed the bus."

Other factors operating against Chamberlain included a general intensification of concern over Labor's continued refusal to work with him, along with the nagging sentiment that responsibility for this lay not entirely with Labor. The deepening danger seemed to demand a unity of purpose and a marshalling of talent that could be achieved only through National government, and this was impossible under Chamberlain. In addition, changes in the structure of defense (a reorganization of the Military Co-ordination Committee, ironically but unavoidably initiated by Chamberlain) permitted Churchill and his great talents to advance to the fore. The convergence of all these forces pointed in the direction of a change in leadership.

The change was triggered by Britain's failure to halt the German advance into Norway. Determined to enforce Scandinavian neutrality, the British laid mine fields in Norwegian waters in early April. Germany retaliated with a long-prepared invasion of Denmark and Norway. Though British expectations were high and Chamberlain spoke for a time with confidence, by early May British forces had been ousted from nearly all of Norway. Narvik and Trondheim were added to the list of place names connoting frustration or failure to disturbed and dejected Englishmen. German operations on the sea had not been checked nor had adequate air cover been provided for British troops. These two deadly failures raised urgent questions in the House of Commons: Was the country being equipped for total war? Was the Chamberlain Government capable of doing it?

The debate of May 7–8 was decisive. Chamberlain's defense of the conduct of operations, the structure of the War Cabinet, and other related issues was matter-of-fact and, on the surface, reasonable. But once again (shades of March 15, 1939) he utterly failed to appreciate and meet the feeling in the House. To say that British failures reflected that the nation was not yet strong enough was very true indeed, but it hardly engendered enthusiasm. To explain the attempt on Trondheim as a sort of afterthought scarcely fostered confidence. And to hint obscurely about possible changes in the character and structure of the Government without having anything positive to offer only invited reproof. His explication was simply not the kind his listeners—grave, troubled, anxious, apprehensive as they were—could quietly abide. It appeared to betray a dangerous resignation, a tragic loss of that aggressive spirit to which Britain owed her glory. No one gave expression to that better than Sir Roger Keyes, who, resplendent in his admiral's uniform, seemed to speak for all who believed that the political leaders had let the servicemen down. But it remained to Leo Amery, a lifelong Chamberlain friend and colleague, to deliver the decisive blow. In an intensely moving philippic which caught the mood of the House, he exposed the Government's weaknesses with devastating cogency, pleading at length (in Cromwellian words) for a "real National Government" to replace the one which had already sat too long. The corner thus was turned. Chamberlain did his own cause no good when, upon hearing the call for a division on the second day, he rose in anger and besought "his friends" to support him in the lobby. He did not yet sense the depth of feeling that had been stirred—or, sensing it, he could not accept, while under attack, the spreading sentiment that he was unfit for leadership in wartime. His unfortunate appeal to party or personal loyalty seemed quite beneath the dignity required by the occasion and probably helped to clinch the issue for some uncertain listeners.[13]

Chamberlain's majority of 81 represented a very great loss of support.[14] Thirty-three of his regular supporters voted against him; almost twice that number abstained. The figure would probably have been worse had not word circulated beforehand that Chamberlain was planning reconstruction. Ex-ministers Duff Cooper, Amery, Hore-Belisha, and Winterton voted against the Government, as did a number of the dissident Conservatives earlier clustered around Churchill and Eden. So the point was clear to all, the Prime Minister included: Chamberlain did not have the kind of support required to face the deepening crisis.

To his credit, Chamberlain resisted any idea of skirting the immediate issue and asking for a straight vote of confidence. Instead, he contemplated resignation at once. First consulting Halifax and Churchill, he approached the Labor leaders (May 9) to ask whether they would serve in a National government with him, or if not, with someone else. The word which Attlee and Greenwood brought back (May 10) from Bournemouth (where the Labor Party was in conference) was that they would serve, but not with him. This was not surprising; indeed he had sought official confirmation largely to justify resignation to his own party. Meanwhile, in a session with Halifax, Churchill, and Margesson (Chief Conservative Whip), Chamberlain posed the question of a successor, noting that the choice lay between the first two of these men. Halifax firmly excused himself from the running, and Chamberlain reluctantly accepted his view.[15] Churchill—toward whom both Parliamentary and public sentiment definitely was pointing—was left as the logical choice, and when Labor gave its approval the issue was swiftly settled.

The German invasion of Holland on May 10 tempted Chamberlain to delay his resignation and thus avoid at that moment the confusion of a change of government. But he was quickly dissuaded, one of his old and trusted colleagues (Kingsley Wood) impressing upon him that Germany's action made the formation of a National government not less but more imperative. So Chamberlain went promptly to the Palace (evening, May 10) and offered his resignation. In broadcasting to the nation that night, he said that his "duty was plain." He could not achieve "essential unity," so the nation must rally behind a new leader.[16]

Reviewing the episode on May 11, Chamberlain was not inclined to see his loss of support in the House of Commons in terms of his own shortcomings. Rather, he attributed it to a combination of other factors best summarized in his own words:

The long period of waiting without any real setback to German prestige, and then the sudden and bitter disappointment over the hopes that had been so recklessly and unjustifiably fostered by the press, just boiled up, with the accumulated mass of grievances, to find expression. The serving members were acutely conscious of various deficiencies, not realizing apparently that, though you can double your Territorial Army with a stroke of the pen, you can't do the same thing with its equipment. The Amerys, Duff Coopers, and their lot are consciously, or unconsciously, swayed by a sense of frustration because they can only look on, and finally the personal dislike of Simon and Hoare had reached a pitch which I find it difficult to understand, but which undoubtedly had a great deal to do with the rebellion.[17]

His decision to step down quickly was statesmanlike, crucial in avoiding domestic turmoil, and in that sense, a real act of self-sacrifice and public-spiritedness. But his failure to consider that his own shortcomings might have been involved in his fall—his willingness to accept uncritically the polite assurances of some of those who voted against the Government that they had nothing against him personally—evidenced a kind of arrogance and inability to appreciate subtleties which were a definite part of his character.

Willing to serve with Churchill if he wanted him, but also prepared to recede into the background, Chamberlain became Lord President in the reconstituted Government. He also retained, by agreement with Churchill, the party leadership. The Exchequer he apparently ruled out himself—his relations with Labor would not permit it; and when Churchill's proposal that he lead the House of Commons was balked by Labor opposition, Chamberlain gave it up "without a sigh." Buoyed by Churchill's acknowledgment that "to a very large extent I am in your hands—and I feel no fear of that," he was content to play the role of elder statesman, offering advice and administrative talents whenever and wherever called upon to do so. Indeed, he soon came to think it providential perhaps that the revolution which overturned him coincided with the beginning of "real" war in western Europe.

For a time he worked effectively, even impressing—to his obvious satisfaction—some of his bitterest critics (Sinclair and Attlee, for example) with the value of his counsel and his businesslike manner.[18] As chairman of the Lord President's Committee, he led a small group of senior ministers in dealing with a wide range of matters, especially domestic problems, outside of the full Cabinet. Pushed by German advances in western Europe to accept the need for total action, he was instrumental in securing enactment of the Emergency Powers Bill, which placed in effect every Englishman's service and property at the disposal of the state. At Churchill's request, he pursued special assignments, such as the secret (and unsuccessful) attempt to persuade Eire to abandon neutrality. Churchill looked to him for advice and help on a number of thorny domestic problems: railway fares, rating problems in war-damaged areas, and war damage compensation among them. In a quieter way, he contributed to Cabinet unity by soothing ruffled Conservatives who found it hard to work in coalition with long-time partisan foes, and by demonstrating to others that he was not the die-hard Tory they had always felt him to be. Evidence of his own spirit of compromise in this regard appears in his reluctant consent to work even with Lloyd George, when Churchill contemplated (but did not carry out) his appointment to the Cabinet.

In time, however, Chamberlain's spirits—and thus his effectiveness—were numbed by dual misfortune. One was the nation's peril as it came to stand alone against the onslaught of German force. The other was his rapidly-developing physical affliction. Which of these tormented him more is very hard—and indeed unnecessary—to say; in combination they tore at him ruthlessly as the summer months went by.

Though shaken by the turn of political events, Chamberlain could not but feel relieved that final responsibility was off him. Consequently, it was not the fall of his Government which shattered his spirits so much as the fall of France (which destroyed the breathing space on which British planners had always relied and rudely disrupted their strategy), the Italian declaration of war, and the expected invasion of Britain. Never did he openly entertain the spectre of defeat. Indeed his faith in Britain's cause and his confidence in eventual triumph remained steady to the end.[19] But the enormity of the task confronting the country, and the untold mutilation, agony, and death it would surely entail, sickened his mind and soul. His depression was compounded by the fact that in the face of these events his political reputation sank to a new low. There were many who could not forget Munich and who saw the nation's distress as stemming directly from it. The *Guilty Men* pamphlets, which castigated anew the "Men of Munich," were widely circulated. Bitter attacks in the leftist press labeled him the one great barrier to national unity and seemed intent on driving him from office altogether. Even in the War Cabinet, things came to such a pass that Churchill detained the group after one of its regular meetings to exhort certain ministers to suspend their heresy hunt against members of the previous Government and get on with the pressing business at hand. None of this made Chamberlain doubt (as he wrote to Baldwin a few weeks before his death) the rightness of what he had done at Munich, or believe that he could have done more than he had to prepare the nation for war. But his pride was seared, and his sensitivity precluded easy acceptance of abuse which, to his mind, was entirely unjustified and altogether untrue.

Even this might not have fazed him greatly had he been able to work on—and perhaps fight back—as he had always done. But his "physical machine" (his term) was running down, slowly at first, then with mounting suddenness. Before his fall, gout and other minor ailments were working, along with the one great malady of war, to make him tired, irritable, and depressed. But serious illness came only after his resignation—opening the way for possible (though pointless here) speculation about the extent to which his political downfall helped to bring it on. Mid-June found him with "considerable pain in the abdomen," the first real sign of serious trouble. X-rays revealed a partial intestinal stricture, and an exploratory operation, followed by a major operation, ensued in late July. He took it well, and for a time his spirits were high. Recuperating at Heckfield in Hampshire, he found comfort in reading, encouragement in many notes from colleagues and friends, and hope in his scheduled brief guardianship of the Foreign Office while Halifax took a rest. Acknowledging, upon his return to London in early September, that he must adjust to the new life of a "partially crippled man," he nonetheless hoped "to go on working in my present capacity till the end of the war. . . ." [20] But before ten days had passed, a relapse forced him back to Heckfield. It was then that he wrote his resignation from office, which Churchill graciously laid aside for the moment, but at length accepted on September 30.

Numerous honors followed, including an offer of the Garter. He declined it, as he had declined a peerage some time before. He preferred to remain "plain Mr. Chamberlain" like his father before him. Tributes to his character and service arrived in great number from all manner of men. They certainly cheered him and helped him to combat infrequent moments of depression over the seeming lack of public understanding of the "human tragedy" which lay behind him.

Chamberlain knew by now that his cancerous affliction was incurable, and pressing his doctor for an opinion, learned that he had not long to live. This knowledge he found "very helpful and encouraging"; "it would be a terrible prospect," he wrote in his diary, "if I had to wait indefinitely for the end, while going through such daily miseries as I am enduring now." [21] The next few weeks were spent in a stoical arrangement of his personal affairs, cherished correspondence with old colleagues and friends, and a confident following of the course of the war. Death came on November 9. Five days later his ashes were buried at Westminster Abbey. His record of service was now thrown open to the verdict of history.

CHAPTER XVIII

What Manner of Man?

CHAMBERLAIN'S RECORD WILL SURELY BE DEBATED FOR MANY YEARS to come. There is no cause for despair in that, for if history is to live and have meaning, re-examination and re-evaluation are essential to its life. No "final judgment" on Chamberlain will be attempted here; indeed, it must be said from the outset (and this is true for most men) that any assessment offered depends in part upon which facets of his life and character the evaluator chooses to concentrate and the circumstances of the time in which the judgment is made. What can appropriately be undertaken in these pages is an effort to facilitate "seeing the man again" in the light of a generation passed, by pointing up certain aspects of his character and career which are pertinent to any evaluation of his place in history.

Like most men, Chamberlain was imbued with qualities, characteristics, and attitudes the strength or weakness of which depended upon the nature of their use. Some of these sprang from heredity, some from early experience, others from continuing circumstance. Without making any particular effort to determine their source or origin, it is perhaps worthwhile to indicate a few of them here.

Throughout much of his life Chamberlain was among the most self-reliant of men. He could arrive at conclusions, formulate plans of action, and push ahead with their implementation without relying heavily on the aid or advice of others. Whether facing a challenge in the Bahamas or at Berchtesgaden, he did so with complete confidence in his own ability and judgment, seldom flinching for lack of courage to face the task. This made him a man who was able to confront problems directly and without timid procrastination. It also made him rather unresponsive to the ideas and views of others, especially the annoying suggestion that he might sometimes be wrong.

Whether the cause or effect of his self-reliance, he was also highly self-contained. He had few intimates outside his family, and came to be thought of as coldly detached and aloof. His relations with political friends and colleagues were correct and businesslike rather than warm and familiar. He was widely respected, but in a manner divorced from sentimentality. Sufficient evidence has been brought to light (especially from his personal papers) to suggest quite clearly that underneath his stern exterior was a sympathetic, sensitive, and oftentimes generous heart. But it was seldom apparent to those around him, save perhaps for a limited few. According to a story, a Chamberlain supporter in Ladywood once offered this explanation for his seeming unpopularity in his own constituency: "If the b—— was cut in half neither part would bleed."

A deadening shyness (perhaps inborn), combined with a lack of affability and a dislike of humbug, made him considerably less than personable in the eyes of opponents and supporters alike. He joked with difficulty, and the humor he displayed on rare occasions was self-conscious and studied, sometimes even tasteless. He did not take criticism well, especially that of political opponents, which he was inclined to interpret in intensely personal terms. The result was often counterattack in which he would castigate his critics with succinct and smashing invective which of course did nothing to ease the strain between them. In one sense, these factors detracted considerably from his personal stature; but in another sense, they added greatly to his reputation—especially within his own party—as a serious, austere man who would accept responsibility, face difficult situations boldly, and fight vigorously for what he believed to be right.

In almost all that he did, Chamberlain was impressively efficient and highly systematic. His efficiency, so often noted before, needs little elaboration here. Whether operating an industrial plant, running a city government, developing plans for a national ministry, or keeping in touch with all the activity around him as prime minister, Chamberlain exhibited a mastery of detail, devotion to careful and accurate accounting, and familiarity with a wide range of problem areas which few other men could show. A man of regular personal habits and great self-discipline, he approached everything—from casting a fishing fly to emptying his Cabinet boxes to pursuing appeasement—according to an operational timetable (both in terms of schedule and method) which he deemed necessary for best results. This made him a creature of habit and left him appearing dull and unimaginative in the eyes of many—a sort of efficiency expert who placed greater value on the effectiveness of operation than on creativity. At the same time, there were many who believed that the times and conditions demanded the leadership of this steady and efficacious, if unspectacular, kind of man.

Put in another way, Chamberlain did not rise to political prominence on the basis of surging personal popularity or appeal. He did so by a quiet, steady demonstration of energy and skill. At no point in his career did he blossom forth as a "man of destiny," as one of those historical figures who appear occasionally in conditions which seem to suggest that Fate had decreed their arrival at that particular point in time. Even during Munich he was widely regarded as "plain old Neville," an honest, conscientious "common man" plugging away in an effort to bring order out of chaos, but without any unusual gifts or powers at his command by which to accomplish his ends. It is also a fact that many of the posts which Chamberlain held had first been declined by other men. In a limited sense, his party often turned to him because it could not escape him; he was always there, ready to do his best (oftentimes in positions little coveted by others), and his administrative talents seemed so frequently needed in the kinds of jobs which demanded attention. Some have concluded from this that Chamberlain's rise in national government was due at least as much to a dearth of good men to whom the party could turn as to any positive attributes of his own. If reference is made to personality (or personal appeal) alone, there is much to support this point of view. But it should not be accepted without condition, for Chamberlain did have qualities and skills which placed him in the "highly useful" if not the "indispensable" category of men.

One of Chamberlain's greatest assets was his remarkable skill in going to the root of any problem. He could in a few minutes strip a question of all that was incidental and get right down to its basic facts. He had little use for theory divorced from reality; it was the practical aspect of any question that appealed to him, and he came to take great pride in himself as a practical man. Nor did he often make the common mistake of assuming that analysis was remedy. Widely recognized as a man of integrity ("the whole sum of a series of consecutive values"), Chamberlain's measure of that particular quality took the form of requiring a conclusion to be followed by positive action. For those willing and able to discuss anything at all, but utterly skeptical of acting, Chamberlain felt only contempt. Though he grew fond of Baldwin as a person, he was always irritated by Baldwin's gift for contemplative reflection. This is not to say that Chamberlain had no time or use for meditation. He could contemplate and reflect. He read widely and thoroughly enjoyed quiet listening to good

music. Throughout his life he took great pleasure in ornithology
and fishing—and sometimes longed to "get away from it all" in
order to pursue these interests more fully. But the temptation of
positive action, coupled with his immense powers of industry,
made him a "driver," one who pushed incessantly to get things
done. Naturally, this aspect of his character was approved or condemned according to a wide range of judgments on the nature
and value of what he proposed to do.

In many ways Chamberlain was a man of simple tastes, and he
exuded a tranquility which seemed to spring from this stern self-
discipline. He was a moralist, not in a deeply religious sense, but
in his adherence to long-standing family and national values for
which he was perfectly willing to fight. His simplicity and morality, in combination with his skill in analysis and his penchant for
action, led him to think in positive terms of right and wrong,
with little room for neutral or middle positions. Thus it was usually obvious where he stood on a question, and his firmness of
conviction and self-confidence in expressing it pointed back in
the direction of simplicity—and stubbornness—again.

In domestic politics Chamberlain was something of a utilitar-
ian—prepared to act for the greatest good of the greatest number.
He described himself in 1923 as a socialist, and spoke some eight
years later of "that odious title of Conservative." He was actively
interested in the welfare of all Englishmen, especially those in the
working classes. Yet he did not get along well with the Labor
Party, and their mutual dislike eventually came close to being
pathological. Part of the explanation for this lies in Chamberlain's personality—in what Labor saw as his aristocratic, pater-
nalistic, and solicitous attitude toward the workingman. But part
of it also rested in their somewhat artificial evaluation of his
method. Chamberlain sought to raise the material standard of the
nation through the active intervention of the state. Government
by regulation was likely to produce quickest results, and the
transference of local power from smaller areas to larger ones
would facilitate the implementation of governmental order. In
short, this meant increasing centralization. In all of this, Chamberlain assumed that power, concentrated and centralized, would
always be used for good purposes, such as the abolition of slums
and the reduction of disease. Any other use would be unthinka-
ble. But his opponents feared that concentrated and centralized
power, wielded by this Prime Minister, could just as easily be
used for evil purposes, as in Fascist Italy or Nazi Germany; and
since Chamberlain had something of the natural autocrat in him,

the fear was compounded. Herein lay the basis of the occasional charge, entirely unfounded but partisanly plausible, that Chamberlain was truckling to the dictators, adopting their techniques, even conspiring with them. There was a certain ambiguity in this, for the elevation of living standards through state intervention was something the Labor Party itself espoused. But distrusting Chamberlain personally and suspicious of his "style," Laborites were prone to condemn his methods, however alike their own (at least in broad conception) they might have been. And this distrustful questioning of his best intentions did not prompt Chamberlain to charitable response.

The overtones of method aside, it is ironic to note that had Chamberlain retired in 1937, he might well have gone down in English history as a great administrator and social reformer.[1] At the Ministry of Health he was progressive and decisive, leaving behind a record of legislative and administrative achievement perhaps unequalled. In the old tradition of radical reform, he was often willing to consider novel and comprehensive remedies for national ailments. His tenure at the Treasury found him turning more conservatively orthodox, yet his efforts were often crowned with success. But as it turned out, all this was but a prelude to the most historically prominent phase of his life.

The extent to which Chamberlain's attitude toward the use of centralized power at home colored his foreign policy and paved the way for his deception—if deception it was—by Hitler and Mussolini is at best a matter for speculation. Insofar as a connection existed, it was surely one of practical politics rather than devotion to an ideology, blind and prejudiced commitment to a system, or conscious effort at the manipulation of political power for the sake of power itself. But the question is pertinent by way of opening up for consideration the important matter of Chamberlain's foreign policy, for which he is best—in fact, in the minds of many, exclusively—remembered, and on which his political reputation has come to rest.

That Chamberlain made grave errors of judgment while pursuing the policy of appeasement is, of course, hardly open to question. Among them were his evaluation of Hitler and Mussolini as appeasable men; his seeming belief that Sudeten self-determination was the basic issue in the Czech crisis; his reliance on the desire for peace among the German people (as opposed to Nazi leaders) as a deterrent against war; his dismissal of Russia as an insignificant force in European affairs; his underestimation of the willingness of his own countrymen to accept, and do something about, unpleasant reality; and his apparent conviction that, while Nazism endangered central Europe, Britain had little to fear for herself. But it is a mistake to think that his errors were predetermined by all his previous life and thought. There is sharp divergence between certain of his actions as Prime Minister and his ideas and attitudes in preceding years, and historical accuracy seems to demand that these be assessed as separate and distinct periods in his life. For years before 1937, Chamberlain held and gave expression to many of what the later critics of appeasement would have called "right" ideas about the kind of action needed to meet the totalitarian threat in Europe. But once he was entrusted with leading the nation through international turmoil, his ideas and tactics changed. Put in bluntest form, this is simply to say that, for better or for worse, Chamberlain was not the appeaser prior to 1937 that he was in 1938–1939. The sobering experience of full responsibility for his nation's welfare, changing circumstances in central Europe, and a number of associated factors altered his outlook appreciably.

It has often been said that Chamberlain was ignorant of foreign affairs when he assumed his nation's highest office. This is accurate in the sense that he had no real "touch" for a diplomatic situation, that he did not always grasp the full implications of what he was doing, and that his confidence in his own judgment alone was at times misplaced and naive. It is not accurate with reference to his previous exposure to and experience in foreign affairs. While stationed at the Treasury, 1931–1937, he had followed foreign affairs closely and had participated in policy-making on major issues. His "awareness" of Germany was of long-standing. "Detesting" (his own word) Germans in World War I, and confessing in 1930 that he still "loathed" them, he took a lead in urging the abolition of reparations in the hope of strengthening the anti-Nazi forces. The first year of Hitler's rule was enough to convince him that Germany was "up to her old tricks," and the assassination of the Austrian Chancellor Dollfuss (July, 1934) intensified his hatred of Nazism. Persuaded that Britain must rearm, he was instrumental in urging appropriate action in the Cabinet, 1934–1936. Since force was the only thing that Germany understood, Chamberlain was dissatisfied that Britain did not shape her policy accordingly. He grumbled at the weakness of Sir John Simon at the Foreign Office, and later held that sanctions against Italy, once threatened, should be enforced. Consistently he showed himself to be alert to potential totalitarian dangers, and as anxious for rearmament as anyone in the British Government—

or outside it. Some would point to his negative attitude toward the Foreign Office and his questionable operations outside of it as evidence of his ignorance. But his action in this regard came not from unfamiliarity with past procedures but a determination to alter them. Even the Birmingham businessman jibe, as an assertion of his nescient condition, is misleading; businessmen in Birmingham were capable of many things, and the one who served as his model (his own father) hardly fits the stereotype.

It would be convenient to argue that Chamberlain was an appeaser by nature. Much has been made—and rightly so—of his "businessman's approach," his belief that the best way to settle problems in international diplomacy was to utilize the tested techniques of settling difficulties between business enterprises or between management and labor, that is by sitting down amicably together and negotiating in a spirit of good will until a compromise solution was reached. But evidence abounds that Chamberlain could be a stern, uncompromising man—and none more potent than his stubborn refusal to budge from appeasement as a viable approach to the dictators until long after its ineffectiveness had become painfully clear to all but the most die-hard supporters of the policy. So the explanation of appeasement must be sought in factors beyond a simple description of Chamberlain's nature and business background alone, although both of these undoubtedly contributed to his bent of mind.

Some have held that Chamberlain's commitment to appeasement is to be explained in terms of a class-oriented yearning to preserve the capitalistic advantages enjoyed by a few (his group) from the onslaught of creeping socialism, to protect aristocratic privileges from the assault of social democracy, to thwart and isolate Soviet Russia as a means of enfeebling the world-wide communist menace—and a concomitant belief that all this could be accomplished only "in alliance" with Nazi Germany. Such suppositions do not hold up under intensive analysis. His hostility toward the Soviets, his suspicion of their methods and goals, are altogether clear, and they undoubtedly affected his attitude toward cooperation with Russia in resisting Germany. It is probable, as a widely-rumored story had it, that he would gladly have stood aside had Hitler chosen Russia as his victim. But to try to explain Chamberlain's policy in terms of this or any other equally simplistic and doctrinaire view alone is to miss a most essential point about the man. He was not a genuine crusader for any cause save that of British democracy and the avoidance of conflict by rational solutions to war-inducing crises. Neither was he blindly anti-anything or anybody except insofar as practical political considerations, as he saw them, made him so. Rather, to be understood at all, he must be seen as a well-meaning, if sometimes imprudent and myopic man working within the complex, ambivalent, and *ad hoc* characteristics of human activity. He made some grave and regrettable errors, but they were not predetermined in accordance with some fixed and conscious objective which can be defined in terms of ideological or doctrinal prejudice.

From what point in time it is hard to say, but surely long before he became Prime Minister, Chamberlain was convinced that policy must depend upon power. Consequently he was hung on a nasty dilemma. Prepared to believe that force was necessary to counter the dictators, he had also to recognize that force was something Britain did not possess. Neither did France nor the League of Nations, whose value as an organization for preserving peace had been reduced to almost nothing in Chamberlain's mind by its failure in the Abyssinian affair of 1935. To make matters worse, Chamberlain experienced only modest success at best in his attempts to strengthen British power through rearmament. And his efforts were hampered by his own mental reservations about the extent to which the sacrifice of the nation's resources on the altar of the military establishment was compatible with the most basic needs and interests of his countrymen. Perhaps there was another way out. Indeed, there must be another way out, and he set about the business of looking for it.

It follows then that Chamberlain was right in making an initial effort to see whether appeasement would provide an answer to the explosive international problems which were threatening the peace of Europe. The principle of appeasement (in the pre-Munich meaning of the term) was entirely in line with the canons of civilized life in the Western world, and equally important, it was still uncertain whether the dictators were in fact appeasable. In one sense, the policy involved a defiance of probabilities inasmuch as Hitler and Mussolini had hardly demonstrated generosity and reasonableness in their actions of previous years; yet any practical estimate of the diplomatic situation in which Chamberlain found himself seemed to point to the fact that appeasement —at least of a limited and exploratory kind—was worth a try. Thus Chamberlain's general policy toward the crisis in Czechoslovakia, even his actions which led to the much-despised Munich Agreement, are not only understandable but defensible in the light of Britain's own military posture, the strong warning

against war which came from the British Chiefs of Staff, the lack
of support from the Dominions, the obvious irresolution of
France, the potency of the German argument for Sudeten self-
determination, and so on. He was negotiating from a position of
weakness and he knew it.

Chamberlain's great miscalculation was not that he tried appeasement in the first place, but that he clung to it so tenaciously
in spite of overpowering evidence that it was not accomplishing
the purpose he had in view. The point at which he becomes most
vulnerable to criticism is in his attitude *after* Munich, when he
went on blithely preaching appeasement and confidently trusting
—or at least behaving as if he trusted—in the imminent arrival of
the "new era" despite all the ugly signs of totalitarian force and
lawlessness, when he went on acting as if he still had faith in the
dictators despite all his harrowing experiences of September at
Hitler's hands. In this he did a great disservice to the English
people in deluding them about the real nature of the Nazi menace. He undermined his own credibility about the urgency of rearmament and blunted a revival of moral and martial vigor and
a will to resist further totalitarian encroachment to which the
practical political sensibilities of many Englishmen now pointed
as manifestly essential.

It has long been argued, and with considerable force, that Munich was in effect dictated by the "peace psychosis" of the English
people. There is no question that Chamberlain had the great majority of Englishmen behind him until early September, 1938,
and by that time there was little chance of turning back on the
course of events which led inexorably to Munich. It is likewise
true that the great majority of Englishmen, too emotionally overcome by relief from war to ask questions about its cost or its implications for the future, welcomed Chamberlain home from Munich as the savior of peace and civilization. Stuart Hodgson ex-
presses the nature of Chamberlain's rapport with the English
people in a passage worth quoting intact:

> There are some men, like Napoleon and Caesar, who seem to hew out
> for themselves their own opportunities, often out of the most seemingly
> unpromising circumstances. There are others who are so completely the
> product of their time, like Cromwell and Lincoln, that it is hard to be-
> lieve that in any other they would have risen to the eminence they did,
> or even to any eminence at all. But there is a third class of men with no
> particularly striking gifts who are forced to the front of the stage cer-
> tainly without any desire of their own, to face with their modest equip-
> ment enormous dangers. If they are not immediately swept away, such

men stand against the darkening sky like tragic little epitomes of mankind pitting their meagre resources against the monstrous forces of destiny. If they bear themselves at all gallantly, if they shoulder, however sorrowfully, the burden of their tremendous responsibilities, the crowd loves these better than any other "great man." It understands them so much better; there is no barrier of genius between them; it sees its own sorrows and fears and anxieties reflected in theirs, and when they triumph it triumphs with them.[2]

Chamberlain stood in the ranks of this third class of men.

It is equally true, however, that the hysteria of Chamberlain's return from Munich lasted only a few days. As the threat of personal danger receded and the debate in the House of Commons, October 3–6, pointed the way toward a serious and thoughtful review of the situation, it began to dawn on many Englishmen how curious it was that Munich had been received with much greater enthusiasm by the "losers" in London and Paris than by the "winners" in Berlin and Rome. There was soon room for guilt, humiliation, even shame along with the sense of relief, and the recollection of September experiences in digging slit trenches and trying on gas masks created a powerful undercurrent of anxiety and concern for the future on which a more astute statesman might well have capitalized. Bluntly, the immediate post-Munich period would have been an opportune time for Chamberlain to have taken some new initiative, some more positive action, to meet the growing totalitarian threat to European peace and security which by then should have been perfectly obvious to any man who prided himself on his realism. In failing to do so, he left the British nation devoid of leadership at a time when it was desperately needed. He failed to expose the British electorate to the German peril and lulled it back to the slumber of false security when it should have been rapidly awakening to stark reality.

The German seizure of Prague in March, 1939, brought about a change of policy which resulted in the guarantee to Poland. Many factors account for this, Chamberlain's own indignation and his rising confidence in Britain's military capabilities among them. But the stiffening of Britain's attitude originated with a sudden, widespread, and insistent demand for action in Parliament and the press, and with the wrath of a disillusioned public. Chamberlain was swept along by the tide—propelled somewhat no doubt by the widespread suggestion that unless his policy changed he himself must go—and at length produced the guarantee in a moment of crisis when he appeared boxed in with no alternative before him. He had to act, irrespective of practical diplomatic or military considerations.

The extent to which the guarantee actually represented a change in policy rather than a tactical maneuver is not entirely clear. Having no military justification (how could Britain come to Poland's aid except through Russia?), it was in essence a political creation devoid of effective preparation for general war. It was, in a way, a bluff in every sense of the word save one—that Britain and France were now committed to crying halt to Hitler whatever the circumstances. Chamberlain appears to have thought of it as a warning, not a threat—a warning which might incline Hitler more readily to accept appeasement as a reasonable man. There was still a hope, as A. J. P. Taylor has so aptly put it, "of conciliating Hitler under the determination to resist him just as previously there had been an inclination to resist under the top layer of appeasement." [3]

That Chamberlain was slow to accept the idea of cooperation with Russia in the summer of 1939 is something of an understatement. Whether he was unduly so depends upon an estimate of Russian policy and intentions, and on this there is great uncertainty. It can be argued that the outcome of the Anglo-Russian negotiations was decided the moment the Germans began to talk with Russia, for they simply had more to offer. But this can also be taken to emphasize the importance of timing, and leaves unanswered all questions about the possible effect of an earlier willingness (during 1938) to consult with the Soviets. It can be held that Britain would probably have been double-crossed by Russia even had there been an earlier agreement, for Russia desperately needed a continuation of peace (she was not yet prepared for war) and was bent upon assuring it for herself in any way she could. This cannot, of course, move beyond the realm of speculation. The wisdom of hindsight might provide support for Chamberlain's doubt of Russia's motives in eastern Europe and his argument that as the protector of small states, Britain could not force upon them (especially Poland and Romania) conditions to which they strenuously objected. Yet it may be asked why he was so concerned with the "feelings" of Poland and Romania when he had cared so little about the feelings of Czechoslovakia. It is hard to escape the conclusion that he neither shared nor understood Russia's fear of a war in which she might have to fight alone and receive the German attack on Russian soil instead of going out to meet it in the Baltic states, Poland, and Romania. Indeed, he seems to have operated on the assumption that Britain had nothing to fear for herself, and that she still had the latent power to assert herself as the arbiter of Europe should the need arise. Britain did not yet need Russia to such a degree as to warrant the paying of a very high price for her assistance. In this, of course, Chamberlain was badly mistaken.

Chamberlain's staunch commitment to appeasement despite all the setbacks the policy suffered raises the question whether he was in fact fooled by Hitler and Mussolini. On this point the evidence is conflicting and so are the opinions of those who have written about it. Some of those closest to him (Sir Samuel Hoare, for instance) hold that Chamberlain considered Hitler a paranoiac and was certain from the first that he was partially mad. Frequent reference to Hitler in the Inner Cabinet as "the madman" lends credence to that view. On the other hand, there are those who counter that Chamberlain could not possibly have adopted his mellow attitudes toward the dictators unless he was victimized by gross misjudgment of their aims and methods. In either case Chamberlain does not fare well. If he did indeed misjudge them, he is open to the charge of disastrous naiveté and political myopia of very dangerous proportions. If he did assess them correctly, he is guilty of a stubborn refusal to face facts and a blind adherence to wishful thinking. Few would defend a policy of attempting to construct a basis for peace in Europe on trust and friendship with a madman.

While there is no direct answer to the question, several observations may cast some light upon it. For Chamberlain the dividing line between hope and belief was so indistinguishable as to be practically non-existent. Though he may on occasion have believed the worst, he so ardently hoped for the best that the two became inseparably intertwined. And in that situation, the nature of the man was such that hope predominated. Consequently, he deliberately closed his eyes to unpalatably pessimistic views convincingly expounded by British statesmen with greater experience and understanding of foreign affairs than his own, and took immense risks on the strength of his belief in the superiority of his own judgment.

Further, Chamberlain seemed to believe that there was an affinity between himself and the dictators entirely denied to other men. He could not believe that he could not influence them by his patience, understanding, and reasonableness. Whether this is to be explained in terms of his inborn character, a sense of Chamberlain family "mission," his lifelong training and experience, his sympathy for the dictatorial mentality (which he did not really understand), or some other kind of factor, the effect was still the same. When once reminded of Hitler's long and monotonous trail of violated pledges, he is said to have remarked: "Ah, but this time he has given his pledge to me."

Finally, the vital question may concern Chamberlain's judgment of Nazism rather than Hitler. Here he definitely fell short, apparently believing that Hitler was an isolated phenomenon, never really grasping the extent to which he was, on the contrary, the symbol and spearhead of a vast new force in German life. To the end he seemed to believe that his policy had failed largely through the accident of his having encountered a fanatic. Of course he was not alone in this, for not very many Englishmen— or others—grasped the full implications of the new totalitarian forces at work in Europe until very late in the day. But Chamberlain had more resolution, more courage or audacity (depending upon how one wishes to view it) in pronouncing his views, and this, along with the fact of his political leadership, served to enhance his ultimate failure and to promote the idea that he alone had failed.

Chamberlain's place in history will inevitably be based upon his actions in the realm of foreign affairs during the years in which he was Prime Minister. The times were that important, the stakes that large, the consequences that significant. But it is a great mistake of historical judgment to think that appeasement constitutes the sum total of the man's record or exemplifies the full story of his existence, thereby permitting a dismissal of the first 67 years of his life on that ground. Whatever the estimate of his character and ability, his contributions to other aspects of English life were too noteworthy for that.

When caught in the web of totalitarian ruthlessness, his limited vision and inability to grasp the moving essence of totalitarianism, combined with his genuine commitment to the cause of humanity, led him to major miscalculations. These misjudgments, and the consequences which sprang in part from them, constitute a sorry episode in history. But the things for which he stood—and thus in a sense the substance of the man himself—do not. Perhaps the distinction is artificial, yet it must perforce be made. Without it historical accuracy suffers and misconceptions thrive.

Notes

CHAPTER I

1. Iain Macleod, *Neville Chamberlain* (London, 1961), p. 16.
2. This story is told in detail in J. L. Garvin, *The Life of Joseph Chamberlain*, 4 vols. (London, 1933–1935), I, *passim*.
3. Sir Charles Petrie (ed.), *The Life and Letters of The Right Hon. Sir Austen Chamberlain*, 2 vols. (London, 1939, 1940), I, 5–6.
4. Keith Feiling, *The Life of Neville Chamberlain* (London, 1947), p. 4.
5. Macleod, *Chamberlain*, pp. 18, 21.
6. Feiling, *Chamberlain*, p. 3.
7. Quoted in Macleod, *Chamberlain*, p. 20.
8. Feiling, *Chamberlain*, p. 7.
9. *Ibid.*, p. 10.
10. Macleod, *Chamberlain*, p. 19.
11. Feiling, *Chamberlain*, pp. 15–16.

CHAPTER II

1. Five shillings per acre for the first 10,000 acres, with an option of 10,000 more acres, at 16s.8d. per acre, to be exercised at the end of ten years. The governor would build a wharf which the Chamberlains could use freely, and would limit the sale of Crown lands for sisal-growing to 100,000 acres so as to confine the market. Macleod, *Chamberlain*, pp. 28–29.
2. He kept extensive notes about his work, reported regularly to his father, and wrote descriptive letters to his sisters. Revealing excerpts from these appear in Feiling, *Chamberlain*, pp. 19–31, and Macleod, *Chamberlain*, pp. 29–36.
3. Petrie, *Life and Letters of Austen Chamberlain*, I, 38–39.
4. Feiling, *Chamberlain*, p. 25.
5. *Ibid.*
6. Macleod, *Chamberlain*, p. 32.
7. *Ibid.*, p. 33.
8. *Ibid.*, p. 36.
9. Feiling, *Chamberlain*, p. 30.
10. *Ibid.*

CHAPTER III

1. A vivid, if somewhat satirical description of Birmingham and "Birmingham men" may be found in George B. Harris, "Mr. Chamberlain and Birmingham—The Political Riddle," *The Fortnightly*, LXXX (July, 1906), 18–32.
2. This idea is emphasized in Duncan Keith-Shaw, *Prime Minister Neville Chamberlain* (London, n.d.), *passim*.
3. Feiling, *Chamberlain*, p. 34.

4. *Ibid.*, p. 41.

5. *Ibid.*, p. 48.

6. Macleod, *Chamberlain* (p. 45), contains more information on Anne Cole's family background.

7. Stuart Hodgson, *The Man Who Made the Peace: Neville Chamberlain* (New York, 1938), p. 33.

8. Sir Charles Petrie, *The Chamberlain Tradition* (New York, 1938), p. 242.

9. Feiling, *Chamberlain,* p. 51.

CHAPTER IV

1. See Report of the special housing inquiry committee for presentation at the monthly meeting of the Council on Tuesday, the 20th of October, 1914. Birmingham, 1914.

2. Petrie, *Life and Letters of Austen Chamberlain,* I, 356.

3. Macleod, *Chamberlain,* p. 47.

4. *Ibid.*

5. Feiling, *Chamberlain,* p. 58.

6. Further elaboration of Neville's views on these points can be found in Macleod, *Chamberlain,* pp. 50–53.

CHAPTER V

1. Feiling, *Chamberlain,* p. 62. A good account of the circumstances of Neville's appointment appears in Petrie, *Life and Letters of Austen Chamberlain,* II, 63–65.

2. Feiling, *Chamberlain,* p. 62.

3. Great Britain, *Parliamentary Debates, House of Commons,* Fifth Series (hereinafter cited as *Parl. Debs., HC*), December 19, 1916, vol. 88, 1352.

4. Macleod, *Chamberlain,* p. 57.

5. *Parl. Debs., HC,* February 27, 1917, vol. 90, 1902.

6. L. Raskay, *Neville Chamberlain* (London, n.d.), p. 9. Lloyd George's account of this whole episode appears in *War Memoirs of David Lloyd George.* 6 vols. (Boston, 1933–1937), III, 273–85. There he describes Chamberlain as a "man of rigid competency . . . indispensable for filling subordinate posts . . . but . . . lost in any emergency or in creative tasks. . . ."

7. Keith-Shaw, *Chamberlain,* pp. 58–59.

8. Feiling, *Chamberlain,* p. 74.

9. Macleod, *Chamberlain,* p. 71.

10. Feiling, *Chamberlain,* p. 77.

11. *Ibid.*, p. 81.

12. The term "coupon" refers to the endorsement provided by Lloyd George and Bonar Law to all candidates classed as loyal to the Coalition.

CHAPTER VI

1. Petrie, *The Chamberlain Tradition,* p. 252.

2. Feiling, *Chamberlain,* p. 89.

3. *Ibid.*, p. 85.

4. Macleod, *Chamberlain,* p. 83.

5. Feiling, *Chamberlain,* p. 97.

6. Austen's account in Petrie, *Life and Letters of Austen Chamberlain* (II, 207), is very similar to Neville's account in Feiling, *Chamberlain* (p. 101).

7. Feiling, *Chamberlain,* pp. 110–11.

8. Petrie, *Life and Letters of Austen Chamberlain,* II, 227.

9. This involved the sensational publication, five days before the election, of a letter from the head of the Comintern (Third Communist International) inviting British workers to engage in subversive activities. Its debated authenticity could not be determined before election day.

10. Macleod, *Chamberlain,* p. 109.

CHAPTER VII

1. Feiling, *Chamberlain,* p. 117.

2. In October, 1925, Austen was instrumental in bringing about the Locarno Agreements, which included frontier guarantees along Germany's western border and bilateral arbitration conventions between Germany on one hand and France, Belgium, Poland, and Czechoslovakia on the other. The Locarno Treaties appeared to herald a new era of international cooperation among Britain, France, and Germany.

3. In the British general strike of May 4–12, 1926, the Trades Union Congress called out transport workers, builders, printers, and workers in heavy industries (and later engineers) to support the grievances of British miners. The Baldwin Government was able, by emergency measures, to avoid paralysis of the nation. But the affair left a legacy of bitterness on both sides.

4. Macleod, *Chamberlain,* p. 119.

5. Feiling, *Chamberlain,* p. 142.

6. *Ibid.,* p. 150.

7. See Charles Loch Mowat, *Britain Between the Wars, 1918–1940* (Chicago, 1955), pp. 338–41.

8. This is the view of A. J. P. Taylor in *English History, 1914–1945* (New York, 1965), p. 221.

9. Feiling, *Chamberlain,* p. 127.

CHAPTER VIII

1. Beaverbrook was an extraordinary (somewhat maverick) personality whose voice in Conservative affairs commanded attention because of his forceful disposition, his experience in politics and government, his friendship with leading political figures, and his influence as a major newspaper controller.

2. Feiling, *Chamberlain,* p. 173.

3. *Ibid.,* p. 192; Macleod, *Chamberlain,* p. 150.

4. Feiling, *Chamberlain,* p. 200.

CHAPTER IX

1. Petrie, *The Chamberlain Tradition,* p. 23.

2. *Parl. Debs., HC,* February 4, 1932, vol. 261, 296.

3. See Mowat, *Britain Between the Wars,* p. 432, for example.

4. In the period 1925–1931, a £700 million expenditure on public works had at no time found employment for more than 100,000 men.

5. Feiling, *Chamberlain,* p. 251.

6. *Ibid.,* p. 253.

7. *Ibid.,* p. 254.

8. Macleod, *Chamberlain,* p. 179; Feiling, *Chamberlain,* p. 240.

9. Viscount Templewood, *Nine Troubled Years* (London, 1954), pp. 36–37.

CHAPTER X

1. Germany undertook to keep her navy to the ratio of 35 percent of the British fleet, although within that limitation she could build submarines to the total tonnage of the Commonwealth.

2. With reference to the need to "hurry on our own rearmament," he thought in terms of spending "an extra £120 million or more" in so doing over the next 4 or 5 years. Feiling, *Chamberlain*, p. 266; Macleod, *Chamberlain*, p. 182.

3. Macleod, *Chamberlain*, p. 183.

4. Feiling, *Chamberlain*, p. 265.

5. *Ibid.*, p. 268.

6. Hoare's account of his speech in his memoirs allows room for the interpretation that it constituted a kind of bluff. Templewood, *Nine Troubled Years*, p. 166. The extent to which Neville shared this view is uncertain.

7. L. S. Amery, *My Political Life.* 3 vols. (London, 1955), III, 174.

8. Macleod, *Chamberlain*, pp. 187–88.

9. Feiling, *Chamberlain*, p. 274.

10. "I know no one that I would trust to hold the balance between rigid orthodoxy and a fatal disregard of sound principles and the rights of posterity," he had written his sister several months before. *Ibid.*, p. 275.

11. *Ibid.*, p. 279.

12. *Ibid.*

13. *Ibid.*, pp. 295–96.

14. *Ibid.*, p. 284; Macleod, *Chamberlain*, p. 191.

15. Macleod, *Chamberlain*, p. 198. He recognized, however, that renunciation of the marriage was the solution the general public wanted.

16. Neville was by this time tending to the view that the air force and navy should take precedence over the army. See Duff Cooper, *Old Men Forget* (London, 1954), p. 205.

CHAPTER XI

1. Macleod, *Chamberlain*, p. 205; Feiling, *Chamberlain*, p. 307.

2. Martin Gilbert and Richard Gott, *The Appeasers* (London, 1963), p. 23.

3. A number of recent works have sought to analyze the bases of appeasement, among them: Gilbert and Gott, *The Appeasers;* Martin Gilbert, *The Roots of Appeasement* (London, 1966); Margaret George, *The Warped Vision: British Foreign Policy, 1933–1939* (Pittsburgh, 1965); A. L. Rowse, *Appeasement: A Study in Political Decline, 1933–1939* (New York, 1961); and Donald Lammers, *Explaining Munich: The Search for Motive in British Policy* (Stanford, 1966). The emphases and conclusions vary considerably, especially on the question of class attitudes and prejudices as an element in appeasement. Lammers' work explodes the view that a blind anti-Soviet bias was a significant determining factor.

4. Feiling, *Chamberlain*, p. 324.

5. See William R. Rock, *Appeasement on Trial: British Foreign Policy and Its Critics, 1938–1939* (Hamden, 1966), pp. 8–9.

6. *Parl. Debs., HC,* February 21, 1938, vol. 332, 64.

7. Neville Chamberlain, *In Search of Peace* (New York, 1939), p. 29.

8. For an estimate of Wilson's role and influence, see Gilbert and Gott, *The Appeasers,* p. 69.

9. Feiling, *Chamberlain*, p. 329.

10. A thorough account of the background of Halifax's visit appears in Earl of Avon, *The Memoirs of Anthony Eden: Facing the Dictators, 1923–1938* (Cambridge, 1962), pp. 576ff.

11. The Earl of Birkenhead, *Halifax: The Life of Lord Halifax* (London, 1965), pp. 365–74, contains a detailed account of Halifax's visit and the conversations which he had with Hitler.

12. Feiling, *Chamberlain*, pp. 332–33.

CHAPTER XII

1. At the Nyon Conference, held in late summer, 1937, in response to a mysterious outbreak of submarine piracy against British, French, and Russian shipping in the western Mediterranean (Italian submarines were suspected), the three injured parties agreed that submarines attacking any non-Spanish merchant vessel would be counterattacked by ships from the British and French fleets. Italy refused to attend the conference, but was later persuaded to adhere to the agreement. No further acts of piracy were reported.

2. Quoted in Keith-Shaw, *Chamberlain*, pp. 78–79.

3. Macleod, *Chamberlain*, p. 212.

4. *Foreign Relations of the United States: Diplomatic Papers, 1938* (hereinafter cited as *U. S. For. Rel.*), I, 118–20.

5. Nine or ten of the principal ministers whom Chamberlain summoned on urgent international problems, thus tending to by-pass the full Cabinet. See Templewood, *Nine Troubled Years*, pp. 290–91.

6. Chamberlain's version of this episode, taken from his diary, is available in Macleod, *Chamberlain*, pp. 211–13. Eden's extensive explanation appears in *Facing the Dictators*, pp. 621ff.

7. See Templewood, *Nine Troubled Years*, p. 278, for an explanation.

8. Macleod, *Chamberlain*, p. 214; Feiling, *Chamberlain*, pp. 337–38.

9. The fullest accounts of this meeting appear in Grandi's highly colored but substantially accurate report to Ciano, *Ciano's Diplomatic Papers*, edited by Malcolm Muggeridge (London, 1948), pp. 165–83, and Eden's memoirs, *Facing the Dictators*, pp. 659–63. The material from Chamberlain's diary in Macleod, *Chamberlain*, is summary in nature (p. 215).

10. The question is moot as to whether Chamberlain might have reached the point of removing Eden had the Foreign Secretary not offered to resign. There had been some muffled talk of "kicking Eden upstairs" a week or two before, and it is known that Sir John Simon had awkwardly besought Eden to go on a six-months' holiday for reasons of health. But it is yet unknown whether Chamberlain had a hand in any of this.

11. *Parl. Debs., HC*, February 21, 1938, vol. 332, 53–63.

12. *Ibid.*, February 21–22, 1938, vol. 332, 45–155, 209–332. This debate is analyzed in Rock, *Appeasement on Trial*, pp. 31–38.

13. Press reaction is described in some detail in Rock, *Appeasement on Trial*, pp. 40–44.

14. A March 3 conversation which Nevile Henderson, the British ambassador in Berlin, had with Hitler (in pursuance of instructions drafted by the Foreign Office) attests to this. *Documents on German Foreign Policy, 1918–1945*, Series D (hereinafter cited as *G. D.*), I, 240–49.

15. Feiling, *Chamberlain*, pp. 341–42.

16. *Parl. Debs., HC*, March 14, 1938, vol. 333, 47–52.

17. Feiling, *Chamberlain*, pp. 347–48.

18. *Documents on British Foreign Policy, 1919–1939*, Third Series (hereinafter cited as *B. D.*), I, 62–64.

19. See Rock, *Appeasement on Trial*, pp. 56–58.

20. *Parl. Debs., HC*, March 24, 1938, vol. 333, 1399–1413.

CHAPTER XIII

1. Spain, confirmation of the Mediterranean agreement of 1937, extension of the articles concerning the status quo in the Mediterranean to other Mediterranean powers, Italian forces in Libya, exchange of military information, naval treaty, Palestine, Syria, Arabia, propaganda, and Abyssinia.

2. See Rock, *Appeasement on Trial*, pp. 67–69.

3. Feiling, *Chamberlain*, p. 350.

4. *Parl. Debs., HC*, May 2, 1938, vol. 335, 533–45.

5. Feiling, *Chamberlain*, p. 351.

6. *League of Nations, Official Journal, 1938* (London, 1938), XIX, pt. 1, 335–47.

7. *U. S. For. Rel., 1938*, I, 215.

8. *Parl. Debs., HC*, June 14, 1938, vol. 337, 41–44.

9. Macleod, *Chamberlain*, p. 222.

10. *U. S. For. Rel., 1938*, I, 56–57.

11. Noteworthy among the detailed treatments of the Czech crisis of 1938 are the following: R. G. D. Laffan, *The Crisis Over Czechoslovakia, January to September, 1938* ("Survey of International Affairs," II [for the year 1938]), (London, 1951); John W. Wheeler-Bennett, *Munich: Prologue to Tragedy* (London, 1948); Keith Eubank, *Munich* (Norman, 1963); and Boris Celovsky, *Das Münchener Abkommen von 1938* (Stuttgart, 1958).

12. *B. D.*, I, 212–32.

13. *Ibid.*, I, 55–56.

14. The more regular participants in these weekend gatherings, mainly those favorable to appeasement, came to be called "the Cliveden set," a term of opprobrium used by political opponents and critics in general.

15. It was flatly stated that France had obligations to Czechoslovakia and would be forced to intervene should a conflict arise. Britain could not guarantee that she would stand aside. *B. D.*, I, 332, 334–35, 341. Playing both sides, however, Halifax shortly thereafter warned the French not to assume that this meant Britain was prepared at once to take joint military action with them to preserve Czechoslovakia against German aggression. *Ibid.*, I, 347.

16. One writer pictures Chamberlain as "furious with Halifax" for the line he had taken. Arthur H. Furnia, *The Diplomacy of Appeasement: Anglo-French Relations and the Prelude to World War II, 1931–1938* (Washington, 1960), p. 315. However, evidence on the point is lacking.

17. Macleod, *Chamberlain*, p. 232; Feiling, *Chamberlain*, p. 354.

18. *B. D.*, I, 355; *G. D.*, II, 322–23.

19. Runciman was less than enthusiastic. "You are setting me adrift in a small boat in mid-Atlantic," he is reported to have said. Lord Strang, *Home and Abroad* (London, 1956), p. 139.

20. Templewood, *Nine Troubled Years*, p. 298.

21. *Parl. Debs., HC*, July 26, 1938, vol. 338, 2959.

22. Interesting detail on Runciman's work appears in F. T. A. Ashton-Gwatkin, "The Personal Story of the Runciman Mission," *The Listener*, XL (October 21, 1948), 595–97. Thorough accounts may be found in Laffan, *The*

Crisis Over Czechoslovakia, pp. 211–62, and Wheeler-Bennett, *Munich,* pp. 84–92.

23. Central figures in these contacts were Erich and Theodor Kordt, Ribbentrop's *chef de cabinet* and the Counsellor of the German embassy in London respectively; Ernst von Weizsäcker, Secretary of State in the German Foreign Office; and Ewald von Kleist and Lieutenant-Colonel Hans Boehm-Tettlebach, emissaries for anti-Hitler German generals. For further information, see Erich Kordt, *Nicht aus den Akten, Die Wilhelmstrasse in Frieden und Krieg: Erlebnisse, Begegnungen, und Eindrücke, 1928–1945* (Stuttgart, 1950), pp. 250, 279–81; Ernst von Weizsäcker, *Memoirs of Ernst von Weizsäcker* (Chicago, 1951), pp. 144–45; John W. Wheeler-Bennett, *The Nemesis of Power: The German Army in Politics, 1918–1945* (London, 1953), p. 445; Walter Goerlitz, *History of the German General Staff* (New York, 1954), pp. 333–38; Winston S. Churchill, *The Gathering Storm* (Boston, 1948), pp. 311–13; and *B. D.,* II, 242, 683–89, 689–92.

24. Harold Temperley's *Foreign Policy of Canning.*

25. Feiling, *Chamberlain,* p. 360.

26. P. K. Kemp, *Key to Victory: The Triumph of British Sea Power in World War II* (Boston, 1957), p. 26.

27. Feiling, *Chamberlain,* p. 362.

28. See in particular D. C. Watt, *Personalities and Policies: Studies in the Formulation of British Foreign Policy in the Twentieth Century* (Notre Dame, 1965), pp. 159–74, and Nicholas Mansergh, *Survey of British Commonwealth Affairs: Problems of External Policy, 1931–1939* (London, 1952), pp. 437–44. Pertinent materials on Commonwealth opinion may be found in Nicholas Mansergh (ed.), *Documents and Speeches on British Commonwealth Affairs, 1931–1952,* 2 vols. (London, 1953), I; and Gwendolyn M. Carter, *The British Commonwealth and International Security: The Role of the Dominions, 1919–1939* (Toronto, 1947).

29. Feiling, *Chamberlain,* p. 357.

30. "If these tortured creatures [the Sudeten Germans] do not receive justice and help, they can get both from us," Hitler bellowed. Norman H. Baynes (ed.), *The Speeches of Adolf Hitler, April 1922–August 1939,* 2 vols. (London, 1942), II, 1487–90.

31. Feiling, *Chamberlain,* p. 364.

32. See Rock, *Appeasement on Trial,* pp. 118–19.

CHAPTER XIV

1. Note in particular Wheeler-Bennett, *Munich;* Laffan, *The Crisis Over Czechoslovakia;* Eubank, *Munich;* and Gilbert and Gott, *The Appeasers.*

2. Eubank holds that Chamberlain had been prompted by Henderson to exclude Ribbentrop, who was desirous of war and would harm the discussions. *Munich,* p. 133.

3. Chamberlain's accounts of his Berchtesgaden conversation with Hitler may be found in *B. D.,* II, 338–51; Feiling, *Chamberlain,* pp. 366–68; Macleod, *Chamberlain,* pp. 234–39.

4. See *B. D.,* II, 482–83.

5. *U. S. For. Rel., 1938,* I, 621–22.

6. This appears in *B. D.,* II, 463–73, 499–508. In addition, Kirkpatrick provides color and commentary in his memoirs, *The Inner Circle* (London, 1959), pp. 112ff.

7. *B. D.,* II, 482–83.

8. Templewood, *Nine Troubled Years*, p. 312.

9. Duff Cooper, *Old Men Forget*, p. 234.

10. Birkenhead, *Halifax*, p. 399.

11. See *Ibid.*, pp. 399–401. According to Macleod, Chamberlain's own papers are silent on the point. He was not keeping a diary, and the pressure of events had forced a two-week gap in his correspondence. *Chamberlain*, p. 247.

12. See *B. D.*, II, 520–35.

13. Macleod, *Chamberlain* (p. 248), takes this view.

14. Chamberlain, *In Search of Peace*, pp. 174–75.

15. Kirkpatrick, who accompanied Wilson on both these visits to Hitler, provides a graphic description of what occurred. *The Inner Circle*, pp. 122–26.

16. It has often been suggested that the glum and silent reception given by the German people to a propaganda march of German troops through Berlin on September 27 helped to influence Hitler. Certainly there were also other factors which help to explain his modified attitude. On this point, see Eubank, *Munich*, pp. 204–05.

17. *B. D.*, II, 587.

18. It is nowhere clear (as Macleod, *Chamberlain*, p. 249, and Feiling, *Chamberlain*, p. 373, suggest) that Mussolini's support was a benefit reaped from the Anglo-Italian Agreement. Mussolini appears to have acted on the basis of very practical considerations, such as the desire to avoid being dragged into war.

19. Feiling, *Chamberlain*, p. 376. It has been suggested that the timing of the announcement was all but a put-up job. Chamberlain's flair for the dramatic, as well as certain circumstantial evidence, would seem to make this plausible, but there is no conclusive evidence of a "fix."

20. Accounts of the conference appear in *B. D.*, II, 630–35, and *G. D.*, II, 1003–08, 1011, 1014.

21. See Macleod, *Chamberlain* (p. 253), for a summary of differences as some saw them at the time.

22. *B. D.*, II, 635–40.

23. Macleod, *Chamberlain*, p. 256.

24. Templewood, *Nine Troubled Years*, pp. 320–21.

25. See Rock, *Appeasement on Trial*, pp. 140–41.

26. *Parl. Debs., HC*, October 6, 1938, vol. 339, 40–50, 547–58.

27. For a summary reassessment of the question, written ten years after Munich, see Cyril Falls, "Should the Democracies Have Fought in 1938?" *The Listener*, XL (November 11, 1948), 717–18.

28. Feiling, *Chamberlain*, p. 365.

CHAPTER XV

1. Dissident Conservatives had been meeting informally since Eden's resignation. There were two groups, one centered around Churchill, the other around Eden. The Czech crisis spurred their gatherings, and Munich gave increased impetus to their efforts to alter the course of British foreign policy. See Churchill, *The Gathering Storm*, p. 309, and Amery, *My Political Life*, III, 277–78.

2. L. B. Namier, "Munich Survey: A Summing Up," *The Listener*, XL (December 2, 1948), 836.

3. Feiling, *Chamberlain*, p. 385.

4. *Ibid.*, p. 389.

5. *Ibid.*

6. Munich had brutally clarified Halifax's earlier nebulous outlook on Europe, and his thinking about policies and procedures had undergone considerable revision. See Birkenhead, *Halifax*, pp. 394, 420–21, 425.

7. See *B. D.*, III, 285–311, for a record of the conversation.

8. See Rock, *Appeasement on Trial*, pp. 173–74, 185–86.

9. Feiling, *Chamberlain*, p. 389.

10. Taken together, the by-elections held in the months following Munich did not indicate a significant trend against the Government, but neither did they encourage it to believe it had an enthusiastic country behind it. See Rock, *Appeasement on Trial*, pp. 200–02.

11. *Parl. Debs., HC*, December 19, 1938, vol. 342, 2517–18.

12. It was decided to bring into London from Lichfield an anti-aircraft regiment which, when stationed in Wellington Barracks, could readily be seen from the German embassy. See Kirkpatrick, *The Inner Circle*, pp. 138–39.

13. See *B. D.*, III, 517–30.

14. *The Ciano Diaries: The Complete Unabridged Diaries of Count Galeazzo Ciano, Italian Minister for Foreign Affairs, 1939–1943*, edited by Hugh Gibson (New York, 1946), pp. 9–10.

15. *Ibid.*

16. Ciano recorded in his diary: "The Duce approved it and commented, 'I believe this is the first time that the head of the British Government submits to a foreign government the outline of one of his speeches. It's a bad sign for them.'" *Ibid.*, p. 17.

17. *Parl. Debs., HC*, January 31, 1939, vol. 343, 37–40. Hitler had remarked: "In the future we shall not tolerate the Western Powers attempting to interfere in certain matters which concern nobody except ourselves in order to hinder natural and reasonable solutions by their intervention." But Chamberlain refused to place a sinister construction upon these words.

18. This point is made effectively in Macleod, *Chamberlain*, p. 272.

19. See Gilbert and Gott, *The Appeasers* (pp. 191–206), on economic appeasement.

20. For details on the developments in British rearmament during these months, see M. M. Postan, *British War Production* (London, 1952), and Robin Higham, *Armed Forces in Peacetime: Britain, 1918–1940, A Case Study* (Hamden, 1962). Hoare also devotes a chapter of his memoirs to the subject. Templewood, *Nine Troubled Years*, pp. 327–40.

21. Feiling, *Chamberlain*, p. 394; Macleod, *Chamberlain*, p. 272.

22. *German White Book: Documents on the Events Preceding the Outbreak of the War* (New York, 1940), p. 259.

23. Feiling, *Chamberlain*, p. 396.

CHAPTER XVI

1. The immediate background of the destruction of Czechoslovakia is detailed in R. G. D. Laffan *et al.*, *Survey of International Affairs, 1938*, III (London, 1953), 247–69.

2. *Parl. Debs., HC*, March 15, 1939, vol. 345, 435–40.

3. *Ibid.*, March 15, 1939, vol. 345, 435–564.

4. Among the British arguments were assertions that in the circumstances the Government could hardly send a responsible minister to take part in a conference, and that it was dangerous to hold a conference without the certainty of success. *B. D.*, IV, 392–93.

5. Feiling, *Chamberlain*, p. 401.

6. For confirmation of this opinion concerning the comparative military power of Poland and Russia, see Lord Halifax, *Fullness of Days* (New York, 1957), p. 210; Templewood, *Nine Troubled Years,* pp. 342–45; Strang, *Home and Abroad,* p. 167; Amery, *My Political Life,* III, 309.

7. For detail, see Rock, *Appeasement on Trial,* pp. 222–28.

8. See *B. D.,* IV, 516, 541.

9. *Parl. Debs., HC,* March 31, 1939, vol. 345, 2415.

10. For a full discussion of the guarantee, see William R. Rock, "The British Guarantee to Poland, March, 1939: A Problem in Diplomatic Decision-Making," *The South Atlantic Quarterly,* LXV, No. 2 (Spring, 1966), 229–40.

11. The draft of the telegram to Warsaw is in Chamberlain's handwriting, with additions by Halifax and Cadogan. *B. D.,* IV, 546fn.

12. Strang, *Home and Abroad,* p. 161.

13. Halifax, *Fullness of Days,* p. 209.

14. *Parl. Debs., HC,* April 3, 1939, vol. 345, 2482.

15. *Ibid.,* April 3, 1939, vol. 345, 2481–86.

16. *Ibid.,* April 3, 1939, vol. 345, 2486.

17. Feiling, *Chamberlain,* p. 404.

18. *Parl. Debs., HC,* April 13, 1939, vol. 346, 15.

19. Feiling, *Chamberlain,* p. 406.

20. Note the following in particular: Arnold J. and Veronica Toynbee (eds.), *The Eve of War, 1939* ("Survey of International Affairs," 1939–1946, x; London, 1958); L. B. Namier, *Diplomatic Prelude, 1938–1939* (London, 1948); Wheeler-Bennett, *Munich;* W. P. and Zelda K. Coates, *A History of Anglo-Soviet Relations* (London, 1944); David J. Dallin, *Soviet Russia's Foreign Policy, 1939–1942* (New Haven, 1942); Max Beloff, *The Foreign Policy of Soviet Russia, 1929–1941* (London, 1949), vol. II; A. J. P. Taylor, *Englishmen and Others* (London, 1956); and William R. Rock, "Grand Alliance or Daisy Chain: British Opinion and Policy Toward Russia, April-August, 1939," in Lillian Wallace and William Askew (eds.), *Power, Public Opinion, and Diplomacy* (Durham, 1959).

21. Feiling, *Chamberlain,* p. 403.

22. *Ibid.,* p. 408.

23. *Parl. Debs., HC,* April 13, 1939, vol. 346, 15.

24. See Rock, *Appeasement on Trial,* pp. 255–56.

25. *B. D.,* V, 215.

26. *Parl. Debs., HC,* May 2, 1939, vol. 346, 1698.

27. *Ibid.,* May 5, 1939, vol. 346, 2220–22.

28. Feiling, *Chamberlain,* p. 407.

29. *Parl. Debs., HC,* May 19, 1939, vol. 347, 1812–86. See Rock, *Appeasement on Trial,* pp. 264–68.

30. *B. D.,* V, 679–80.

31. So he told the American ambassador, Joseph Kennedy. *U. S. For. Rel., 1939,* I, 272.

32. *Ibid.,* I, 276.

33. *Ibid.* A letter from Strang to Sir Orme Sargent of the Foreign Office, July 20, gives eloquent testimony to this pressure on the British Government and its effect upon the negotiations with Russia. *B. D.,* VI, 422–26.

34. Records of these conversations may be found in *B. D.,* VI, 389–91; *G. D.,* VI, 977–83; and *Documents and Materials Relating to the Eve of the Second World War,* 2 vols. (New York, 1948), II, 67–72.

35. Feiling, *Chamberlain,* p. 409.

36. *Ibid.,* p. 407.

37. See *B. D.,* VII, 558–614, for minutes and other materials relating to the military conversations.

38. Strang (*Home and Abroad,* p. 166) and Kirkpatrick (*The Inner Circle,* pp. 142–43) are among those who doubt that anything would have altered the outcome, particularly after the Germans entered the bidding. Eden (*The Memoirs of Anthony Eden: The Reckoning* [Boston, 1965], pp. 65–66) is less inclined to accept that view. Lord Vansittart ("A Morally Indefensible Agreement," *The Listener,* XL [November 4, 1948], 676) believes the question academic, inasmuch as Russia probably would have double-crossed Britain later even had there been an agreement between them. Historians have not, of course, been able to answer the question with certainty, and the tentative suggestions they have offered fall on both sides of the issue.

39. *The British War Blue Book: Documents Concerning German-Polish Relations and the Outbreak of Hostilities Between Great Britain and Germany on September 3, 1939* (New York, 1939), pp. 125–27.

40. Major-General Sir Edward Spears, Conservative M. P., records that members of the House were on the watch to detect, and resent, any sign of weakness in Chamberlain's statement. *Assignment to Catastrophe,* 2 vols. (New York, 1954), I, 13. They did not find it.

41. Dahlerus gives his own account in *The Last Attempt* (London, 1947).

42. Feiling, *Chamberlain,* pp. 416–17.

43. In a very dramatic episode, Fritz Hesse, German press attaché in London, apparently carried to Horace Wilson Hitler's offer to withdraw from Poland and permit Britain to mediate the German-Polish conflict, in return for the assurance of certain concessions from Poland. See Fritz Hesse, *Das Spiel um Deutschland* (Munich, 1953), pp. 211–16. A brief summary appears in Rock, *Appeasement on Trial,* pp. 318–19.

44. Feiling, *Chamberlain,* p. 416.

CHAPTER XVII

1. Feiling, *Chamberlain,* p. 417.

2. Macleod, *Chamberlain,* p. 281.

3. On this point see Harold Macmillan, *The Blast of War, 1939–1945* (London, 1967), pp. 4–8, and Amery, *My Political Life,* III, 328–29. Chamberlain had demonstrated this sort of thinking before. In the hectic days which preceded Munich, he had responded to a query from Walter Citrine (a Labor leader) as to whether he believed Hitler wanted a peaceful solution in these words: "If we accept the challenge now it means war. If we delay a decision something might happen. Hitler may die." Lord Citrine, *Life and Work: An Autobiography* (London, 1964), p. 365.

4. Macleod, *Chamberlain,* p. 279.

5. *Ibid.,* p. 281.

6. After the fall of Poland, Hitler proposed in a Reichstag speech a European conference to deal with problems arising from Poland's collapse, Germany's colonial claims, and disarmament. Dahlerus was also still active.

7. Feiling, *Chamberlain,* p. 424.

8. Churchill's role in Chamberlain's wartime Cabinet, as well as his relationship with the Prime Minister, is detailed in the former's memoirs. *The Gathering Storm,* pp. 405ff. Despite their long political relationship, only once did

they have an intimate social conversation—on which occasion (in November, 1939) Chamberlain reminisced at length about his early experience on Andros Island.

9. A full account of this episode appears in R. J. Minney, *The Private Papers of Hore-Belisha* (New York, 1961), pp. 266–86. Chamberlain had regularly assured Hore-Belisha of his confidence in him, but bent under the force of "resentment" and "prejudice" against the Secretary in the War Office and the Army Command in France.

10. One of the critics, L. S. Amery, a long-time Conservative colleague of the Chamberlains, later described the early War Cabinet as an "ill-defined blend of an administrative and a policy Cabinet" which resulted in a "planless muddle" characterized by lack of decision. *My Political Life*, III, 327–28. Likewise, Eden found the military direction of the war "not happily organized." *The Reckoning*, pp. 74, 104.

11. For more detail on Chamberlain and military matters, the following might be consulted: Churchill, *The Gathering Storm*, pp. 405ff.; Minney, *The Private Papers of Hore-Belisha*, pp. 232ff.; Colonel Roderick Macleod and Denis Kelly (eds.), *The Ironside Diaries, 1937–1940* (London, 1962), pp. 97ff.; and General Lord Ismay, *The Memoirs of General Lord Ismay* (New York, 1960), pp. 100ff.

12. See Macmillan, *The Blast of War*, pp. 65–66; Amery, *My Political Life*, III, 339, 358.

13. The drama of this debate is effectively reconstructed in Amery, *My Political Life*, III, 358–69 and Macmillan, *The Blast of War*, pp. 67–75. That Chamberlain did not give up easily is attested by the overnight activity of his closest adherents, who approached individual members of dissident groups to convey the message that, if they would vote for the Government in the division, Chamberlain would see them next day to discuss their requirements in a generous spirit.

14. With a majority of approximately 250 seats in the Commons, Chamberlain's majority in House divisions had run consistently close to that figure.

15. An interesting account of this session, as seen through Halifax's eyes, appears in Birkenhead, *Halifax*, pp. 454–55. Churchill gives his version in *The Gathering Storm*, pp. 662–63. See also Halifax, *Fullness of Days*, pp. 223–24.

16. These political maneuvers of May 9–10 are chronicled, sometimes in informative detail, in the following memoirs: Churchill, *The Gathering Storm*, pp. 660–63; Macmillan, *The Blast of War*, pp. 75–78; Amery, *My Political Life*, III, 370–76; Templewood, *Nine Troubled Years*, pp. 431–33; Eden, *The Reckoning*, pp. 110–12. The Labor Party's attitude and role is described in Dalton, *The Fateful Years*, pp. 304–12, and Attlee, *As It Happened*, pp. 157–59.

17. Feiling, *Chamberlain*, p. 440; Macleod, *Chamberlain*, pp. 290–91.

18. See Clement R. Attlee, *A Prime Minister Remembers* (London, 1961), p. 37, for a retrospective judgment.

19. "People ask me how we are ever going to win this war," he wrote on July 14. "I suppose it is a very natural question, but I don't think the time has come to answer it. We must just go on fighting as hard as we can, in the belief that some time—perhaps sooner than we think—the other side will crack." Feiling, *Chamberlain*, p. 449.

20. *Ibid.*, p. 451.

21. *Ibid.*, p. 454.

CHAPTER XVIII

1. Among others, Harold Macmillan makes this estimate in *Winds of Change, 1914–1939* (New York, 1966), p. 467.

2. Hodgson, *The Man Who Made the Peace*, pp. 16–17.

3. A. J. P. Taylor, *The Origins of the Second World War* (New York, 1962), p. 204.

Bibliographical Essay

A number of diverse biographical studies of Neville Chamberlain have been published. Chief among them are the official biography written by Keith Feiling, *The Life of Neville Chamberlain* (London, 1947), and Iain Macleod, *Neville Chamberlain* (London, 1961). Feiling's work is thorough, sophisticated, and sometimes brilliantly (though sometimes obscurely) written. It is dated to some extent, but its value has not significantly declined. The Macleod volume is a semi-apologia which drops off abruptly after Munich; but it has merit as a clear, concise, and straight-forward piece of work. These are the only biographers who have had access to Chamberlain's personal papers. They quote extensively from them, and their works are thus indispensable to a study of this kind. Most other biographical studies of Chamberlain appeared between the time of Munich and the end of the year in which he died (1940). They are thus written in the light of special contexts and are generally less scholarly and balanced. Among the more useful ones are the following: Derek Walker-Smith, *Neville Chamberlain, Man of Peace* (London, 1940); Duncan Keith-Shaw, *Prime Minister Neville Chamberlain* (London, n.d.); Stuart Hodgson, *The Man Who Made the Peace: Neville Chamberlain* (New York, 1938); and L. Raskay, *Neville Chamberlain* (London, n.d.). Broader works which contain helpful biographical material include Sir Charles Petrie, *The Chamberlain Tradition* (New York, 1938); W. N. Medlicott, "Neville Chamberlain," in *British Prime Ministers: A Portrait Gallery Introduced by Duff Cooper* (New York, n.d.); and Joseph Condurier de Chassaigne, *Les trois Chamberlain: une famille de grands parlementaires anglais* (Paris, 1939).

Material on Chamberlain's early life is not abundant. In addition to that which appears in the better biographies, J. L. Garvin's *The Life of Joseph Chamberlain*, 4 vols. (London, 1933–1935, 1951), provides much information on Neville's father and the general circumstances in which Neville grew to manhood. Sir Austen Chamberlain, *Politics from Inside: An Epistolary Chronicle, 1906–1914* (New Haven, 1937), and Sir Charles Petrie (ed.), *The Life and Letters of the Right Hon. Sir Austen Chamberlain*, 2 vols. (London, 1939–1940), include a variety of references to Neville by his elder half-brother. On Neville's interest and activities in Birmingham, the following shed some light: William Haygood, *The Development of Birmingham: An Essay* [introduced by Neville Chamberlain] (Birmingham, 1918); *Birmingham Commercial and Industrial Official Handbook* [introduced by Neville Chamberlain] (Cheltenham and London, 1921); George B. Harris, "Mr. Chamberlain and Birmingham—the Political Riddle," *The Fortnightly*, LXXX (July, 1906); Report of the Special housing inquiry committee for presentation at the monthly meeting of the Council on Tuesday, the 20th October, 1914 (Birmingham, 1914). With regard to aspects of his early activity as a Member of Parliament, the following are useful: Interim report of the Committee appointed by the minister of health to consider and advise on the principles to be followed in dealing with unhealthy areas (London, 1920); Second and final report of the committee appointed by the minister of health to consider and advise on the principles to be followed in dealing with unhealthy areas (London, 1921); Second interim report of the Committee on inland waterways (London, 1921).

That part of Chamberlain's life which found him serving in national government is rich in materials for study, especially the period of the latter 1930s, when he occupied the office of prime minister during a most crucial time.

The memoirs of British (and other) statesmen who were Chamberlain's colleagues and/or contemporaries vary greatly in depth of coverage, directness of approach, and consequent usefulness. Those which were most helpful in this study include the following: Alfred Duff Cooper, *Old Men Forget: The Autobiography of Duff Cooper* (London, 1953), which provides some valuable Cabinet revelations; Viscount Templewood (Sir Samuel Hoare), *Nine Troubled Years* (London, 1954), defensive in nature and sometimes inaccurate in detail, but revealing on the outlook of the appeasers; L. S. Amery, *My Political Life*, 3 vols. (London, 1955), which contains the hard-hitting viewpoints of one who was long a Chamberlain supporter but finally choked on appeasement; the Earl of Avon, *The Memoirs of Anthony Eden: Facing the Dictators* (Cambridge, 1962), especially good on Chamberlain and the question of negotiations with Italy; Sir William Strang, *Home and Abroad* (London, 1956), in which a key participant reviews the negotiations with Russia in 1939; Sir Ivone Kirkpatrick, *The Inner Circle* (London, 1959), in which Chamberlain's visits to Godesberg and Munich are thrust into bold relief by one who assisted him there; Winston S. Churchill, *The Gathering Storm* (Boston, 1948), the interwar account of one who was for a time Chamberlain's colleague, then a consistent critic of appeasement; Hugh Dalton, *The Fateful Years: Memoirs, 1931–1945* (London, 1957), which documents Labor's view of and relations with Chamberlain; Thomas Jones, *A Diary with Letters, 1931–1950* (London, 1954), especially revealing with regard to the roots of appeasement; Georges Bonnet, *Défense de la Paix*, 2 vols. (Geneva, 1946–1948), recollections of the French Foreign Minister which must be used with caution; and Herbert von Dirksen, *Moscow, Tokyo, London: Twenty Years of German Foreign Policy* (Norman, 1952), the sometimes revealing, though occasionally questionable, account of the German ambassador in London.

Other memoirs, generally less valuable to this study, but worthy of mention because of their contribution on certain issues, include: Lord Halifax, *Fullness of Days* (New York, 1957); Viscount (John) Simon, *Retrospect: The Memoirs of the Rt. Hon. Viscount Simon* (London, 1952); Sir Nevile Henderson, *Failure of a Mission: Berlin, 1937–1939* (New York, 1940); Lord Vansittart, *The Mist Procession: The Autobiography of Lord Vansittart* (London, 1958); B. H. Liddell Hart, *Memoirs*, 2 vols. (London, 1965); The Rt. Hon. Earl Winterton, *Orders of the Day* (London, 1953); General Lord Ismay, *The Memoirs of General Lord Ismay* (New York, 1960); The Earl of Woolton, *The Memoirs of the Rt. Hon. Earl of Woolton* (London, 1959); Clement Attlee, *As It Happened* (New York, 1954); Clement Attlee, *A Prime Minister Remembers* (London, 1961); the Earl of Avon, *The Memoirs of Anthony Eden: The Reckoning* (Cambridge, 1965); Harold Macmillan, *Winds of Change, 1914–1939* (New York, 1966); Harold Macmillan, *The Blast of War, 1939–1945* (London, 1967); Vernon Bartlett, *And Now, Tomorrow* (London, 1960); Lord Citrine, *Men and Work: An Autobiography* (London, 1964); Viscount (Herbert) Samuel, *Memoirs* (London, 1945); David Low, *Low's Autobiography* (New York, 1957); Sir

Hughe Knatchbull-Hugessen, *Diplomat: In Peace and War* (London, 1949); Sir Walford Selby, *Diplomatic Twilight, 1930–1940* (London, 1943); Lieutenant Commander P. K. Kemp, *Key to Victory: The Triumph of British Sea Power in World War II* (Boston, 1957); Sir John Slessor, *The Central Blue: The Autobiography of Sir John Slessor, Marshal of the RAF* (New York, 1957); Rt. Hon. Josiah C. Wedgwood, *Memoirs of a Fighting Life* (London, 1951); Fritz Hesse, *Das Spiel um Deutschland* (Munich, 1953); Ivan Maisky, *Who Helped Hitler?* (London, 1964); Colonel Jozef Beck, *Final Report* (New York, 1957); Robert Coulondre, *De Staline á Hitler: souvenirs de deux ambassades, 1936–1939* (Paris, 1950); André Francois-Poncet, *The Fateful Years: Memoirs of a French Ambassador in Berlin, 1931–1938* (New York, 1949); Birger Dahlerus, *The Last Attempt* (London, 1947); Erich Kordt, *Nicht aus den Akten, Die Wilhelmstrasse in Frieden und Krieg Erlebnisse, Begegnungen, und Eindrücke, 1928–1945* (Stuttgart, 1950); Paul Reynaud, *La France a sauvé l' Europe,* 2 vols. (Paris, 1947); Paul Schmidt, *Hitler's Interpreter* (New York, 1951); Ernst von Weizsäcker, *Memoirs of Ernst von Weizsäcker* (Chicago, 1951).

The more useful published collections of papers and speeches include Hugh Gibson (ed.), *Ciano's Hidden Diary, 1937–1938* (New York, 1953), *The Ciano Diaries, 1939–1943* (New York, 1956), and Malcolm Muggeridge (ed.), *Ciano's Diplomatic Papers* (London, 1948), all of which contain the pertinent, if sometimes slanted, observations of the Italian Foreign Minister in the 1930s; Neville Chamberlain, *In Search of Peace* (New York, 1939), a collection of Chamberlain's speeches; Norman H. Baynes (ed.), *The Speeches of Adolf Hitler, April 1922–August 1939,* 2 vols. (London, 1942); R. J. Minney, *The Private Papers of Hore-Belisha* (New York, 1961), a narrative based on the papers of Chamberlain's Secretary of State for War; Colonel Roderick Macleod and Denis Kelly (eds.), *The Ironside Diaries, 1937–1940* (London, 1962), extracts from the daily account of the Chief of the Imperial General Staff; H. H. E. Craster (ed.), *Speeches on Foreign Policy by Viscount Halifax* (London, 1940).

Among the official documents and publications useful in this study, the following are especially noteworthy: *Parliamentary Debates* (Great Britain), Fifth Series; *Documents on British Foreign Policy, 1919–1939,* edited by E. L. Woodward and Rohan Butler, Third Series (London, 1949–1955); *Documents on German Foreign Policy, 1918–1945,* Series D (Washington, 1949–1956); *Foreign Relations of the United States: Diplomatic Papers, 1937, 1938, 1939* (Washington, 1954–1957); *Documents and Materials Relating to the Eve of the Second World War,* 2 vols. (New York, 1948); *Documents on International Affairs, 1928—* (London, 1929—); *League of Nations, Official Journal* (London, 1921–1939); *The French Yellow Book: Diplomatic Documents, 1938–1939* (New York, 1940); *Trial of the Major War Criminals Before the International Military Tribunal,* 42 vols. (Nuremberg, 1947–1949).

Of the many newspapers which contain information on a wide variety of matters, *The Times* (London), the *Manchester Guardian,* and the *Birmingham Daily Post* proved most valuable to this work.

A host of both general and specialized secondary works touch upon facets of Chamberlain's later public career. For the general background of British history, Charles L. Mowat, *Britain Between the Wars, 1918–1940* (Chicago, 1955), and A. J. P. Taylor, *English History, 1914–1945* (New York, 1965), are full, well-organized accounts. Robert Graves and Alan Hodge, *The Long Weekend: A Social History of Great Britain, 1918–1939* (London, n.d.), and the *History of The Times,* 4 vols. (London, 1954), are also useful in a general way.

With more specific reference to British foreign policy, noteworthy volumes include John Connell, The "Office": A Study in British Foreign Policy and Its Makers, 1919–1951 (London, 1958); F. S. Northedge, The Troubled Giant: Britain Among the Great Powers, 1916–1939 (New York, 1966); Arnold Wolfers, Britain and France Between Two Wars: Conflicting Strategies of Peace Since Versailles (New York, 1940); W. M. Jordan, Great Britain, France, and the German Problem, 1918–1939 (London, 1943); D. C. Watt, Personalities and Policies: Studies in the Formulation of British Foreign Policy in the Twentieth Century (Notre Dame, 1965); and A. J. P. Taylor, The Origins of the Second World War (New York, 1962).

Among those volumes which concentrate largely or entirely on appeasement are John W. Wheeler-Bennett, Munich: Prologue to Tragedy (London, 1948), by now an "old standard"; Martin Gilbert and Richard Gott, The Appeasers (London, 1963); Martin Gilbert, The Roots of Appeasement (London, 1966); Margaret George, The Warped Vision: British Foreign Policy, 1933–1939 (Pittsburgh, 1965); A. L. Rowse, Appeasement: A Study in Political Decline, 1933–1939 (New York, 1961); Arthur H. Furnia, The Diplomacy of Appeasement: Anglo-French Relations and the Prelude to World War II, 1931–1938 (Washington, 1960); Boris Celovsky, Das Münchener Abkommen von 1938 (Stuttgart, 1958); Henri Noguères Munich: Peace For Our Time (New York, 1965); Keith Eubank, Munich (Norman, 1963); William R. Rock, Appeasement on Trial: British Foreign Policy and Its Critics, 1938–1939 (Hamden, 1966); and Donald Lammers, Explaining Munich: The Search for Motive in British Policy (Stanford, 1966).

Additional works dealing with pertinent foreign policy topics are R. G. D. Laffan, The Crisis Over Czechoslovakia, January to September, 1938, "Survey of International Affairs," II [for the year 1938] (London, 1951); Arnold J. Toynbee and Frank Ashton-Gwatkin (eds.), The World in March, 1939, "Survey of International Affairs," I [for the years 1939–1946] (London, 1952); Arnold J. and Veronica Toynbee (eds.), The Eve of War, 1939, "Survey of International Affairs," X [for the years 1939–1946] (London, 1958); L. B. Namier, Diplomatic Prelude, 1938–1939 (London, 1948); L. B. Namier, Europe in Decay: A Study in Disintegration, 1936–1940 (London, 1950); Max Beloff, The Foreign Policy of Soviet Russia, 1929–1941, 2 vols. (London, 1949); A. J. P. Taylor, Englishmen and Others (London, 1956); and William R. Rock, "Grand Alliance or Daisy Chain: British Opinion and Policy Toward Russia, April–August, 1939," in Lillian Wallace and William Askew (eds.), Power, Public Opinion, and Diplomacy (Durham, 1959).

In the wake of Munich, a number of shorter works about Chamberlain, some of them quite polemical in nature, appeared both in England and elsewhere. Some of those worth consulting in order to gather contemporary opinions about Chamberlain are Steven MacGregor, Truth and Mr. Chamberlain (London, 1939); Allen Hurt, Gordon Schaffer, and George Darling, "Peace For Our Time"; Mr. Chamberlain and Munich: The Truth About a Policy (London, 1938); Colin Brooks, Can Chamberlain Save Britain? The Lesson of Munich (London, 1938); Rómulo González Irigoyen, Chamberlain: El apóstol de la paz o el gestor de la guerra? (Mexico City, 1941); György Pálóczi Horváth, Chamberlain, a felelös; Európa két éve (Budapest, 1939); Waldemar Müller-Eberhart, Chamberlain, neuordnung der völker (Landsberg W., 1939); and Otto Kriegk, Die englischen kriegshetzer (Berlin, 1940).

With respect to the problem of rearmament as Chamberlain confronted it, two volumes are particularly useful: M. M. Postan, British War Production (London, 1952), and Robin Higham, Armed Forces in Peacetime: Britain,

1918–1940, A Case Study (Hamden, 1962). British Commonwealth policy and opinion are treated in Nicholas Mansergh, *Survey of British Commonwealth Affairs: Problems of External Policy, 1931–1939* (London, 1952), and Gwendolyn M. Carter, *The British Commonwealth and International Security: The Role of the Dominions, 1919–1939* (Toronto, 1947).

Other secondary works which touch upon various aspects of Chamberlain's life and times include the Earl of Birkenhead, *Halifax: The Life of Lord Halifax* (London, 1965), a full biography of Chamberlain's Foreign Secretary; John Evelyn Wrench, *Geoffrey Dawson and Our Times* (London, 1955), the story of the editor of *The Times,* who was a close friend of Chamberlain; Ian Colvin, *Vansittart in Office* (London, 1965), an account of Chamberlain's much-ignored Chief Diplomatic Advisor; Harold Nicolson, *King George V* (London, 1952); John W. Wheeler-Bennett, *King George VI: His Life and Reign* (New York, 1958); and G. M. Young, *Stanley Baldwin* (London, 1952).

Periodical articles of particular use in this study include the following: Frank T. A. Ashton-Gwatkin, "The Personal Story of the Runciman Mission," *The Listener,* XL (October 21, 1948); W. L. Burn, "Neville Chamberlain," *The Nineteenth Century and After,* CXLI (May, 1947); Robert Bernays, "After Mr. Baldwin—What Next?" *The Fortnightly,* CXLI (February, 1937); Neville Chamberlain, "Local Government," *The Nineteenth Century and After,* CV (January, 1929); Cyril Falls, "Should the Democracies Have Fought in 1938?" *The Listener,* XL (November 11, 1948); Agnes Headlam-Morley, "Was Neville Chamberlain's Policy Wrong?" *The Listener,* XL (October 14, 1948); Sir Robert Bruce Lockhart, "September Crisis—And After," *The Listener,* XL (October 28, 1948); L. B. Namier, "Munich Survey: A Summing Up," *The Listener,* XL (December 2, 1948); Harold Nicolson, "The Commons and the 1938 Crisis," *The Listener,* XL (November 25, 1948); S. K. Ratcliffe, "The Chamberlain Family in British Politics," *Current History,* XXXVII (January, 1933); William R. Rock, "The British Guarantee to Poland, March, 1939: A Problem in Diplomatic Decision-Making," *South Atlantic Quarterly,* LXV, No. 2, (Spring 1966); Lord Vansittart, "A Morally Indefensible Agreement," *The Listener,* XL (November 4, 1948).

Among the pamphlets used in this study are these: Imperial Conference, London, 1937, *Summary of Proceedings* (London, 1937); Report of the Postgraduate medical education committee (London, 1930); Statement by the chancellor of the Exchequer at the Monetary and economic conference on 14th June, 1933 (London, 1933); Widows', orphans', and old age pensions: Speech by the Rt. Hon. Neville Chamberlain, M. P., minister of health, broadcast from the Birmingham station of the British broadcasting company on Tuesday, 22nd September, 1925 (London, 1925).

Index